# The Dark Side of Alice in Wonderland

# The Dark Side of Alice in Wonderland

Angela Youngman

PEN & SWORD
HISTORY

AN IMPRINT OF PEN & SWORD BOOKS LTD.
YORKSHIRE - PHILADELPHIA

First published in Great Britain in 2021 by
Pen & Sword History
An imprint of
Pen & Sword Books Ltd
Yorkshire - Philadelphia

Copyright © Angela Youngman, 2021

ISBN 978 1 52678 581 7

The right of Angela Youngman to be identified as the Author of this work has been asserted by her in accordance with the Copyright, Designs and Patents Act 1988.

A CIP catalogue record for this book is available from the British Library.

All rights reserved. No part of this book may be reproduced or transmitted in any form or by any means, electronic or mechanical including photocopying, recording or by any information storage and retrieval system, without permission from the Publisher in writing.

Printed and bound in the UK by CPI Group (UK) Ltd, Croydon, CR0 4YY

Pen & Sword Books Ltd incorporates the Imprints of Pen & Sword Archaeology, Atlas, Aviation, Battleground, Discovery, Family History, History, Maritime, Military, Naval, Politics, Railways, Select, Transport, True Crime, Fiction, Frontline Books, Leo Cooper, Praetorian Press, Seaforth Publishing, Wharncliffe and White Owl.

For a complete list of Pen & Sword titles please contact

**PEN & SWORD BOOKS LIMITED**
47 Church Street, Barnsley, South Yorkshire, S70 2AS, England
E-mail: enquiries@pen-and-sword.co.uk
Website: www.pen-and-sword.co.uk

or

**PEN AND SWORD BOOKS**
1950 Lawrence Rd, Havertown, PA 19083, USA
E-mail: uspen-and-sword@casematepublishers.com
Website: www.penandswordbooks.com

# Contents

| | | |
|---|---|---|
| **Chapter 1** | Who is Alice? | 1 |
| **Chapter 2** | The Real Alice | 5 |
| **Chapter 3** | Women & Child Friend Alice | 16 |
| **Chapter 4** | Photo Alice | 38 |
| **Chapter 5** | Lolita Alice | 56 |
| **Chapter 6** | X-Rated & Banned Alice | 66 |
| **Chapter 7** | Ripper Alice | 80 |
| **Chapter 8** | Murder Mystery Alice | 95 |
| **Chapter 9** | Mad Alice | 107 |
| **Chapter 10** | Drug Alice | 126 |
| **Chapter 11** | Surreal Alice | 134 |
| **Chapter 12** | Horror Alice | 146 |
| **Chapter 13** | Occult Alice | 158 |
| **Chapter 14** | Bizarre Alice | 168 |
| **Chapter 15** | The Last Mystery | 178 |
| *Resources* | | 183 |
| *Index* | | 184 |

*Chapter 1*

# Who is Alice?

'Who in the world am I? Ah, that's the great puzzle.'
*Alice in Wonderland*

This is the question that Alice asks herself just after she has become a giant and frightened away the White Rabbit.

Was Alice a figment of Lewis Carroll's imagination or a real girl? It is a question that can never entirely be answered, given the vast array of views and concepts that have used, and continue to use, these stories over the decades. In the 159 years since Lewis Carroll created this iconic story, the historical Alice has emerged in the form of Alice Liddell. Alice has been transformed into incredibly scary versions, turned into a Lolita figure, become a fashion icon, political commentator, the victim of pornography, eroticised and involved in countless murders. Alice has even been turned into a revolutionary within an immersive theatre concept in which the audience realise they are acting out her identity. She has been psychoanalysed, linked to hallucinogenic drugs and turned into medical conditions. Add to that the mysteries that continually surround her creator with suggestions of child abuse, paedophilia and madness – even suggestions of links to Jack the Ripper – and a beloved childhood story takes on a much darker appearance.

The story of Alice begins on 4 July 1862 with a trip on the river Isis, a branch of the River Thames running through the centre of Oxford. Charles Lutwidge Dodgson, a mathematics lecturer at Christ Church College, Oxford and his friend, the Reverend Robinson Duckworth, took Alice, Lorina and Edith Liddell – daughters of the Dean of Christ Church – on a boating trip towards Godstow. It was a hot, sunny afternoon and Alice – just ten years old – quickly became bored. Alice later recalled what happened next:

'The beginning of Alice was told to me one summer afternoon when the sun was so hot we landed in meadows down the river, deserting the boat to take refuge in the only bit of shade to be found, which was under a newly made hayrick.'

2   The Dark Side of Alice in Wonderland

To entertain Alice and her sisters, Charles Dodgson began to tell a story about a bored girl who followed a White Rabbit down a rabbit hole into Wonderland, meeting all kinds of crazy creatures such as the Mad Hatter, the March Hare, Playing Card gardeners painting white roses red, babies turning into pigs and a Queen of Hearts peremptorily ordering executions. Duckworth was so surprised by the story, that he turned round and asked where Dodgson had found it. Dodgson answered, quite simply, 'I'm inventing it as we go along.'

The children too were enthralled and at the end of the day, Alice requested that Dodgson should write down the story for her as a memento of her 'golden afternoon'.

It was two years before Dodgson completed his written version of the story. On 26 November 1864, Dodgson visited the Liddells' home and gave Alice a handwritten manuscript containing the story – *Alice's Adventures Under Ground* – complete with his own hand-drawn illustrations. One year later, the story appeared in print for the first time from Macdonald publishers; printed at Dodgson's own expense and using his established pseudonym of Lewis Carroll, under which he had already published poetry such as the romantic poem *Solitude* in 1856. Dodgson had even personally commissioned and paid for the leading illustrator of the day – Sir John Tenniel – to undertake the illustrations for *Alice in Wonderland*. Dodgson never expected to make much money on the books and considered it might even make a loss.

*Alice in Wonderland* proved to be a success, popular with adults and children. One reviewer described it as 'a children's feast of triumph and nonsense; it is nonsense with bonbons and flags … never inhuman, never inelegant … Never tedious'. Queen Victoria wrote to him saying how much she admired it, and that she looked forward to his next book. Despite its publicity, the story did not make Dodgson a rich man. The extra income generated by the book never brought in more than around £1,000 a year, and there was only a limited amount of merchandising ever created such as a stamp box container and a biscuit tin. Although Dodgson considered turning the story into a theatre production, and even approached Arthur Sullivan about the possibility of composing some music, it came to nothing. It was only 20 years after the publication of *Alice's Adventures in Wonderland* that producer Henry Saville Clarke was given permission to adapt the book on condition that 'the production should contain nothing of coarseness, or anything suggestive of coarseness'.

*Alice's Adventures in Wonderland* has never been out of print, with millions of copies being sold worldwide. It has been translated into 176 languages making it one of the most read books of all time.

Successive generations have not only enjoyed the story but have used it in ways far removed from anything that Dodgson could ever have imagined. After all, as a clergyman in minor orders, he would have undoubtedly been horrified at the way in which pornographers have put the story to use. Changing cultures and viewpoints have brought new opportunities but have also meant that the story has been analysed and criticised in ways that the original readers would never have anticipated.

Even the book's author has come under considerable scrutiny, with innumerable opinions of his life, character and actions being put forward.

In a talk for the US Ripper Conference in 2000, entitled *Jack Through the Looking Glass (or Wallace in Wonderland)*, Karoline Leach commented:

> '"Lewis Carroll" has always been at the centre of a powerful mythology. His Alice books have tapped into the depths of the collective psyche in ways we cannot and never will fully understand. In some curious way, he seems to have told an allegorical story of what it is to be human, confused and alone in a mad and infinite universe.
>
> 'The "shy clergyman" at the heart of this story has become that strange and inexplicable thing – an icon. He was seen as a 'scholar-saint' who avoided the adult world, a 'perpetual child' who could only relate to children; a tragic deviant whose lifelong passion for a child – Alice Liddell – fired his burning creativity. As an icon to 'otherness' did "Carroll" become famous and infamous. After his death, he was simply rebuilt in a different, 'better', image. For the Victorians and Edwardians, he became the ultimate symbol of innocence, of the elf-like and unworldly soul of Man before the Fall, whose life must be seen to have been beyond the taint of adult corruption.
>
> 'For the modern world, he became the symbol of hypocrisy, of secret appetites, the disordered sage, the patron saint of Freudian deviancy. All of these images – of Carroll as saint, or Carroll as Dennis Potter's sweaty palmed deviant, or indeed Carroll as the Whitechapel murderer – are about the triumph of imagination over reality.'

4   The Dark Side of Alice in Wonderland

So, take a step into the world of Alice, and discover the many unexpected, darker aspects of this iconic character and her creator whether it be a Japanese cute Lolita, an erotic girl child, an Alice of nightmares, a child abused or not abused. Looking at this darker world of *Alice in Wonderland* reveals a world of surprises, a world far removed from the Tenniel drawing or, indeed, the universally familiar Walt Disney version.

As Charles Dodgson points out within the books:

'"And what is the use of a book," thought Alice, "without pictures or conversation?"'

'Why, sometimes I've believed as many as six impossible things before breakfast.'

'It's no use going back to yesterday, because I was a different person then.'

'Curiouser and curiouser!'

'We're all mad here.'

This is the mad, dark world of Charles Lutwidge Dodgson/Lewis Carroll and *Alice in Wonderland.*

*Chapter 2*

# The Real Alice

'What wert thou, Dream Alice, in thy foster-father's eyes?'

C.L. Dodgson

In November 1865, a storybook entitled *Alice's Adventures in Wonderland* arrived at bookshops in England and proved to be an instant success, much to the surprise of the author, C.L. Dodgson aka Lewis Carroll. His first venture into publishing the book some months earlier in June had proved disappointing. The publishers had printed 2,000 copies but on seeing it, the illustrator John Tenniel was so disappointed with the book's quality that he requested that every copy should be recalled, and the entire book reprinted. Dodgson wrote in his diary that all the copies would be 'sold as waste paper.' It represented a major expense for Dodgson, since he had funded all the printing and illustration costs himself. Five thousand revised copies were printed the second time, and he anticipated again losing money, but hoped to make a small profit if it reached a second edition.

So popular has the book become that it has never been out of print since that date. Although he never made a fortune from it, he did get a steady income which proved to be a useful supplement to the payments for lecturing and tutoring at Christ Church College, Oxford. *Alice in Wonderland* was soon being translated into other languages, with French and German editions appearing as early as 1869, soon followed by Dutch, Swedish, Russian and Italian.

Virtually everyone who read the book believed that the central character, Alice, was just a figment of the author's imagination, a convenient name around which to fit the storyline.

Years passed. Charles Lutwidge Dodgson died in January 1898. Yet the popularity of *Alice in Wonderland* continued to grow, being translated into yet more languages including Finnish, Irish, Norwegian, Serbian, Spanish, Japanese and Hebrew. It became an iconic story, an essential part of childhood, with the first film version appearing as early as 1903.

6　The Dark Side of Alice in Wonderland

Then, one day in 1928, a lady named Alice Hargreaves contacted Sotheby's Auction House with a manuscript. She wanted to know whether it was worth selling. Having lost two of her sons in the First World War, experienced the recent death of her husband and facing the spendthrift ways of her third son, she was now in need of money. Opening the manuscript, the auctioneers were astonished to discover that it was a green handwritten book entitled *Alice's Adventures Under Ground*, with illustrations by Dodgson himself. Not only that, there was a handwritten dedication to Alice: 'A Christmas Gift to a Dear Child in Memory of a Summer's Day'.

When asked about the manuscript and the associated memorabilia, Mrs Hargreaves explained. She was born Alice Liddell and her father had been Dean of Christ Church College. In 1862, Charles Dodgson took her sisters Lorina and Edith together with herself on a boat trip along the river Isis in Oxford. At her request, Dodgson had made up a story to keep her and her sisters entertained. She had enjoyed it so much, she had asked him to write down for her. The book was the result. He had brought it to her home as a gift in 1864.

News of the discovery quickly spread worldwide. At the auction, the price was nearly four times the reserve that had been placed on it by Sothebys. An American collector, Dr A.S.W. Rosenbach, who subsequently became known as 'the man who bought Alice', purchased the book for £15,400. Taking it back to America in his trunk led to a moment of total horror. He wrote that he boarded the boat with the manuscript packed carefully in his trunk:

> '... with instructions to place it in my cabin on the Steamer *Majestic* ... Imagine my shock to find ... that the trunk was not in my stateroom. Cold chills ran up and down my spine ... Finally after spending a sleepless night the baggage master informed me the next day that the missing trunk had been found under the bed in the stateroom of a prominent banker.'

After selling it for £30,000 to Eldridge Johnson, the inventor of the Victrola (a talking machine), Rosenbach later repurchased it when Johnson's family sold it to pay death duties and wrote in the book that it was 'purchased by me'. In 1948, the Alice Fund was set up to buy the book back from Rosenbach and return it to the UK as a gift in recognition of the efforts made by the British people during the Second World War: 'as an expression of thanks to a noble people who held Hitler at bay for a long period single-handed'.

It was not only the presence of that signed book that attracted global attention, but the story of Alice, the girl who was the inspiration behind that iconic story. It was the first time that Alice Hargreaves had ever referred publicly to her links with Charles Dodgson. Even though the Liddells continued living at the Deanery, contact between Charles Dodgson and the Liddell family had all but ceased in 1862, just after that memorable journey. She had not acknowledged any receipt of that handwritten book, nor had he attended her wedding even though he had sent her a wedding gift. That too had not been acknowledged. The only public acknowledgement she made of her connection to Dodgson was in 1892, when he wrote to her, telling of the book's success as it had by that point sold over 120,000 copies. She responded with a polite, but cool letter. An invitation to tea when she visited Oxford in 1878 resulted in a short, courteous visit accompanied by her sister. Alice did not attend his funeral in 1898.

Charles Dodgson was already living at Christ Church when the Liddell family arrived in Oxford following Henry Liddell's appointment as Dean of Christ Church College in 1856. Until that point, Liddell had been the headmaster of Westminster School, as well as having been appointed the domestic chaplain to Prince Albert and preaching at church services at Windsor. Liddell was a notable scholar, having jointly edited a Greek/English lexicon with a fellow academic Robert Scott. This was the first time such a lexicon had been created and it proved extremely popular, being reprinted several times. By 1869 there had been six editions, creating 48,000 copies overall. The seventh edition resulted in additional profits of £1,650 for Dean Liddell, a massive sum in those days. As Headmaster of Westminster School, he was credited with transforming it from a failing school to a highly successful one, attracting the attention of the Royal Family. The Liddells were successful and wealthy. Mrs Liddell was responsible for organising their social life, ensuring they attended all the most appropriate society events and functions, as well as being responsible for the general welfare of the Westminster school boys.

Alice Pleasance Liddell was born on 4 May 1852 and was their fourth child. Her older siblings were Harry (born 1847), Lorina (born 1849) and Arthur, who was born in 1850, dying in 1853. Edith was born two years after

8    The Dark Side of Alice in Wonderland

Alice, in 1854. Another five children were born after the Liddells moved to Oxford, including Alice's favourite brother Frederick, who later became a lawyer and senior civil servant.

Before taking up residence at Christ Church College, the Liddells rebuilt the Dean's House to create a house which was suitable for their ever-increasing family, as well as their status in society. It became the focal point for Oxford society, and Christ Church became an increasingly popular college for the aristocracy. In 1858, the Prince of Wales (later King Edward VII) came to study at Christ Church College and the following year, his mother Queen Victoria came for a visit. In 1870, Dean Liddell received further preferment, being appointed Vice-Chancellor of Oxford University.

The Liddell children were placed in the daily care of a young local woman who also acted as their governess. Her name was Mary Prickett. She provided children with an elementary education and later, when the girls were older, special teachers were brought in to teach Art, French, German, Italian and Music. The boys were eventually sent away to boarding school, but the girls continued to be educated at home. The Liddell family enjoyed summer holidays in the fashionable Victorian resort of Llandudno, North Wales.

Alice and her siblings often played in the garden of The Deanery. It was in that garden that they were first seen by Charles Dodgson, whose college rooms were nearby in Tom Quad. Initially, Dodgson became involved with Harry Liddell, using him as photographic subject and also helping him with his mathematics. Contact with the remainder of the family steadily widened, and Dodgson frequently took them on outings, including journeys on the river. He also photographed them. Alice later recalled being taken to his rooms for the photographic sessions:

> 'We used to sit on the big sofa on each side of him, while he told us stories, illustrating them by pen and ink drawings as he went along. When we were thoroughly happy and amused at his stories, he used to pose us, and expose the plates before the right mood had passed.'

In due course, Alice became one of his child friends, with the first specific reference to her being made in his diary on 1 May 1857. Dodgson wrote, 'I went to the Deanery in the afternoon, partly to give little Alice a birthday present, and stayed for tea.'

Dodgson and his lifelong friend Reginald Southey (who had also studied at Christ Church) often used to take the children on the river Isis during the summer days. It was on one of those boat journeys that he first told the story which has since become known as *Alice in Wonderland.*

The relationship came to an abrupt end in the autumn of 1863. No reasons were ever given, although it did arouse some gossip at the time. There have been numerous suggestions as to why this change occurred. In 2015, a BBC TV programme, *The Secret World of Lewis Carroll* suggested that there may be links to the nude photograph they found in the Musée Cantini, Marseilles, which might be an image of Lorina Liddell.

On 26 November 1864, Dodgson visited the Deanery to present the handwritten manuscript of *Alice's Adventures Under Ground* to Alice. In 1865, he delivered the very first printed copy of *Alice's Adventures in Wonderland*, bound up in white vellum, to the deanery. There was little response. The breach between the Liddell family and Dodgson was virtually complete, with Mrs Liddell having forced Alice to burn all Dodgson's correspondence with her. Copies of subsequent editions including various translations were delivered at intervals during the next few years.

Despite the lack of contact, Alice appears to have remained a constant muse. Many years later, in 1887, Dodgson wrote in *'Alice' on the Stage*:

'What wert thou, dream-Alice, in thy foster-father's eyes? How shall he picture thee? Loving, first, loving and gentle; loving as a dog (forgive the prosaic simile, but I know no earthly love so pure and perfect), and gentle as a fawn; then courteous – courteous to all, high or low, grand or grotesque, King or caterpillar, even as though she herself were a King's daughter, and her clothing of wrought gold: then trustful, ready to accept the wildest impossibilities with all utter trust that only dreamers know; and lastly, curious – wildly curious, and with the eager enjoyment of Life that comes only in the happy hours of childhood, when all is new and fair, and when Sin and Sorrow are but lost names – empty words signifying nothing.'

Researchers also point to an acrostic poem that appears in *Through the Looking Glass.* Quite apart from the way in which it evokes the pleasant

10    The Dark Side of Alice in Wonderland

days with the Liddell children on the river, when the initial letter of each line is read downwards, it spells out Alice's full name:

A boat beneath a sunny sky,
Lingering onward dreamily
In an evening of July –

Children three that nestle near,
Eager eye and willing ear,
Pleased a simple tale to hear –

Long has paled that sunny sky:
Echoes fade and memories die.
Autumn frosts have slain July.

Still she haunts me, phantomwise,
Alice moving under skies
Never seen by waking eyes.

Children yet, the tale to hear,
Eager eye and willing ear,
Lovingly shall nestle near.

In a Wonderland they lie,
Dreaming as the days go by,
Dreaming as the summers die:

Ever drifting down the stream –
Lingering in the golden gleam –
Life, what is it but a dream?

In 1869, the painter Ruskin was appointed the first Slade Professor of Fine Art at Oxford and Alice became his pupil. Ruskin reported that he was pleased with her progress and in 1870 gave her a copy of Sir Walter Scott's *Minstrelsy of the Scottish Border*, in which he wrote 'Alice P Liddell, First Prize for Time Sketch 1870'. Her skill as an artist continued to increase in subsequent years, and she even copied Turners lent to her by Ruskin.

In 1870, Alice was deemed ready to enter society, and in 1872 undertook a grand tour of Europe with her sisters Lorina and Edith. Mrs Liddell was ambitious for her children and wanted them to marry well. Both Dean Liddell and his wife were younger children of aristocratic families and were conscious of their position in society. Alice had become a classic beauty and attracted a lot of attention.

Her first real admirer is believed to have been Prince Leopold, the youngest son of Queen Victoria. Prince Leopold was an undergraduate at Christ Church College, Oxford from 1872 until 1876. It is said that they fell in love and had an intense relationship. But their marriage was deemed impossible by Queen Victoria, as Alice was just a commoner and unrelated to royalty.

Instead, Alice married another Christ Church graduate, Reginald Hargreaves, who had been a one-time student of Dodgson. A notable cricketer and a wealthy man, Reginald Hargreaves was the son of a Lancashire calico mill owner, with estates in Hampshire as well as the north of England. Alice and Reginald married at Westminster Abbey in 1880. Prince Leopold did not attend but sent a wedding present – a horseshoe brooch which she wore on her wedding dress. Three years later, Leopold married a German princess and had a daughter, whom he named Alice.

Following her marriage, Alice went to live at Cuffnells in the Hampshire town of Lyndhurst, located within the New Forest. Dodgson's unacknowledged wedding gift – a watercolour of Tom Quad – hung above the drawing room fireplace for the rest of Alice's life. She became a society hostess, attending balls and soirees, and became the first president of the Emery Down Women's Institute. Alice also continued with her love of art and carved a door panel depicting St Frideswide, Oxford's patron saint, which was donated to the Church of St Frideswide in Oxford.

Alice and Reginald had three children, all boys; Alan, Leopold and Caryl. Prince Leopold was the godfather of her second child. Both Alan and Leopold were killed in action during the First World War. Although Caryl Hargreaves survived the wartime carnage and had a daughter of his own, he was known to be a spendthrift. Whether the name Caryl was a nod to her links with Charles Dodgson, no one will ever know.

From 1880 onwards, there was very little contact between Alice and Charles Dodgson. He sent her a copy of his humorous poetry book *Rhyme? And Reason?* containing reprints of poems such as *The Hunting of The Snark* as well as new ones like *Echoes* and *Fame's Penny-Trumpet*.

12    The Dark Side of Alice in Wonderland

Written inside was an inscription, 'For auld lang syne. I want to send a copy of my new book to one without whose infant patronage I might never have written at all'. In 1885, he wrote again, this time with a request. Could he borrow the original manuscript of *Alice's Adventures* so that he could publish it in facsimile on the basis that he believed many people would love to see the story in its original form, ending the letter, 'Always your friend C.L. Dodgson'. Alice agreed to his request and sent him the original manuscript, although she seems to have had some reservations about the publication of the photo Dodgson had taken of her aged seven. In July, he wrote again, suggesting that the profits for the publication should be given to hospitals and homes for sick children. Alice amended this to children's hospitals and convalescent homes for sick children, a request to which he agreed. Dodgson also sent her copies of various memorabilia that had been produced, such as an ivory-handled parasol, carved in the shape of Tweedledee and Tweedledum, the Alice postage stamp case and the Alice biscuit tin.

Alice saw Dodgson for the last time in December 1891. Her father had decided to retire at Christmas, and she was visiting Oxford. Hearing that Alice was visiting the Deanery, Dodgson wrote inviting her to tea saying:

'My dear Mrs Hargreaves,

'I should be so glad if you could, quite conveniently to yourself, look in for tea any day. You would probably prefer to bring a companion; but I must leave the choice to you, only remarking that if your husband is here he would be most very welcome (I crossed out most because it's ambiguous; most words are, I fear). I met him in our Common Room not long ago. It was hard to realise that he was the husband of one I can scarcely picture to myself, even now, as more than 7 years old!

'Always sincerely yours,
C.L. Dodgson

'Your adventures have had a marvellous success. I have now sold well over 100,000 copies.'

Although Alice did not go to tea, she and her sister Rhoda visited Dodgson for a short time. When Dodgson died, she did not attend his funeral but did send flowers.

The Real Alice    13

Following her identification as the person who inspired *Alice in Wonderland*, she became world famous. The centenary of Lewis Carroll's birth in 1932 brought her yet more attention. She was invited to America to receive an honorary doctorate from Columbia University, New York, in commemoration of the centenary. Just before she set sail on the liner *Berengaria*, she autographed a copy of *Alice's Adventures in Wonderland* for the then Princess Elizabeth (later to become Queen Elizabeth II), inscribing it as 'From the original Alice'. The book was then displayed at St Mary's Hospital Paddington, where a children's ward was being created in memory of Lewis Carroll.

On her arrival in America, Professor J. Enrique Zanetti, Chairman of the Columbia Carroll Centenary Committee went on board the *Berengaria* to welcome her. He later recalled that she was:

> 'of medium height and build, grain-haired and had charming old fashioned manners ... She spoke in low tones and had a quaint sense of humour. She wore a blue flowered dress, a black camel's hair coat with a squirrel collar and black hat with feather. A large bunch of orchids was attached to her coat. She used two canes for walking.'

The University provided accommodation for her at the luxury Waldorf Astoria Hotel and she was given a special tour of New York. Vast crowds gathered to see her, and a police escort was needed everywhere she went. Interviewed by WABC Columbia, she remarked 'America and New York City are such exciting places that they take me back to Wonderland'. She went on to talk about the memorial funds for children's hospitals on both sides of the Atlantic, read letters she had received from Dodgson concerning the facsimile edition and his request that funds be donated to hospitals, ending with the acrostic bearing their names which he had given to the Liddell children in their copy of Holiday House for Christmas 1861.

The acrostic reads:

> Little maidens, when you look
> On this little story-book,
> Reading with attentive eye
> Its enticing history,
> Never think that hours of play

14   The Dark Side of Alice in Wonderland

Are your only HOLIDAY,
And that in a HOUSE of joy
Lessons serve but to annoy.
If in any HOUSE you find
Children of a gentle mind,
Each the others pleasing ever
Each the others vexing news
Daily work and pastime daily
In their order taking gaily –
Then be very sure that they
Have a life of HOLIDAY.

When receiving her doctorate in a private ceremony, she commented:

'I shall remember it and prize it for the rest of my days, which may not be very long. I love to think, however unworthy I am, that Mr Dodgson – Lewis Carroll – knows and rejoices with me.'

During the Centennial Celebrations, a short recording of one of her speeches was made on an aluminium disk. She recalls her childhood friend, and commented, 'I have often wondered what wonderful stories the world has missed because he never wrote anything down.' She also commented that 'If Lewis Carroll had told me the story which I am living today it would have seemed as strange as the whimsical stories which he used to tell me, using me as his "Alice".'

On 15 November 1934, Alice Hargreaves died at her home in Lyndhurst. She was 82 years old. On 27 November, Menella Dodgson (Charles Dodgson's niece) wrote, 'So Mrs Hargreaves has gone. I wonder how long she will be remembered.'

Since 1934, the memory of Alice Liddell has lived on through the words of *Alice in Wonderland*. Her identity has become almost confused at times with the Alice of the story, a confusion which seemed to begin almost immediately after her death. Reporting on her death, the *Evening Standard* headline read: 'Alice in Wonderland is dead'. Her obituary in *The Times* was headed 'Mrs Hargreaves', while underneath in smaller letters were the words 'Alice in Wonderland'. Buried in the family tomb at St Michael and All Angels Church, Lyndhurst, the grave initially read simply 'Hargreaves'.

Later, an unknown person added the words: 'The grave of Mrs Reginald Hargreaves. The "Alice" in Lewis Carroll's Alice in Wonderland.'

Memorabilia relating to Alice Liddell and *Alice in Wonderland* continues to attract considerable attention. In 1998 at an auction in New York, a picture of the six-year-old Alice Liddell sold for $62,000 while Lewis Carroll's own personal copy of the story raised $1.54m. Even rarer are the few copies that still remain of that first-ever edition that Tenniel asked to be destroyed. One of those copies came up for auction at Christies in 2016, and was expected to raise up to $3m, but failed to reach its reserve price.

*Chapter 3*

# Women & Child Friend Alice

'Dodo-Dodgson'
'An entirely confirmed old bachelor'

C.L. Dodgson

Charles Lutwidge Dodgson wrote one of the most imaginative and well-loved children's books of all time. It has been translated into 174 languages, turned into films, musicals, an opera and even a ballet as well as being used as inspiration for works by countless authors, playwrights and artists. Yet he never married or had children of his own. He remained solitary his entire life – although he did have countless female friends and child friends, relationships which have raised questions over the years. Even during his lifetime, there was considerable gossip regarding his female relationships. According to biographer Jenny Woolf:

'From at least his twenties, when he was supposed to be chasing Alice's governess, right until the end of his life, he was dodging tittle-tattle. The older he became, the more lady friends he acquired, and the more obtrusive the gossip became.'

His background was nothing unusual for the period. He was born on January 27, 1832. His father, Charles Dodgson, was a graduate of Christ Church Oxford who had chosen to enter the church, becoming a curate, ministering to a congregation at All Saints Church, Daresbury in Cheshire. This was a conventional career for university graduates, as there were few other alternative occupations open to gentlemen which would allow them to marry and have a family. Daresbury was a remote location and Dodgson and his ten siblings formed a close-knit group. Charles was the third child, but the first son to be born.

He had seven sisters and three brothers: Edwin, Wilfred and Skeffington. During those early years in Daresbury, Charles Dodgson's imagination led to the creation of a back garden railway of wheelbarrows and barrels in which they played. Their education was left to their parents, Charles Dodgson and Frances (née Lutwidge).

In 1836, Charles Dodgson took on the extra role of Examining Chaplain to an old friend, C.T. Longley, who was the Bishop of Ripon. As a result, when a more important living under the control of the Crown became available in 1843, the Bishop wrote to the Prime Minister, Sir Robert Peel, recommending his friend for the position of Rector at Crofton-on-Tees.

Other clerical appointments soon followed, including that of the Archdeacon of Richmond, and a Canon of Ripon Cathedral, Yorkshire. As a result, the children's lives changed dramatically. Aged 11, Charles Lutwidge Dodgson was enrolled in a small boarding school in Richmond, Yorkshire, where he stayed for three years, before being sent to Rugby School, Warwickshire, one of the oldest independent public schools in England. Academically inclined, he then obtained a place at his father's old college, Christ Church, at the University of Oxford.

Being a student at Oxford in the mid-Victorian period did not necessarily involve an academic background. Many of his fellow students were members of the aristocracy, sent to Oxford to round off their education and were more interested in hunting and social pleasures than going to lectures. There are accounts of such students bringing packs of dogs into college for use when they went hunting and clerics having to stop the dogs from entering the college chapels. The behaviour of many of these students was described by Oxford clerics as 'loutish'. The more academically inclined students were fewer in number but included people who would eventually become extremely influential like future prime minister William Gladstone, the artist John Ruskin and Robert Gascoyne-Cecil (later Lord Salisbury, another future prime minister). Charles Dodgson was a model student, enjoying his studies and obtaining a first in mathematics.

He was then nominated for a studentship at Christ Church College – this was the equivalent of a fellowship – which brought with it the right to stay at the college forever, enjoying an income of £25 a year. Dodgson became a college lecturer in mathematics. Although the position provided security, it also meant that he had to take minor orders and become a member of the clergy. Under the regulations of the College at that time, lecturers could not marry but had to remain celibate as if living in a monastery. If they chose to marry, they had to leave and seek employment elsewhere. Such employment usually meant taking up a position in a parish as a clergyman – just as his father had done. Under University rules, he was supposed

18   The Dark Side of Alice in Wonderland

to eventually become fully ordained, but this he avoided throughout his career and, eventually, Dean Liddell gave him an exemption. There have been many suggestions as to why he chose not to accept ordination, which would have given him the opportunity to have a family of his own. Possible reasons that have been mooted include differing religious views, his love of the theatre – unlike the Bishop of Oxford who fervently disapproved of the theatre and did not want priests to attend theatrical performances.

One of the most likely reasons was the simple fact that he suffered from a speech impediment. His nephew and first biographer, Stuart Dodgson Collingwood, wrote that his uncle 'saw that the impediment of speech from which he suffered would greatly interfere with the proper performance of clerical duties'.

Dodgson's long-standing friend, May Barber, commented:

> 'Those stammering bouts were rather terrifying. It wasn't exactly a stammer because there was no noise, he just opened his mouth … When he was in the middle of telling a story … He suddenly stopped and you wondered if you had done anything wrong. Then you looked at him and you knew that you hadn't, it was all right. You got used to it after a bit. He fought it wonderfully.'

If he had accepted full ordination, Dodgson would have been required to preach regularly. This would have been a total nightmare, and virtually impossible to accomplish. As a deacon, Dodgson generally avoided any invitations to preach. The scale of the problem he faced when preaching can be seen in his recollection of the rare occasions when he did actually accept an invitation to preach. He recalled:

> 'I got through it all with great success, till I came to read out the first verse where the two words, "strife, strengthened" coming together were too much for me, and I had to leave the verse unfinished.'

Speaking to biographer Florence Becker Lennon in 1930, Lorina Liddell recalled an equally unpleasant occasion when his stuttering affected his speech. She said:

> 'He stuttered badly at times. As the Students were, in those days, allowed to choose a senior Student to read the lessons in Chapel,

they always chose him for the lesson 13th Chapter of the Acts of the Apostles 9th verse, where Saul's name is changed to Paul and it was a long time before P-P-P could be got into Paul.'

In 1861, he sought the help of James Hunt who was regarded to be the foremost speech therapist in the country, dealing with issues of stammering and stuttering. James Hunt is believed to have treated 1,700 people possessing a stuttering problem using a method designed to encourage people to speak consciously in a way that other people spoke unconsciously. Dodgson undertook speech therapy sessions, but although it helped, the problem clearly remained, since by 1873 he was seeking help from James Hunt's brother-in-law Henry F. Rivers, who taken over the practice following Hunt's death. Dodgson was seeking help with the sounds he found particularly difficult:

'My difficulties with "p" in such combinations as "impossible", "patience", "the power", "spake" which combinations have lately beaten me when trying to read in the presence of others, in spite of my feeling quite cool, and trying my best to do it "on rule".'

Dodgson went to note, 'These failures have rather deferred the hope I had formed of being very soon able to help in Church again, for if I break down in reading to only one or two, I should be all the worse, I fear for the presence of a congregation.' Despite all his attempts, the situation was never fully overcome, as by 1890 he informed a Miss Alice Cooper that he could not give an address at her school because his speech defect made it too difficult to give a public speech.

Under the University rules, he had to take vows within four years of taking his MA or lose his position and income. He eventually took the vows of a deacon at the last possible moment on 22 December 1861. His soul-searching continued and eventually, after a long discussion with Dean Liddell, he was given an unusual exemption from having to take final vows, remaining as a deacon, with permission to remain at Christ Church for the rest of his life.

The requirement to be celibate became a mixed blessing for Dodgson. He enjoyed female company but could not afford to allow any relationship to develop that might result in marriage. The death of his father in 1868 left him with responsibility for his seven sisters and the need to help support

20    The Dark Side of Alice in Wonderland

them. Although he was responsible for administering the trust set up by his father to maintain his daughters, Dodgson did provide extra payments from time to time, and gave financial help to cover his costs whenever he went to stay with them at their house.

He certainly enjoyed female companionship. His childhood resulted in the development of close relationships with his sisters. He was imaginative, gentle and kindly by nature. He was not a man's man, being totally uninterested in the typical Victorian shooting, hunting, fishing country pursuits common to people of his class. Dodgson remained clean shaven and a non-smoker at a time when the majority of gentlemen had facial hair and smoked pipes.

Victorian women were expected to make a good marriage, preferably with status and wealth. Careers were not an option. Around the age of 17 to 18, they were brought out into society with the aim of attracting a good match and were introduced to suitable men at balls, concerts, and house parties. If the family was sufficiently aristocratic or had enough money, girls were expected to take part in a London Season where they would meet the right people. Chastity was expected until their wedding night. Being seen unchaperoned in the wrong company, being kissed by an adult male, or seen with a male companion who was not a member of the family could result in dishonour and seriously damage their position within the marriage market, making it difficult, if not impossible, to obtain a suitable husband.

Such attitudes would undoubtedly have made it difficult for unattached males such as Dodgson to enjoy the company of respectable women. Biographer Jenny Woolf believes that he may have had at least one love affair during his life. Although there is no specific proof of this, there are lots of hints and suggestions contained within his diaries and letters and Woolf believes that it was a relationship that became a disaster. The soul searching over his ordination coincides with a period when there were no entries in his diaries. It is also a time when he wrote and published the only serious love poetry of his life – and many of these poems were signed not with his nom de plume of Lewis Carroll, but with his own initials C.L.D.

His poem, 'Stolen Waters', relates to this period and deals with the issue of love, not just sex and extra marital affairs. As a man who possessed deep religious beliefs including the sanctity of marriage, affairs would have affected him deeply. Jenny Woolf points to the fact that there are no diaries or letters for the period between 1858-1862, and that when he began writing his diary again in 1862, it began with a prayer:

> 'Help me to overcome temptation, help me to live as in thy sight, help me to remember the coming hour of death. For of myself I am utterly weak, and vile and selfish. Lord, I believe that Thou canst do all things; oh deliver me from the chains of sin. For Christ's sake, Amen.'

A few weeks later, on 13 March, he wrote again an entry simply saying 'Amen, Amen'. These are the only times within his diaries that he expressed such a level of despair, although there is no indication as to what caused it. From this time onwards, there was an increased focus on his relationships with children, and eventually women, on what has been described as an 'avuncular' basis. Moral redemption was regarded as important, with little girls offering the prospect of redemption by respecting their innocence.

In order to do so, he deliberately set out to present himself as a person who presented no threat to women by adopting the role of an 'uncle', firstly to children, then to adult women. By stressing his age, it made him more acceptable to parents, allowing him to take out children or young women unchaperoned, and to enjoy privileges such as loving kisses. His brother Wilfred later commented that Dodgson:

> 'adopted this avuncular position with a view to the time when his "nieces" began to grow out of the teens ... and no longer be treated with anything like intimate affection except by "uncles" and such-like relations. I know of a very charming married lady who says that one of the conditions she made when she accepted her husband was that she might continue to be kissed by "uncle Charles".'

Dodgson even sometimes introduced himself as being 'Dodo-Dodgson', referring to the extinct animal. In *Alice in Wonderland*, there is a scene where Alice takes part in a caucus race, running in circles with an elderly dodo and other animals and birds. The Dodo is said to be Dodgson himself. The race ends with the Dodo asking Alice if she has anything she could give as a prize. She hands over a thimble, which the Dodo then returns to her saying, 'We beg your acceptance of this elegant thimble.'

## 22  The Dark Side of Alice in Wonderland

He always sought the permission of parents before taking a woman on an outing. In 1884, he wrote to a Mr Alderson asking if he could take Alderson's 22-year-old daughter Helen on a visit saying:

'As yet I do not know if you would sanction any such expedition, without other chaperon but ... I am an entirely confirmed old bachelor who is now well over 50 ... so why should Mrs Grundy object to my having what is so pleasant to me, the friendship of my child friends? So many of my friends ... have allowed me to chaperone my quondam child friends – at all ages from 15 to 25 and upwards?'

The phrase 'Mrs Grundy' was often used in Victorian times, as a personification of conventional propriety, possessing a somewhat priggish attitude. Dodgson referred to Mrs Grundy many times in his letters, highlighting his awareness of the differences between conventional views and his own, unconventional activities.

Not everyone accepted his viewpoint. There was a steady flow of gossip especially within Oxford society. Theatrical designer Laurence Irving noted that there were people in Oxford who regarded Dodgson as 'a greying satyr in sheep's clothing' who took young women out for trips and for private meals. Talk of one young woman's outings – including a weekend away – with Dodgson led her father to call on Dodgson, but there is no record of the subsequent conversation. Dodgson's nephew and biographer Stuart Collingwood acknowledged that his uncle had a Bohemian or unconventional attitude towards young women and girls.

Such gossip was not eased by the fact that Dodgson could be flirtatious and irresponsible on occasions. In 1886 he wrote to the 18-year-old Marion Miller saying:

'My Dear Mary,

'Here is the photo. Looking at it, however, it is not much of a substitute for the live Mary. I wish you would come back again; I need not point out how cruel it is of you to be away so many weeks while I am here, for no doubt you are already feeling a little ashamed of your heartless conduct.'

Several years later in 1893, he wrote to 22-year-old Edith Lucy:

'My dearest Edith

'Why will you insist on my beginning when you know what a lot of Ediths I know … And how awfully hard it is to decide which of them is the dearest!'

On 13 September 1893, a letter to a 10-year-old child friend Enid contained details of an outing he had just enjoyed with 23-year-old May Miller. They had intended to visit Henrietta, Dodgson's sister, in Brighton and took a steamer from Eastbourne. The sea was quite rough, and the duo deliberately got themselves drenched by the waves. Dodgson described the resultant sensation as being 'slapped by a large warm blanket'. By the time they reached Brighton, they were totally soaked. As a result, they changed their plans and returned immediately to Eastbourne, where they went to Dodgson's rooms. May changed into the maid's clothes while her own costume dried out, and they had a private dinner together. Such behaviour would have been verging on scandalous within the constraints of Victorian society.

By stressing his age, he ventured to take girls on holiday with him. When asked for their permission, parents allowed this, on the basis that the girls had their own bedroom, a maid to look after them and were supervised by Dodgson's landlady, Mrs Dyer. In September 1890, he invited the 21-year-old Gertrude Chataway to visit him in Eastbourne. He wrote, saying:

'If I live to next January, I shall be 59 years old. So it's not like a man of 30, or even a man of 40, proposing such a thing. I should hold it quite out of the question in either case. I never thought of such a thing, myself, until 5 years ago. Then, feeling I really had accumulated a lot of years, I ventured to invite a little girl of 10, who was lent without the least demure. The next year I had one 12 staying here for a week. The next year I invited one of 14, quite expecting a refusal, that time, on the ground of her being too old. To my surprise, and delight, her mother simply wrote, "Irene may come to you for a week, or a fortnight. What day would like to have her?" After taking her back, I boldly invited an elder sister of

24    The Dark Side of Alice in Wonderland

hers, aged 18. She came quite readily. I've had another 18 year old since and feel quite reckless now, as to ages: and so far as I know, "Mrs Grundy" has made no remarks at all.'

At the end of the letter, he added, 'At present, there is, lying on the sofa by the open window of my tiny little sitting-room, a girl-friend from Oxford, aged 17. She came yesterday, and will stay perhaps a week.'

By September 1893, the gossip regarding Dodgson's relationships with women was sufficiently strong that Dodgson's sister Mary, wrote to him expressing her concern. He wrote back commenting:

'The only two tests I know apply to such a question as to having some particular girl-friend as a guest are first, my own conscience, to settle whether I feel it to be entirely innocent and right, in the sight of God; secondly the parents of my friend to settle whether I have their full approval for what I do.

'You need not be shocked at my being spoken against. Anybody, who has spoken about at all, is sure to be spoken against by somebody, and any action, however innocent in itself, is liable, and not at all unlikely, to be blamed by somebody.'

The issues around Dodgson's sexuality have continued to cause controversy. Over the years since his death, biographers and researchers have highlighted quotations from his letters, diaries and other writings suggesting that he had problems relating to his celibate status, which he described as 'the inclinations of my sinful heart'. The introduction to his *Curiosa Mathematica, Part II* includes the unusual comment that by concentrating on mathematics while lying in bed it was possible to ward off 'unholy thoughts, which torture with their hateful presence, the fancy that would fain be pure'.

It was not just his relationships with adult women that resulted in controversy, the role of his child-friends was equally controversial. He sought the company of children of his own social class or those close to it such as those he met through his theatre contacts. He rarely became involved with uneducated children – they had to be able to talk to him and appreciate his humour, and his cultural activities. His diaries contain many references

Women & Child Friend Alice   25

to spotting children that he thought might offer pleasant company. He would then seek to discover their identities, and who their parents were. Having done so, he would then present his card at their parents' home and a note asking if he could get to know the children. After the publication of *Alice in Wonderland*, his identity as the author made him particularly acceptable. The parents would consider his request and decide whether to grant it. Sometimes they imposed certain restrictions such as any contact must be chaperoned by the mother or two older sisters, or by people with specific religious views.

His letters indicate his awareness of the potential problems and sensitivity concerning gentlemen friends. He wrote to his friend Beatrice Hatch on 16 February 1894:

> 'I should like to know, for curiosity, who that sweet-looking girl was. Aged 12 ... speaking to you when I came up to wish you good night. I fear I must be content with her name only; the social gulf between us was probably too wide for it to be wise to make friends. Some of my little actress friends are only of a rather lower status than myself. But below a certain line, it is hardly wise to let a girl have a "gentleman friend" – even one of 62.'

Dodgson enjoyed the company of children, especially little girls. He had, after all, grown up among a close group of siblings, mostly female. Dodgson told his colleague Arthur Girdlestone that 'Children were three-fourths of my life. I cannot understand how anyone could be bored by little children'. On 24 October 1879, he wrote to Kathleen Eschwege saying, 'I am fond of children (except boys), and have more child-friends than I could possibly count on my fingers, even if I were a centipede'. He preferred individual visits from children rather than in groups as he could then give them his personal attention, often taking them on outings to the theatre, afternoon tea, trips on the river or for walks. With no interest in traditional Victorian manly pursuits, art and culture were much more attractive and he enjoyed sharing such experiences with his female friends. When he was with little girls, he could do simple things, play games, enjoy jokes, relax and regain elements of his own childhood.

A typical letter written to parents seeking permission to take children to the theatre is that which he wrote in May 1875 to his friend Lord

26    The Dark Side of Alice in Wonderland

Salisbury, referring to the need for legislation on the subject of vivisection before adding:

> 'I have another motive for writing today. I have just heard from Miss Ellen Terry (the much-talked-of Portia in the Merchant of Venice, now acting at the Prince of Wales' Theatre): she says "when you can come to town, please let me know if you would care to take two nice children to see the affair, and then I will send you the best box in the house." Now I wrote to Gwenny some days ago to ask if she and Maud would come there with me on the 17th or 18th (I have accepted a box for one of those nights, whichever she can most conveniently give). If they *may* come, or if (supposing Maud to be considered too old, or myself too young, for *her* to come) then if Gwenny and Jem may come, I shall be delighted to take them. If *not*, I should like to know at once, that I may find two other children. May I beg the favour of a line by return of post – not of course from one so busy as your Lordship, but from one who perhaps can spare a minute from her "Comic Sections!"'

Maud was the oldest of Lord Salisbury's children and 17 years old at the time of this letter, Gwendolen was the second oldest, aged 15 and James (Jem) was 14.

Most children enjoyed his company. Bert Coote, one of the few boys with which he became friendly, later commented:

> 'My sister and I were regular young imps and nothing delighted us more than to give imitations ... But we never gave imitations of Lewis Carroll, or shared any joke in which he could not join – he was one of us, and never a grown-up pretending to be a child.'

Ellie Bickersteth commented that he had 'so gentle and kindly a nature, whose friendship enriched my childhood'.

There is no evidence that he ever romped with them, or upset them. If a child did not want his company, then he never forced it on them. A good example of this is his relationship with Edith 'Dolly' Blaeman. He met the child while on holiday in Eastbourne. He offered her a present but she ran away, and when her family encouraged her to say thank you, Dodgson noted that she had 'a fit of almost hysterical crying', while during another visit he made to the family Dolly 'cried the whole time'. Dodgson told her mother, 'I will gladly do without ever seeing her again, if only she will be happy again, poor little thing'. He put forward some suggestions as to how to deal with her hysterical crying telling her mother that 'I wonder if you noticed, as I did, that when she thought you were not petting her, quite enough, she roared a little louder to recall your attention'. With time, Dolly did agree to become friends with him, and it was to be a friendship that lasted throughout his life.

One of his child friends was actress Isa Bowman, who stayed unchaperoned with him for weeks at a time. As she grew older, her visits to Dodgson involved behaving and acting as though she were younger. On one occasion when aged 18 and unchaperoned, she attended a dinner party held by Dodgson. Throughout the event, she acted as if she were only 12 years old. Another of Dodgson's child friends, Ruth Waterstone, who was aged 10 at the time, wrote an account of the dinner party saying:

> 'He was very anxious that I should meet her, but of course, she was on the stage and he was afraid my parents might object … So, in order that my parents might see her for themselves what a nice little girl she was, he invited them to meet her at dinner. Later, my mother said that as a dinner party, it had not been a great success but she and my father had enjoyed it and been very much amused …You can see it all – Mr Dodgson, ever happy in the society of grownups – the poor stage girl of twelve and my parents doing their best, to make themselves agreeable.'

Questions have been raised as to whether Dodgson was a 'repressed paedophile'.

Critics such as Robert Douglas-Fairhurst in his book *The Story of Alice: Lewis Carroll and the Secret History of Wonderland* highlighted the ambiguities of his relationship with children, especially little girls. He writes:

> 'His pleasure in receiving kisses and the use of words such as dearest and darling, especially in his letters commenting that it can 'encourage a form of flirting, by allowing the private to be smuggled in under the guise of the public, like someone who can only speak their true feelings when they are hiding behind a mask'.

28    The Dark Side of Alice in Wonderland

Douglas-Fairhurst points to the continual play on words, offering verbal protection as a fall-back if any awkwardness should arise. A typical example was Alice Liddell telling her mother that Dodgson had requested a lock of her hair. When she provided one, he turned it into a joke saying that he hadn't really wanted it.

Dodgson was very keen on receiving kisses, referring often to them in his letters. In July 1876, he wrote to Gertrude Chataway saying, 'I send you 7 kisses (to last a week)'. In October that year, he wrote another letter making fun of the need for kisses. He wrote that he had gone to a doctor to complain he was tired. The doctor came to the conclusion that this was caused by his lips:

> '"Of course" I said, "That's exactly what it is!" Then he looked very grave indeed, and said, "I think you must have been giving too many kisses". "Well," I said, "I did give one kiss to a baby-child, a little friend of mine." "Think again," he said, "are you sure it was only one?" I thought again, and said "Perhaps it was eleven times." Then the Doctor said, "You must not give her any more until your lips are quite rested again." "But what am I to do?" I said, "because, you see, I owe her a hundred and eighty-two more." Then he looked so grave that the tears ran down his cheeks, and he said "You may send them to her in a box." Then I remembered a little box that I once brought at Dover and thought that I would give it to some little girl or other. So I have packed them all in it very carefully: tell me if they come safe, or if any are lost on the way.'

Dodgson frequently had kisses available. In November 1879, he wrote to Agnes Hull 'No end of love and kisses to Evie and Jessie. I suppose there's no use in saying "and the same to you," for, if I never leave off kissing them, how in the world can I begin on you?' Writing to Mary Mileham in September 1885, he commented, 'Thank you very much indeed for the peaches. They were delicious. Eating one was almost as nice as kissing you.'

Other writers have taken a different approach and point to the fact that many of the child-friends, and their families, remained on good terms with Dodgson throughout their lives and have only good memories of the relationship. Annie Henderson was one of the children photographed nude by Charles Dodgson. Her daughter, Diana Barrington, later recalled that her mother had been annoyed at the constant suggestions about his unhealthy attitude towards young girls. Annie Henderson had believed strongly that there was no such problem, and that their relationship was a happy one, in which both children and Dodgson could enjoy affection without feeling evil and threatened. Dodgson wrote, 'When I get letters signed your loving, I always kiss the signature. You see I'm a sentimental old fogey.'

Biographer Jenny Woolf argues that 'rather than being a closet paedophile, it seems that the intensity of Carroll's pursuit of little girls reflects the extent to which he sought an antidote to his feelings for women. With his loving child friends, he could obtain loving, beautiful feminine company which was neither tempting nor sinful.'

Above all, it is the relationship with Alice Liddell that has attracted the most attention due to her connection with the *Alice in Wonderland* story, as well as the fact that there was a clear break in their relationship; a break for which there has never been any explanation.

It was photography that had brought Charles Dodgson to the attention of the Liddell family in the first place. As a lecturer at Christ Church College, Dodgson was given accommodation on site. His rooms in Tom Quad occupied a corner of the college, close to the dean's private garden. Seeing the children playing in the garden gave him the idea of photographing them.

Alice and her siblings became Dodgson's child friends, and he often took them out on outings as well as using them as subjects for his photography. Initially he focused on the oldest Liddell child, Harry, taking Harry and Lorina (Ina) on trips around Oxford. Later, when Harry was sent away to school, Alice and her younger sister Edith, joined Ina on the various outings. It was one of those outings – a trip in a rowing boat down the river Isis – that inspired the story of *Alice in Wonderland*.

The breakdown in the relationship began just one year after that legendary boat journey on the Isis. On the 25 June 1863, Dodgson accompanied the Dean's family and friends on a boating trip to Nuneham. There were ten people in the party, Alice and her three sisters, Dean Liddell, Mrs Liddell, Alice's grandfather, Viscount Newry, Harcourt and Dodgson:

> 'We had tea under the trees at Nuneham, after which the rest drove home in the carriage (which met them in the park), while Ina, Alice, Edith and I (mirabile dictum!) walked down to Abingdon Road Station, and so home by railway: a pleasant expedition, with a *very* pleasant conclusion.'

## 30  The Dark Side of Alice in Wonderland

During the visit, he told more of what he described as his 'interminable tale of Alice's Adventures,' before adding in his diary 'A very enjoyable expedition – the last, I should think, to which Ina is likely to be allowed to come – her fourteenth time'. Ina was now fourteen years old and growing up fast.

Two days later, the relationship between the Liddell family and Charles Dodgson underwent a total change. He wrote in his diary, 'Wrote to Mrs Liddell, urging her to send the children to be photographed'. The following page of the diary is now missing, having been removed after his death. A note by Dodgson at this point linked the missing page to an entry on 27 May 1857 highlighting rumours about Dodgson and the governess Miss Prickett. From then onwards, there are no further references to the Liddell children until 5 December 1863, when he noted that he had seen the Liddells at the Christ Church theatricals but 'held aloof from them, as I have done all this term'. Although Dodgson visited the Deanery in mid-December for tea and music, their previous friendly relationship had disappeared. When he sought permission to take Alice, Edith and Rhoda on the river in May 1864, the request was rejected. Mrs Liddell would no longer allow any of the children to go out with Charles Dodgson, even with a chaperone in attendance.

It was a situation which immediately gave rise to gossip within the confines of local society. The most popular reason put forward for this change of attitude was that he had proposed to Alice and been told to go away. This is by far the most commonly held reason. Although Alice was still a child at the time, it was not unknown for Victorian men to speak to parents about a child reaching puberty, in order to arrange for a marriage to take a place a few years later.

Other suggestions frequently made were that he had unsuccessfully courted the children's governess or had sought to marry Alice's older sister, Lorina. There have even been suggestions that he was using his visits to Alice and her sisters to hide his affair with their mother. In 1996, researcher Karoline Leach discovered a document which has since become known as the 'Cut Pages in Diary'. This is a note believed to be written by Charles Dodgson's niece, Violet Dodgson, summarising a missing page from 27–29 June 1963. The note reads:

> 'L.C. learns from Mrs Liddell that he is supposed to be using the children as a means of paying court to the governess – he is also supposed by some to be courting Ina.'

Whether any such marriage suggestions ever actually arose, is unknown. Charles Dodgson had no money of his own, no prospects and had financial responsibilities towards his sisters. His ability to support a household of his own was extremely limited. In addition, Mrs Liddell was an ambitious mother. She was keen to secure a very different class of husband for her daughters – husbands who were wealthy and powerful. Dodgson was also out of favour due to his opposition to plans for Lord Newry (a protégé of Mrs Liddell) to hold a ball at Oxford – a situation which would have contravened college rules. It seems that Dodgson had opposed the holding of the ball. He wrote in his diary, 'I have been out of her good graces ever since Lord Newry's business'.

Occasional contact between the Liddell children and Charles Dodgson remained; in November 1863, Alice and Edith sought his help in organising their collection of aristocratic calling cards and notepaper crests.

Many years later, in 1930, Lorina was interviewed by a Mrs Becker for a book about Lewis Carroll. Afterwards, Lorina wrote to Alice saying:

> 'On thinking to myself, I think she tried to see if Mr Dodgson ever wanted to marry you! She said he had such a sad face, and she thought he must have had a love affair. I said, "I never heard of one" and it did occur to me at the time what she perhaps was driving at!'

Lorina's next letter to Alice continued,

> 'I suppose you don't remember when Mr Dodgson ceased coming to the Deanery? How old you were? I said his manner became too affectionate to you as you grew older and that mother spoke to him, and that offended him so he ceased coming to visit us again, as one had to give some reason for all intercourse ceasing. I don't think you could have been more than 9 or 10 on account of my age. I must put it a bit differently for Mrs. B's book.'

Having studied Lorina's correspondence with Alice and Mrs Becker, Jenny Woolf suggests that the problem might have been that Lorina was becoming too affectionate towards Charles Dodgson, possibly having a crush on him. Irina preferred to portray herself as much younger than she actually was

## 32   The Dark Side of Alice in Wonderland

and did not want people to realise she might have had feelings towards Charles Dodgson.

Although living so close to Dodgson in Christ Church College, there are few reports of any links between the Liddell family and Dodgson from 1863 onwards. Even when he kept his promise and delivered a copy of *Alice's Adventures Under Ground* to their house, the relationship was never rekindled. Dodgson's final portrait of Alice was made on her mother's instructions in 1870. The portrait shows an elegant girl, head turned away from the camera and seeming to lack the spirit and liveliness of earlier portraits. How far this was due to the changed relationship between the two families, to Alice herself, or to the photographer's demands as to her posture will never be known. She was to join the marriage mart and had no choice in the matter.

Suggestions have arisen that Dodgson was a closet paedophile grooming the children with whom he came into contact. How far this is true is very difficult to judge, particularly when looking at the situation the viewpoint of a very different period in history, and changes in society.

What was acceptable in society at the end of the nineteenth century may well be unacceptable to modern society whether it relates to attitudes concerning work, the role of women in society, health and safety, religion, or child protection. Some reservations were clearly expressed at the time, such as those of Mrs Sidney Owen, and there was certainly gossip about him and his activities, yet overall there appear to be no records that any child or parent who came into contact with Charles Dodgson ever saw him as a potential threat. Many of the child friends remained in contact with him all their lives. Many wrote loyal, loving memoirs.

The rise of psychoanalysis and Freudian research during the 1930s led participants to look at literature from a new viewpoint. It was at this juncture that many of the negative comments about Charles Dodgson and *Alice in Wonderland* began to become common. In 1933, A.M.E Goldschmidt published a book called *Alice in Wonderland Psychoanalysed*. It took the viewpoint that the story was all about sexual frustration reflecting Carroll's desire to have sex with Alice. Falling down the rabbit hole was a symbol of frustration, the door with a golden key was a symbol of coitus while the images of Alice growing and shrinking depending on what she ate and drank reflected a tumescent and detumescent penis. Other writers following his line of thought suggested that the Cheshire Cat reflected emotional detachment from sex.

In *Triple Alice* (1940), American writer George Shelton Hubbell came to the conclusion that:

> 'A bachelor all his days, held by a strict conscience to super-chastity, Lewis Carroll found in a sublimated friendship with little girls the emotional release which most men look for in love and marriage. His letters to children often reveal, but thinly disguised under playful nonsense, the essential spirit of romantic love.'

The exact nature of Dodgson's relationship to Alice, and indeed to any of his child and lady friends remains a topic that is constantly questioned and is unlikely ever to be fully settled. The situation provides considerable scope for authors, scriptwriters, and film producers. In 1992, an opera by Robert (Bob) Wilson, Tom Waits and Paul Schmidt based on *Alice in Wonderland* focused very much on this relationship. The nuances of this approach were quickly picked by reviewers, for example, *Der Spiegel* wrote that:

> 'Bob Wilson ... and his writer Paul Schmidt connect Dodgson's erotic life drama with his famous fairy-tale myths. The show suggests that Dodgson wrote his books only in order to make his sexual object, Alice Liddell, rely on him.'

Talking to the *Theatre Magazine*, Yale School of Drama, Paul Schmidt explained why they settled on this interpretation:

> 'What I thought would be interesting for an adult approach to the work was the situation that generated the Alice books – the infatuation of a young cleric at Oxford for his dean's daughter. By now it's a commonplace of Lewis Carroll studies that he was fixated on little girls, and that photographing them was a constant obsession throughout his life. Nineteenth century views of the relations between grownups and children were highly idealized, but even so, Dodgson's relationship with Alice provoked his eventual split with her family.
>
> 'Mrs Liddell stopped him from coming to see her, and made Alice destroy all Dodgson's letters. There is absolutely no evidence that anything physical ever occurred between Dodgson and Alice, and

34    The Dark Side of Alice in Wonderland

my Alice in no way suggests that. What I was concerned to make clear was that the phenomenon we so easily describe as child "molestation" is a complicated matter. Doesn't all affection have an erotic component? At what time does love and care for a child become harmful? At what point does a grown-up's affection for a child become obsessional? At what point does obsession become dangerous? What must it have been like for a child to be constantly photographed, in an era when the process entailed long periods of holding still, stared at by the camera's eye? What kind of memories would it engender?'

Interviewed on the 2015 BBC TV programme *The Secret World of Lewis Carroll*, Vanessa Tait (Alice Liddell's great granddaughter) said:

'My theory is that Alice's mother was the cause of the split. Carroll's manner grew too affectionate towards Alice. Alice's mother was a dreadful snob. She was known as the King fisher in Oxford and she wanted kings, princes, earls, dukes for her daughters so she stamped on it, and she burned all the letters Alice had received from him in the wastepaper bin in the deanery. My grandfather mentioned that it happened. It was a story in my family.'

Suggestions that Dodgson was in love with Alice have been a continual theme for many years. Alice's son, Caryl Hargreaves, commented that 'he very likely was in love with her …. If he was ever in love with anybody. I have always felt in my bones that was probably the case'. On 3 February 1932, Stuart Dodgson Collingwood wrote to his cousin Menella Dodgson saying:

'In regards to the Liddells it was Alice who was undoubtedly his pet, and it was his intense love for her (though she was only a child) which pulled the trigger and released his genius. Indeed it is quite likely that Alice's marriage to Hargreaves may have seemed to him the greatest tragedy in his life.'

Interviewed by the *Telegraph* in 2015, Vanessa Tait commented, 'My understanding is that he was in love with Alice, but he was so repressed that he would never have transgressed any boundaries.'

There can be no doubt that Dodgson did enjoy the companionship of children and young ladies. It is also clear that he abhorred abuse of any kind. His first biographer, Stuart Collingwood, noted that even while attending school at Rugby, he defended others, writing that, 'long after he left school his name was remembered as that of a boy who knew well how to use his fists in defence of a righteous cause'. Throughout his life, he made numerous payments to charities supporting the ill, unprotected, and vulnerable, people whom Dodgson saw as being 'him that hath no helper'. Among the charities were Homes of Help for 'fallen and friendless young women'; Clerkenwell women's prison for rehabilitated fallen women; the Society for the Rescue of Young Women and children at risk of prostitution; various female refuges and the Society for the Protection of Women and Children which opposed sexual exploitation and child trafficking and undertook legal prosecutions against men who abused children.

Dodgson was undoubtedly aware of the problems caused by prostitution and sexual abuse forced on children. William Gladstone who served for twelve years as prime minister, was a fellow student at Oxford. Gladstone was friends with notorious courtesans such as Lillie Langtry and was also known to walk through the streets of London to meet prostitutes, claiming to be seeking to rehabilitate them. Among the many volumes within his personal library was a copy of Felicia Skene's novel *Hidden Depths*, which was written in 1866. The story contains graphic descriptions of Oxford brothels. He also expressed concern about the propriety of costumes worn in theatrical productions. There is an unpublished essay by Charles Dodgson focusing on theatrical costumes. In this essay, he urges producers not to ask actresses to wear skimpy costumes especially if 'an innocent young person' might see them and 'have sinful feelings roused'. When theatre producer Henry Savile Clarke contacted him regarding the possibility of adapting the Alice stories for a theatrical production, Dodgson agreed on the basis that the play should contain nothing that would 'pander to the tastes of dirty minded youths and men in the Gallery'. Numerous other requests were eventually added concerning the choice of actresses and the method of staging. Some of these requests were accepted by Henry Savile Clark – others were not, such as Dodgson's offer to act as Alice's personal dresser.

In 1878, he attended the trial of two bargemen accused of the rape of a 14-year-old girl. Shortly afterwards, he attended a drama production of *Oliver Twist* which features the murder of Nancy, a young prostitute, and he commented that it was 'too real and ghastly'.

36   The Dark Side of Alice in Wonderland

In 1885, W.T. Stead, editor of the *Pall Mall Gazette*, published four sensationalist pieces of investigative journalism headlined 'The Maiden Tribute of Modern Babylon'. It highlighted the fact that every year, hundreds of girls who were not as socially privileged as Alice Liddell, ended up in a very different type of underworld. This was an underworld that was truly nightmarish, where childhood dreams ended within a network of brothels and locked rooms in all areas of London where, as Stead pointed out, 'young virgins were served up as dainty morsels to minister to the passions of the rich'. One brothel keeper told Stead, 'Oh, Mr.---- is a gentleman who has a great penchant for little girls. I do not know how many I have had to repair after him.' Yet another brothel keeper added, 'A gentleman paid me £13 for the first of her, soon after she came to town. She was asleep when he did it – sound asleep. To tell the truth, she was drugged. It is often done. I gave her a drowse. It is a mixture of laudanum and something else.' There were plenty of children available. Stead was told, 'In the East-end, you can always pick up as many fresh girls as you want. In one street in Dalston, you might buy a dozen. Sometimes the supply is in excess of demand.' Clients came from all walks of life including members of the clergy. Stead was told, 'I once sold a girl twelve years old for £20 to a clergyman, who used to come to my house professedly to distribute tracts.'

In writing up the investigation, one editorial technique that was used to catch attention was the use of a series of asterisks set in a blank space between two paragraphs. This was designed to hint at periods of transformation, for example, when a girl was being raped in a brothel or locked room. For anyone familiar with the stories of *Alice in Wonderland*, this technique would have been instantly recognisable as Dodgson used it to highlight instances when Alice was undergoing a major transformation, growing or shrinking rapidly.

Responding to these reports of child trafficking, Dodgson wrote to his friend, Lord Salisbury, the prime minister, highlighting his concerns. He asked Salisbury if he thought publication 'of the most loathsome details of prostitution, is or is not conducive to public morality'. A few days later, Dodgson wrote a letter to the *St James' Gazette*, signing it Lewis Carroll. The letter was published under the title 'Whoso Shall Offend One of Those Little Ones'. It set out the case for preventing what he described as 'impure scandal' from being reported, commenting that 'forcing the most contaminating subjects to the attention even of those who can get nothing from them but the deadliest injury' and 'I plead for our young men and boys whose imaginations are being excited by highly coloured pictures of vice, by the seducing whisper "read this, and your eyes shall be opened, and you be as gods, knowing good and evil!"' He then went on to 'plead for our pure maidens whose souls are being saddened, if not defiled by the nauseous literature that is thus thrust upon them'.

No one can ever know the exact truth relating to the nature of the relationships between Charles Dodgson and his child and women friends. Much depends on personal viewpoints, and the fact that over the past century or so opinions and views on such issues have changed dramatically. What was deemed acceptable within Victorian society is not necessarily what is acceptable today. Greater awareness of child prostitution, of the prevalence of child pornography, of the existence of those who sexually prey on children and young women means that relationships of any kind are much more carefully scrutinised.

*Chapter 4*

# Photo Alice

'Her arms across her breast she laid
She was more fair than words can say:
Bare-footed came the beggar maid
Before the king Cophetua.'
*King Cophetua & the Beggar Maid,* Alfred, Lord Tennyson

In the 1850s, a new craze swept through Victorian society – photography. Parisian entrepreneur Louis Jacques Mandé Daguerre had created a method of capturing images using Daguerreotype, followed quickly afterwards in 1835 by English landowner William Henry Fox Talbot, who produced the first negative during the summer of 1835. Invention continued apace and in 1851, Frederick Scott Archer developed a wet collodion method which combined the best of Daguerre and Talbot's methods, making it much more accessible to a wider public. Victorian gentlemen, in particular, took up the hobby with glee, persuading friends and colleagues to spend time posing for photographs or travelling the country in search of beautiful views. It was a time of intense experimentation with regard to the techniques of both taking and creating photographs.

One of those photographers was Robert Skeffington Lutwidge, a barrister and Commissioner in Lunacy who was Charles Lutwidge Dodson's uncle. It was through Skeffington Lutwidge's influence that Charles Dodgson became enamoured of this new hobby. Dodgson was naturally creative, having a long-standing interest in art and drawing, and photography provided a new outlet for his skills. On 18 March 1856, he purchased his first mahogany and brass folding camera, marking the start of a lifelong interest. At the time, photography was sometimes regarded as a dark art, simply because it fixed images in a way that portrait artists could not do. Then there was the way in which the images were created, posing different meanings to left and right, along with the upside down focus. The creation of the images would certainly have seemed magical, appearing out of the darkness in the darkroom.

This new craze of photography required patience, creativity and a reasonable income. The equipment was not cheap, and photographers required not just a camera, but all the items and chemicals for developing the images. Everything had to be done by the photographer, immediately after taking the image. Dodgson opted for the wet collodion process. Having identified a subject, or arranged a model in a position in front of the camera, the photographer had to dissolve bromide, chloride or iodide salts in a solution of pyroxylin in ether and alcohol. A carefully polished glass plate was then coated with the mixture and left for a few minutes before being taken into a darkened area and dipped into a silver nitrate solution, which converted the salts into silver bromide, chloride or iodide depending on the chemical used. It was then placed in the camera, the lens cap removed to expose the wet plate. Removing the plate from the camera, the photographer dashed back to his darkroom and immediately developed it using a solution of iron sulphate, acetic acid and alcohol in water. It was important to maintain the chemicals at an exact temperature. Contact prints were then made. Throughout this process, the model had to remain totally still, and was usually helped by having a post or chair of some kind to lean against. Evelyn Hatch was one of Dodgson's child friends and was photographed by him on several occasions. She later recalled that it 'meant much patience, for the photographer was always determined to get his picture "just right"'. The children were often invited into the darkroom to watch as he developed the image. They found it very exciting. Writing in her 1932 memoir, Alice Hargreaves commented 'what can be more thrilling than to see the negative gradually take shape, as he gently rocked it to and fro in the acid bath?'

Initially, Dodgson experimented with a variety of subjects such as landscapes and still life composition as well as portraiture. One of his first portraits was that of Harry Liddell, the 9-year-old son of the Dean of Christ Church college. It was a photograph which was received with great acclaim and pride by Dean Liddell's family.

Photography provided a creative outlet for Dodgson and one in which he possessed considerable skill. His interest in photography grew rapidly, particularly within the area of portraiture, leading him to become one of the leading photographic portraitists in the country. Helmut Gernsheim, a specialist in the history of photography describes him as 'the most outstanding photographer of children in the nineteenth century'.

Using his social connections and his steadily developing skills, he was able to persuade famous people such as the painter Holman Hunt, poet

# 40 The Dark Side of Alice in Wonderland

Alfred, Lord Tennyson, scientist Michael Faraday, actress Ellen Terry, Pre-Raphaelite artist John Everett Millais, writer George Macdonald and Frederick, Crown Prince of Denmark to pose for him. He photographed many landscapes, particularly around Oxford and Yorkshire, including the vicarage at Daresbury, Cheshire in which he was born. There were scientific subjects too, such as images of fish skeletons. Between 1856 and 1880, Dodgson took over 3,000 photographs which he carefully recorded and organised in albums. He became an extremely accomplished photographer, exhibiting his work at major shows. For example, in 1858, his photograph of Agnes Wield as Little Red Riding Hood was shown at the London Photographic Society Exhibition.

The portraits were extremely stylised, with attention paid to creating suitable settings helping to tell a story, or include items relevant to the person. Dodgson used a lot of props in all his portraits, especially vases, sculptures and flowers. He was keen on creating genre images which set out to tell stories or illustrate poems. Although he used his rooms at Christ Church, as well as taking his equipment to various locations, his favourite site was the Liddells' private garden located close to his college rooms.

Not all the photographs in Dodgson's personal collection were taken by him. It is known that he did seek out desirable photographs from friends and acquaintances. On 23 January 1872, he wrote to his friend Anne Isabella Thackeray, the eldest daughter of novelist William Makepeace Thackeray saying:

> 'You would be conferring a great additional favour if you could for love or money get me photographs of those charming little friends of yours, Gaynor and Amy – *especially* (if such a thing exists) one of Amy at 3½ as a sailor. You will think me very greedy, but as the American say, "I'm a whale at" photographs.'

It is known that over the years, Dodgson did take a lot of photographs of adult women, many of whom were semi-clad. Almost all of these have disappeared. Karoline Leach, in *The Shadow of the Dreamchild*, surmises that these photographs may have been contained within the envelopes of material ordered 'to be burned unopened' after Dodgson's death. Alternatively, Dodgson's family may well have decided to destroy the images in order to maintain his reputation. There may still be examples waiting to be found hidden in old photograph albums, originally owned by those women he photographed. He certainly admired the adult female form, for example describing circus performer Louie Webb as being 'beautifully formed'.

Photographs of children became one of Dodgson's favourite subjects – and it has resulted in considerable scrutiny and criticism over the years. In Victorian times, such photography was regarded as acceptable. People wanted photographs and, particularly in the early days, felt it was a honour to be chosen as a subject for a portrait. Everyone wanted a photograph and show albums were highly prized, often being brought out in the evenings to show family and friends. It was a popular entertainment and one in which Dodgson frequently participated, showing his photographs to visitors.

Children were regarded as popular subjects for photographs and were photographed wearing clothes as well as unclothed. There was no sense that it might be indecent, sexual, or abusive towards the child. Victorian society had a very different view on the nakedness of children compared to modern times. Children were seen as being pure and innocent, whether clothed or not, and that if unclothed, possessed an innocent sexuality. They were ignorant of adult life and knowledge, therefore possessed a lack of sexuality and were effectively asexual. Taking photographs of naked or half-naked children was therefore regarded as quite acceptable. Many such photographs taken by Victorian photographers did possess a sensual quality. Dodgson was not the only photographer to create such nude images. Oscar Rejlander created shadowy photographs showing the naked backs and buttocks of children and young girls while another photographer, Julia Margaret Cameron, created numerous naked child portraits which were almost dreamlike in their sensuality. In Victorian times, as Karoline Leach points out, 'One could wear one's admiration for the naked child as a badge of incorruptibility, of an aesthetic perception that existed on a level beyond sexuality.'

Such images were commonplace in all forms of art, not just photography. The Pre-Raphaelite painter Millais created a painting of his young daughter entitled *Cherry Ripe*. The painting showed the little girl sitting beside some fresh fruit, with her hands held palm to palm between her legs. Just above her hands are long black wristlets. Cherry was a well-known colloquial term for virginity.

Dodgson wrote about the practicalities and considerations relating to photographing naked and partially clothed children. Writing in *Lewis*

42   The Dark Side of Alice in Wonderland

*Carroll's Photography & Modern Childhood*, author Diane Waggoner commented:

> 'His writings on partial dress and the nude contain his most explicit statements of his theory and practice on imaging the child's body. Dodgson applied an extreme amount of visual scrutiny to the girl's body and acquired an intimate knowledge of its features – to the point of staring at his illustrators' drawings with a magnifying glass and measuring the proportions of child-figures: he often provided lists of minute corrections to the artist's images ... Dodgson needed to govern the relationship between spectatorship, sexual desire, and the form of the girl to ensure that his representations of nude and partially dressed girls were representations of nonsexual bodies that could only be looked at innocently ... Dodgson evacuated any hint of the "sinful desires" he described in his essay on dress in the theatre from his actions concerning the image of the nude girl – a practice that nevertheless acknowledged the possibility – and danger – of the erotic.'

The Liddell children were frequently photographed during the period 1857-63. Dodgson's first attempt to photograph Harry and Lorina alone was met with instant rejection by Mrs Liddell, who insisted that everyone had to be photographed together in a large group. Eventually she relented and allowed the children to be photographed together on the lawn.

Alice became one of his favourite models, although only eleven images of her on her own were ever created between the period 1857 to 1870. together with seven photographs where she is shown with her brother and sisters. The majority of the photographs show her as a child. The final image resulted as an unexpected request by Mrs Liddell, who arrived at his studio accompanied by Lorina and 18-year-old Alice. Mrs Liddell wanted a portrait of each girl, as Alice was about to be launched into society as an adult woman.

It is the image of Alice as a beggar girl, which has become the most famous of all these photographs – and the one that has raised the most eyebrows. She is shown leaning against the crumbling deanery wall, in a corner of the shrubbery. Her pose is often described as being 'mock seductive' with one arm crooked, while the other is bent at waist level. One foot is treading and breaking some nasturtiums, while the other is brushing against some clematis. The leaves are upturned and appear bruised. She is dressed in rags. Her shoulder, left nipple and chest are exposed. Her dress is tucked down above her waist, while the skirt shows her ankles, legs and feet. She looks directly into the camera lens, with an expression hinting at secret knowledge, often described as being both confident and disturbing at the same time. The broken flowers were often used as a symbol of a broken person.

Simon Winchester points out that the image may well be inspired by Lord Tennyson's poem outlining the meeting between King Cophetua and the beggar maid:

'Her arms across her breast she laid
She was more fair than words can say:
Bare-footed came the beggar maid
Before the king Cophetua.
In robe and crown the king stept down,
To meet and greet her on her way:
"It is no wonder," said the lords,
"She is more beautiful than day."
As shines the moon in clouded skies,
She in her poor attire was seen:
One praised her ankles, one her eyes,
One her dark hair and lovesome mien;
So sweet a face, such angel grace,
In all that land had never been
Cophetua swore a royal oath:
"This beggar maid shall be my queen."'

This photograph is actually part of a pair of images. The previous one taken earlier in the day at the same location, shows Alice in normal everyday clothing. Although the flowers are disturbed, they are not broken. Taken together the two images tell a tale of a well-dressed girl brought low, resulting in losing her status and reputation becoming just another beggar girl.

These photographs of Alice were highly regarded when they were taken. There are records of it being admired by people including Alfred, Lord Tennyson, and it is known that the Liddell family carefully preserved a copy of this photograph.

## 44  The Dark Side of Alice in Wonderland

Although these photographs remain the most talked about, due to Alice's link with the famous story, they do only represent a fraction of Dodgson's extensive photographic collection. The eighteen photographs relating to Alice are far fewer than those taken of Dodgson's other child friends. In his book *The Alice Behind Wonderland*, Simon Winchester points out that when looking at the list of portraits of the Liddell children, it can be seen that in the early days, Edith is photographed occasionally, while Lorina and Harry are frequently photographed. There are photographs of all the children together, or in smaller groups: Lorina and Alice, Edith and Alice, Lorina/Edith/Alice and then just Alice on her own.

There is also another photograph that is held within the Musée Cantini, Marseilles, which was highlighted during a 2015 BBC TV film, *The Secret World of Lewis Carroll*. The image bears a dealer's description attributing it to Lewis Carroll and comprises a full-frontal nude picture of a Victorian girl aged around 13-14 years old. Views differ as to whether this photograph was taken by Dodgson or not – some researchers say no, others yes. After carrying out extensive tests by various photographic specialists and a forensic expert, the BBC team decided that there was a serious possibility that it was a photograph of Lorina Liddell as a young teenager. The paper, albumen residue, and use of the wet collodion process were all consistent with the period during which Dodgson was involved with the Liddell family, and the facial features resembled those found on existing known images of Lorina.

Charles Dodgson's photographic collection includes a vast number of portraits of young girls, including some in which the girls are not wearing clothes. Only four of those images remain, all of which are hand coloured in order to render them fully artistic. He also sketched children nude and talked openly about it.

He was quite open about his interest in nude photography. In June 1876, he wrote to the mother of one of his favourite child friends, Gertrude Chataway, asking 'If you should decide on sending over Gertrude and not coming yourself, would you kindly let me know what is the minimum amount of dress in which you are willing to have her taken?' Gertrude was 'so well-formed a subject for art'. Later that year, he thanked Mrs Chataway for allowing her to be photographed and 'making concessions (much against inclination, I fear) to my rather outré and unconventional notions of art'.

The following year, he wrote to a complete stranger, Mr P.A.W. Henderson, saying that a mutual acquaintance had suggested that Mr Henderson's children would be suitable subjects. Permission granted, Dodgson took numerous photographs of Annie Henderson and her sister, Frances. His letters admit that, although given permission for photographs, he did go further than expected, photographing the children naked even though Mrs Henderson had forbidden it. He wrote to Mrs Henderson on 31 May 1880 saying, 'I felt so confident that, when you told Annie they must not be taken naked because it was too cold, it was your only reason ...' He went on to say that his studio was heated and that the girls ran around his studio in 'their favourite costume' (naked) for three hours. He indicated that he hoped to photograph them in the nude for the next two or three years. As it turned out, he took the last such photographs in June 'mostly in their favourite state of nothing to wear', before giving up photography completely in July.

It is these nude photographs and the numerous images of little girls that have led to suggestions that Dodgson was a closet paedophile. In 2001, the Tate Museum held an exhibition entitled 'Exposed: The Victorian Nude'. One of the images displayed within that exhibition had been taken by Charles Dodgson. Reviewers looked askance at the nude image of the Hatch children, Beatrice, Evelyn and Ethel. In the photo, Beatrice is portrayed sitting on a rock with her knees drawn up. Evelyn lies outstretched on her back, arms behind her head and one leg pushed to one side with her body slightly raised. It has been faintly tinted in flesh colours.

Other studio photographs of the Hatch and Henderson children taken by Dodgson were also tinted by hand to turn them into watercolours, adding more romantic and artistic locations. For example, an 1879 image of Annie Henderson lying naked on the grass reading a book was tinted and placed within a rural waterside setting, while another 1879 image, entitled *Evelyn Hatch as Gipsy sitting by Brook* shows her naked, sitting leaning against a tree, with one leg raised to cover part of her body. In 1877, Dodgson wrote to Mrs Hatch:

> 'You know the photo I did of Birdie, seated in a crouching attitude, side view, with one hand to her chin, in the days before she had learned to consider dress as *de rigour*? [sic] It was a gem the equal of which I have not much hope of doing again: and I should very much like, if possible, to get Miss Bond of Southsea (the best photographic colourist living, (*I* think) to colour a copy. But I am shy of asking her question, people have such different views, and it might be a shock to her feelings if I do so.'

46    The Dark Side of Alice in Wonderland

Mrs Hatch was asked to 'make an overture' to the mother of the child in question to see if it could be allowed.

Victorian society regarded young children as being totally innocent, and such innocence had to be preserved and revered. Often it depended on the age of children as to whether parents would allow photographs to be taken in the nude, or partially unclothed. This was linked to the issue of marriageability and the need to preserve a young woman's reputation.

In 1879, Dodgson wrote to the Mayhew family seeking permission to photograph their three children: Janet (7), Ethel (11), and Ruth (13). He wanted to photograph them unclothed. The Mayhew family were quite happy for Janet to be photographed in this way, but not Ethel or Ruth.

He then wrote a detailed letter to Mrs Mayhew requesting confirmation about the limitations being placed on clothing. He said:

'I should like to know *exactly* what is the minimum of dress I may take her [Janet] in, and I will strictly observe the limits. I hope that, at any rate, we may go as far as a pair of bathing-drawers, though for *my* part I should much prefer doing without, and shall be very glad if you say she may be done "in any way she likes herself"'

before adding what he regarded as a 'much more alarming request' to have the same permission to photograph Ethel.

Dodgson ended the letter saying:

'if I did not believe I could take such pictures without any lower motive than a pure love of Art, I would not ask it; and if thought there was any fear of its lessening *their* beautiful simplicity of character, I would not ask it.'

The next letter again stressed what he would like to achieve; as he tried to persuade the Mayhew's to agree to all his requests:

'First, the permission to go as far as bathing-drawers is very charming, as I presume it includes *Ethel* as well as Janet (otherwise there would be no meaning in bringing more than Janet) though I hardly dare hope that it includes *Ruth*. I can make some very charming groups of Ethel and Janet in bathing drawers, though

I cannot exaggerate how much better they would look without. Also the bathing-drawers would enable me to do a full front view of Ethel, which of course could not be done without them, but why should you object to my doing a *back* view of her without them? It would be a *perfectly* presentable picture, and far more artistic than with them. As to Janet, at her age they are surely unnecessary, whatever view were taken.'

The Mayhews continued to object to this and Dodgson then wrote saying that he had already discussed the potential photographs with the children and that Ethel had indicated she had no objections. He continued, 'Now don't crush all my hopes, by telling me that all that Mrs Mayhew said was merely a *façon* [sic] *de parler*, and that all the time you and Mrs Mayhew object absolutely to the thing, however much the children themselves would like it' before concluding, 'If the worst comes to the worst, and you won't concede any nudities at all, I think you ought to allow *all three* to be done in bathing-drawers, to make up for my disappointment!'

In a postscript he added,

> 'if Ruth and Ethel bring Janet, there is really no need for her [Mrs Mayhew] to come as well – that is if you can trust me to keep my promise of abiding strictly by the limits laid down. If you can't trust my word, then please never bring or send any of the children again.'

This request was quickly followed by another letter from Dodgson saying:

> 'After my last had gone, I wished to recall it and take out the sentence to which I had quite gratuitously suggested the possibility that you might be unwilling to trust me to photograph the children in undress. And now, I am more than ever sorry I wrote it … For I hope you won't think me very fanciful in saying I should have no pleasure in doing any such pictures now that I know I am only permitted such a privilege on condition of being under chaperonage. I had rather do no more pictures of your children except in full dress: please forgive all the trouble I have given you about it.'

## 48 The Dark Side of Alice in Wonderland

A meeting with Mrs Mayhew resulted in a final letter:

'The fact I have so unfortunately learnt, that you consider your presence *essential*, which is the same as saying "I cannot trust you," has taken away all the pleasure I could have in doing any such pictures, and most of my desire to photograph them again in any way. It is not pleasant to know that one is not trusted ... I cannot tell you how sorry I am for the annoyance I have caused you by starting so unlucky a topic.'

Many years later, Margaret Mayhew wrote a brief memoir recalling that:

'my mother raised no objection to my youngest sister, aged about six or seven, being photographed in the nude or in very scanty clothing ... but when permission was asked to photograph her older sister, who was probably about eleven, in a similar state, my mother's strict sense of Victorian propriety was shocked and she refused the request. Mr Dodgson was offended and the friendship ceased.'

Dodgson devoted a lot of attention to his photographic activities, and there have been suggestions that one point he even considered it as a career option. He purchased items of clothing for his sitters to wear and obtained appropriate props for his studio, asking his friend Mrs Kitchin to obtain 'items of female attire for his models, including stockings for young women'. On 10 March 1880, he asked Mrs Kitchin to buy him four sizes of 'young ladies bathing dresses' from a Mr Durrant in Ryde.

Later, he wrote concerning the non-arrival of these dresses saying:

'although I have accepted with all resignation the fact that Zie won't be taken in one, yet there are other damsels in the world, and it is quite possible that I would find one not averse to figure as an acrobat. I must, however, admit that it is less likely I shall find one as beautiful'.

Zie was the 16-year-old daughter of Mrs Kitchin.

On 2 June, he wrote 'the (acrobat) dresses look charming ... It is a pity Zie doesn't like them for a photo ... but ... I've found one young lady of 15 who will come and be done in it.'

Dodgson gave up photography in 1880 and made no more images. No one knows the reason why. He simply put his camera away and never took any further interest, telling friends that he no longer had any time for it. In 1885, he told his friend Gertrude Thomson that 'It is 3 or 4 years now since I have photographed – I have been too busy …' Changes in camera technology, with a move towards dry plate techniques may have contributed to his decision. Judging by his letter to Miss Thomson, dated 9 July 1893, he clearly felt that his familiar collodion method was no longer suitable as he said:

> 'If I had a dry plate camera, and time to work it, and could secure a child of really good figure, either a professional model, or (much better) a child of the upper classes, I would put her into every pretty attitude I could think of, and could get in a single morning 50 or 100 such memoranda.'

However, it is known that in that same year, his conduct was severely criticised by a Mrs Owen, the niece of the University Vice-chancellor. Dodgson had kissed her daughter Henrietta (Atty) Owen, believing that she was a child when she was actually 17 years old and of marriageable age. While kissing a child was acceptable, kissing a girl of marriageable age was most definitely not. He said that the girl had agreed, and sent an apology to her mother promising never to do this again. Mrs Owen was not placated, regarding the situation as being much more serious than Dodgson believed, and a series of angry letters followed. Peace was eventually negotiated via a mutual friend, Mrs Kitchin, who was asked to soothe Mrs Owen's feelings. According to Dodgson, Mrs Kitchin was asked to 'get her consent to forgive me and suggest Beatrice Hatch's mother might agree to share some photographs he had taken the previous summer in which "the style of dress" was "simple and unconventional"'.

In July 1880, Dodgson wrote that:

> 'I met Mr S. a few days ago and he looked like a thundercloud. I fear I am permanently in their black books now, not only by having given fresh offence – apparently – by asking to photograph Atty …… but also by the photos I have done of other people's children. Ladies tell me "people" condemn these photographs in strong language, and when I enquire more particularly, I find that "people" means Mrs Sidney Owen.'

50   The Dark Side of Alice in Wonderland

Judging by correspondence that took place the following year with an old friend, there must still have been some criticism being expressed within Oxford society. In June 1881, Dodgson wrote to Mrs Henderson saying:

'I write to ask if you would like to have any more copies of the full-front photographs of the children. I have 2 or 3 prints of each, but I intend to destroy all but one of each. That is all I want for myself, and (though I consider them perfectly innocent in themselves) there is really no friend to whom I should wish to give photographs which so entirely defy conventional rules. Miss Thomson is the only friend who has even seen them, and even to her I should not think of giving copies.'

A few days later, he was writing again to Mrs Henderson saying:

'If the remarks that have been made caused you any annoyance, I am indeed sorry to have (indirectly) caused them; otherwise for my part, I am not only indifferent to being thus gossiped about, but even regard it as being possibly useful as an advertisement!'

The next he wrote again:

'I would have been glad to hear from you (if you don't object to repeating it) what the terrible remark was which somebody made in Annie's hearing. Possibly it may be easier to write than to repeat viva voce. Her name I don't the least desire to know: I don't think it is good for one to know the name of anyone who has said anything against one. But it might be useful to know what is said – as a warning of the risk incurred by transgressing the conventional rules of Society.

'One thing I will add to the note I left – that your remark that you would even now, but for what has been said by others, have lent me Annie as a model, has gratified me nearly as much as if you were actually to do it. It is a mark of confidence which I sincerely value.'

Victorian society was becoming much more moralistic. Female servants were discouraged from having 'followers' and were required to follow strict codes of conduct. Many famous plays such as those of Shakespeare were cleansed of what was regarded as naughtiness and censored (or bowdlerised) with words deemed inappropriate for children or women removed. Although such censorship had been practised for much of the nineteenth century, it became a much stronger element. This was a time of religious morality, of evangelism, personal improvement and women were expected to do nothing that would affect the respectability of the family.

From this point onwards, Dodgson became increasingly careful with regard to his actions. He wrote to the mother of a 17-year-old girl in 1895 that, while he believed they were on 'kissing terms', if she thought it was better to simply shake hands, he would not be upset. Dodgson had always kissed children, regarding 'any child under twelve is kissable'. He dreaded the moment when he would have to greet a girl by shaking her hand or raising his hat, because this was a sign that she was no longer a child.

Biographer Jenny Woolf believes that:

'every scrap of evidence points to the idea that his little girls offered Carroll elements of the idealised romantic relationships he craved, but without the actual sex – and that was how he wanted it. The little girls who did not take to him – and some did find him boring, soppy or exasperating – never felt threatened. If any of them wanted to continue with him after they grew up – in the right pure spirit of course – then he felt blessed to receive sinless kisses and cuddles from real women. They had always to understand where the boundaries lay, and to him, they must always present themselves as sinless children.'

Dodgson certainly appreciated the beauty of the human form, especially that of children. He told his artist friend Gertrude Thomson that 'One hardly sees why the lovely forms of girls should ever be covered up!' On another occasion, he wrote to Gertrude Thomson saying, 'I confess I do not admire naked boys in pictures. They always seem … to need clothes, whereas one hardly sees why the lovely forms of girls should ever be covered up'. He later wrote, 'A girl of about 12 is my ideal beauty of form'.

After giving up photography, he started to sketch young children. In 1885, he completed four naked sketches of 5-year-old Lilian Henderson, writing that it was 'a new experience in Art' and that 'she has a charming little figure and was a very patient sitter'. On 12 April 1891, he wrote to

52　The Dark Side of Alice in Wonderland

Mrs Henderson, with whom he was again in sporadic contact after the earlier disagreements, saying:

> 'I've been drawing, in Mrs Shute's studio in London, 2 beautiful models, aged 16 and 14: but I'd far rather draw a child of 11 than any number of girls in their teens: the child form has a special loveliness of its own.'

By 1893, the situation had changed as he wrote to Gertrude saying:

> 'I wish no more drawings to be made, for me, of either Iris or Cynthia, naked. I find they are being brought up on a way which I consider injudicious and dangerous for their purity of mind, and I will do nothing which can add to the danger. It is a real sacrifice of inclination ... but if we are to follow the voice of conscience, we cannot always do what we should like!'

Despite this, he remained interested in the concept of drawing and photographing young children. On August 10, 1897, he wrote to Gertrude Thomson saying, 'Your description of the sands, and the naked children playing there, is very tempting ...' He considering visiting her to do some sketching, if Gertrude's landlady was able to provide accommodation saying:

> 'yet it is doubtful if I should not, after all, find I had come in vain – and that it was a hopeless quest to try to make friends with any of the little nudities. A lady might do it: but what would they think of a gentleman daring to address them! And then what an embarrassing thing it would be to begin an acquaintance with a naked little girl!'

As an alternative, he asked Gertrude Thomson if she had a camera, and whether she could make friends with some of these 'girl-fairies' and take photographs for him either as solo images or as group photographs. If she did that on his behalf, he would send each of the girls one of his books; and place under one of the photographs words from a poem by Sir Noel Patton:

> 'And there between the gleaming sands,
> Between the ripples and the rocks,
> Stood, mother-naked in the sun,
> A little maid with gleaming locks.'

Issues surrounding photography, what was acceptable and what was deemed indecent were becoming more apparent within society at this time. The Victorian assumption of children being sweet and asexual was coming under attack. Although psychology was in its infancy, many psychologists were already suggesting that children as young as 3 could display signs of sexual awareness. Deciding where to draw a dividing line was not always easy, as a study by Simon Popple on 'Photography, vice and the moral dilemma in Victorian Britain' indicated. Having studied criminal prosecutions for obscenity during the 1860s and 1870s, Popple pointed out that the case of Henry Evans, trapped by plainclothes policemen for selling obscene photographs actually made for the Ethnological Society, marked a distinct turning point in the relationship between photographers, artists and the law in relation to the question of photographic obscenity in mid to late Victorian Britain. Even images obtained through a respectable firm could be called into question. In 1879, bookseller Henry Evans was summoned before the Lord Mayor of London charged with having obscene photographs in his window showing representations of semi-nude Zulus.

Following the revelations of W.T. Stead in the *Pall Mall Gazette* concerning prostitution within 'The Maiden Tribute of Modern Babylon', there seems to have been an increase in the number of pornographic photographs available. A Leeds based publication, *Toby, The Yorkshire Tyke*, ran a feature entitled 'Literary Filth' soon after Stead's revelations. The feature claimed that:

'A perfect wave of immorality is sweeping over the land, and still the authorities do nothing to check it. On every side and at every corner, go where you will, you are, in Leeds at least, confronted by the sellers of these abominable prints. Further than this, inspired by the immunity from prosecution enjoyed by the sellers of disgusting literature, the vendors of indecent photographs have now entered the lists, and the latter contend with the former in spreading pestilence and corruption around. Urged to such a course by the revelations in a spirited Leeds contemporary, I the other day sought the handcart of a man who wheels around a conveyance about ostensibly selling the portraits of celebrities. Around the cart were gathered, amongst others, young girls, who were laughing in a brazen and loud manner. I soon discovered the cause of their mirth. Upon the cart were displayed photographs of the most lewd and immoral kind, a further description of which

## 54  The Dark Side of Alice in Wonderland

I dare not give under any circumstances. Suffice it that they were obscene in the extreme, and that they were being purchased at a penny each by young lads and girls … If such things as these are to be vended freely and without police interference in the streets, we might as well introduce Rabelais and Boccacio into our schools as reading books at once, for the nastiness contained in them is comparatively harmless when judged by the side of that being sold in Leeds.'

Although Charles Dodgson did not sell his photographs, there were people who were already making a living from what Victorians were describing as dubious photographic practices. Arthur Munby, a photographer creating a study of working women, noted in his diary of 22 March 1861 an encounter with a doorman while seeking a subject for photography. He wrote:

'As I gave the doorman a fee for his trouble, he remarked that he had "another young woman" close at hand – "a beautiful specimen". I asked what he meant; and by way of reply, he plunged into a public house next door and produced in a twinkling the damsel in question, who had evidently been in waiting: a tall pale faced girl in mourning of a fashionable make though somewhat shabby. He set her before me in the passage, adding by way of introduction "she's an envelope maker Sir – there's lots of 'em hereabouts". The girl looked quiet and modest; & what I was expected to do with her I could not conceive. I passed on therefore, simply telling her that she was not the sort of hardworking person whose portrait I wanted. The doorman came forward & whispered that he had brought her "to have a picture taken of her with her clothes up".'

Part of the problem regarding these child photographs, nude photographs and drawings relates to changing attitudes over the years. Dodgson's desire to photograph young children, and children in a state of undress has to be taken in the context of the society in which he lived. This was a period when suppression of sexuality was regarded as a Christian virtue. People could appreciate the beauty of the human body since this was God's handiwork, but to spoil it with thoughts of sex was sinful and to embrace the devil. Although reservations about nudity and nude photographs were emerging, many of the parents involved in the photographs saw no problems with their

Photo Alice   55

children being photographed nude or partially clothed. Such an attitude continued for many decades.

It was in the late twentieth century that attention really began to be focused on the issue of child photographs, in view of the increasing awareness and sensitivity regarding child abuse.

There have been fake photographs circulating, the most famous being that of an image of Charles Dodgson being kissed on the lips by a little girl. This image has been proved to be a forged photograph as having been created by splicing together two separate pictures. One picture is a self portrait of Carroll which was taken in 1857 with the aid of Ina Liddell who was responsible for taking off the lens cap in order to expose the image. The second photograph has been proved to be a fragment of a photograph known as 'Open your mouth and shut your eyes'.

The association between *Alice in Wonderland* and child pornography was made worse by the activities of a global pornography ring broken up by an international police operation in 1998. Named after *Alice in Wonderland*, the Wonderland Club had started in America and grew rapidly due to the availability of the internet. It was described as 'an international network of paedophiles involving the rape of boys and girls live on camera and the traffic in images of the torture of children as young as two months.'

When the ring was initially discovered in America, the police investigators continued the *Alice in Wonderland* theme by setting up Operation Cheshire Cat. In the UK, it was referred to as Operation Cathedral, and ultimately involved thirteen other police forces worldwide.

The resulting prosecutions attracted massive publicity, underlining still further the public perception of links with Dodgson as a repressed paedophile, and the idea of *Alice in Wonderland* as having the potential for a slightly erotic aspect.

*Chapter 5*

# Lolita Alice

"'What do you mean by that?" said the Caterpillar, sternly.
"Explain yourself!"
"I can't explain myself, I'm afraid, Sir," said Alice, "because I am
not myself, you see."'

*Alice in Wonderland*

Told from the perspective of a young girl falling into a world where anything can happen, *Alice in Wonderland* is a story that has attracted attention worldwide. It has been translated into 174 languages, and is particularly popular in Japan, where the story has been enjoyed since 1899 when it was serialised in a children's magazine. Since then, the novels have been translated into Japanese by countless authors including Akutagawa Ryūnosuke and Mishima Yukio, together with illustrations by acclaimed Japanese artists such as Kusama Yukio. So popular has the story become that it has led to a vast range of art work, film, food and forms a key element within a major sub culture – that of Kansaii. Yet this sheer popularity has also led to a cultural collision between East and West regarding the Alice concept.

The situation is summed up in just one word – Lolita. Depending on your cultural viewpoint it can represent innocence and cuteness, a specific type of clothing and outlook – or something very much darker in the form of sex and paedophile fantasies, even pornography in which Lolita is self-assertively sexualised. It has even led to the Victoria & Albert Museum being warned about encouraging the sexualisation of children in its plans for an exhibition on *Alice in Wonderland*. Simply typing in a Google search for Lolita brings up an immediate warning about the illegality of child pornography. So how did these conflicting viewpoints arise?

Japan was one of the first countries worldwide to translate the Alice stories. The fantastical creatures and use of a little girl as the main character immediately resonated with links to Japanese mythology and legends. Japanese readers were all too familiar with a world of shadowy supernatural shapeshifting creatures and inanimate objects such as Yokai, Obake, Yurei and Oni that clearly paralleled Alice's world. The Cheshire Cat, for example, immediately stood out since it could appear and disappear at will, just like the Japanese shapeshifting Nekomata and Bakeneko cat Yokai. The White Rabbit, the March Hare and the Caterpillar also possess similar blends of earthbound and supernatural characters common to Yokai legends.

The popularity of *Alice in Wonderland* within Japan has continued unabated ever since that first translation. There have been over 1,270 different editions of the book, and countless variations on the story by Japanese authors, especially within manga and anime, which are very popular types of Japanese media which have steadily gained popularity elsewhere in the world. Manga refers to a style of comic books and graphic novels read by both adults and children, while anime is a form of film animation. Both manga and anime utilise *Alice in Wonderland* themes and concepts whether in the format of the original stories, as spin offs or as source material, for example, the best-selling Ouran High School Host Club series contains a standalone book entitled *Haruhi in Wonderland*. In the story, Haruhi's dream about entering Ouran High School becomes an illusionary *Alice in Wonderland* fantasy in which other members of the Ouran High School take on roles of characters from the story, while Haruhi is Alice. To take another example of the genre, *Code Geass* is an anime with a storyline called *Nunnally in Wonderland* in which the main character seeks to make his sister happy by using his power to hypnotise other characters into believing they have become characters from *Alice in Wonderland*, with his sister becoming Alice.

The *Alice in Wonderland* theme formed a prominent part of the 2019 British Museum Citi Manga exhibition, a unique exhibition containing the largest collection of Manga ever seen outside Japan. Entering the exhibition, visitors immediately saw a small digital print display relating to *Alice's Adventures in Wonderland*, including several Japanese versions. This was designed to show how a universally popular story can be adapted by manga enthusiasts in many different ways. Visitors then entered what the exhibition described as a 'conceptual rabbit hole and journeys through six thematic sections, accompanied by the exhibition's bespoke mascot avatar, a plucky white rabbit named Mimi-chan'.

Writing in the exhibition catalogue, Amanda Kennell commented that:

'Manga, arguably the premier medium of modern Japanese culture, has produced Alice adaptations of startling ingenuity and

58  The Dark Side of Alice in Wonderland

beauty …That's not to say that you see the same story repeated over and over again; the meaning of Alice can change drastically from creator to creator and manga to manga. Later artists have built on the work of their predecessors to create a wider world of Alice in Wonderland symbolism in Japan today.'

As examples of this she highlights the work of several artists:

'Matsumoto Katsuji's *Alice in Wonderland* Fushigi no kuni no Arisu 1960) is clearly influenced by the large eyes and softly curved lines of Walt Disney's animated *Alice in Wonderland* film. Other Alice adaptations' sources of influence are far less obvious. Take for instance, the March Hare Tea Party Club and their *Alice Book I* and *Alice book II* 1991. With the direct reference to Carroll's Mad Hatter's tea party in the group's name and to Alice herself in the titles, you might assume that these two anthologies were full of Alice in Wonderland manga, but you would be wrong: neither Alice nor Wonderland ever appear in either *Alice I* or *Alice II*.'

The reasons for this lie in the attempts by Japanese female authors and illustrators led by Takemiya Keiko to create a role for themselves as editors and creators since almost all manga books were being commissioned by men.

Amanda Kennell explains how Alice in Wonderland was used as a symbol of freedom for female artists:

'In 1991, Takemiya and a group of her fellow female artists, chafing at the restraints imposed by their editors, created the March Hare Tea Party Club for the express purpose of publishing works that they could not get their editors to green-light. For these artists, Alice functioned as a symbol of a free-wheeling Wonderland where women did not have to submit to male oversight, rather than as the story of one specific young girl.'

Within a few years, another female collective created a very different view of Alice, publishing a book entitled *Miyukichan in the Wonderland*. The storyline follows a poor girl named Miyuki through a Wonderland that is inhabited by lesbians keen to attract the pretty Miyuki, who spends all her time trying to escape Wonderland. Further nods to the traditional

Alice story are provided throughout the story, such as when Miyuki falls into Wonderland through a cloud of rabbits cascading around her amid a kaleidoscope of black and white checks.

Over the decades, the appeal of Wonderland has grown steadily in all forms of the media and Japanese lifestyle. Michelle J. Smith, one of the curators of the Australian Centre for the Moving Image 2018 exhibition on Wonderland explains:

> 'Alice is highly symbolic. Alice's ambiguous nature means we have put her to use to express innumerable hopes and fears. In popular music she has been used to celebrate individuality, embody female sexuality, and, as a metaphor for the search for creative inspiration. In Japan, Alice maps perfectly onto the idealised figure of the "shojo" or girl, who occupies the space between child and adult.'

The shojo is sweet, innocent and devoid of sexuality, a character summed up in the Japanese concept of kawaii (cuteness). Alice became the perfect icon for the shojo, due to the image of eternal innocence and beauty that it evokes. Linked into the world of the shojo is a fashion subculture known as the Sweet Lolita style which began to appear around the 1970s and quickly became evident within street fashion. This style is highly influenced by Victorian and Edwardian children's clothing, creating a cute, sweet appearance with demure, elegant shapes. The emphasis is on doll like perfection. Girls tend to wear costumes involving pretty dresses, often in blue or pink, with white aprons, Peter Pan style collars, white knee or ankle socks often adorned with delicate patterns of hearts or cherries, Mary Jane style shoes. Hair is left loose, or confined by plaits, ribbons, bows and head bands. The skirts are often flounced, A-line or bell shaped and sometimes the girls wear Victorian style drawers underneath their petticoats. Outfits are often adorned with lace, and details such as fairy tale characters, crowns and sweet food such as cakes and ice cream, and accessorised with bonnets and lacy caps, hairclips shaped as teapots or slices of cake, as well as matching bags and parasols. Sometimes the dresses are adorned with Alice inspired images such as scenes from the Mad Hatter's tea party, musical notes, the Cheshire Cat, hearts, chess scenes, clocks and watches, or flowers such as roses.

There are variations on the classical Lolita style. Gothic Lolita is a much darker style, favouring black and dark colours, with exaggerated make-up. Although there is some resemblance to western Goth and punk styles, Gothic Lolitas never wear ripped or dirty clothing, nor do they wear second-hand items. Elegance, neatness and smartness are a priority, often with long sleeved Victorian/Edwardian style dresses or blouses with some frills. Corsets are often worn as part of the outfit but are far less frilly than in the Sweet Lolita style. Typical motifs include keys and crosses. Classic Lolita is very refined, with an emphasis on jewel tones, while Country Lolita style is a cross between *Alice in Wonderland* and the American children's story, *Little House on the Prairie* with its use of gingham, plaids and checks. There is also a Schoolgirl Lolita style dominated by sailor dresses, long sleeved or cap sleeved blouses, short pleated or plaid skirts.

There are matching male versions of each style albeit using different names such as Kodona, which is a dandy look incorporating bowler hats, velvet waistcoats, frilly shirts, corduroy pantaloons or trousers that end at the knee or just above the ankle, socks with brogues or velvet slippers often embroidered with fantastic designs.

The concept has led to a merger of Japanese fascination with the styles of Victorian England and the modern genres of manga and anime, affecting not just female characters but also cartoon characters such as Hello Kitty who experience adventures in wonderland. Characters often wear Lolita style clothing, particularly Schoolgirl, Classic, Sweet or Gothic style.

The Lolita/Alice style has expanded into all aspects of everyday life in Japan. Not only are there Lolita clothing styles, but also accessories, books, films and restaurants. Many Japanese cities including Tokyo, Nagoya and Osaka contain numerous *Alice in Wonderland* themed restaurants such as Alice in a Labyrinth, containing playing card accents on tables, walls and ceiling while even the food is themed with ragout pasta made to resemble the Cheshire Cat, while at the restaurant known as Alice in an Old Castle, there are private booths designed to resemble hedges, and diners can enjoy White Rabbit inspired pasta complete with red cabbage leaves for ears.

In the late 1990s, the Harajuku Bridge (Jingu Bashi) in Tokyo became the main meeting place where young people dressed in all types of Lolita style clothing could meet up.

At the same time, interest and awareness of Lolita fashion along with the popularity of anime and manga spread globally, particularly with the rise of ComicCons and the use of Cosplay (costume play) in which participants dress up as their favourite characters from anime, manga books, films or gaming character. The Japanese publisher Tokyopop even began publishing *The Gothic & Lolita Bible* of street fashion, which has since been translated into English and is sold widely within the English-speaking world.

Lolita style fashion is now sold worldwide, with followers of this style of clothing to be found in most countries around the globe. In Thailand, jewellery manufacturer Beauty Gems transformed an old warehouse into an imaginary Alice in the Diamond Land event, involving models wearing *Alice in Wonderland*-themed clothing.

Even the Japanese government has become involved. In 2009, the Ministry of Foreign Affairs appointed models to spread Japanese culture. These models were awarded the tile of Kawaa Taishi – ambassadors of cuteness. One of those models was Misako Aoki, representing the Lolita style of frills and lace. Tourists visiting Japan are encouraged to explore the Harajuku Walk as a way of discovering the city's fashion hub and cute Kawaii fashion such as the Lolita style, by strolling through key fashion areas such as Cat Street, Omotesando Dori and Takeshita Dori involving numerous winding streets and alleyways.

Back in the West, a very different view of Lolita has emerged. In 1925. writer Valdimir Nabokov translated *Alice's Adventures in Wonderland* into Russian. Discovering the world of Wonderland fascinated him, along with the story of Alice and Lewis Carroll. So strong was the influence that it led him to write his own novel, a story that has also become a literary classic. Initially published in France during 1955, it became an underground literary sensation even though some described it as being scandalous trash. Attracted by the increasing acclaim for the book, an American edition was eventually published three years later and became a best seller.

Often described as an erotic novel, *Lolita* tells the story of how Humbert Humbert, a tutor in his mid-thirties, seduces a 12-year-old child Dolores (also known as Lolita), using his gift of spinning spellbinding stories. As with the *Alice in Wonderland* stories, there are lots of puns and word games but the book is much darker in content, focusing on the themes of sex and desire. Humbert is obsessed with Lolita, and even though he marries her mother, he regards this as a way of enabling him to remain in contact with Dolores/Lolita. He writes about his paedophiliac longings in his journal which is found by Lolita's mother. Although he denies everything, she is determined to leave him and storms out of the house, only to be fatally hit by a car. Lolita learns to manipulate him and his desires. Having lost

62 The Dark Side of Alice in Wonderland

Lolita to a stalker named Quilty, Humber remains obsessed with sexually aware young girls, whom he describes as nymphets. Humbert eventually finds Lolita again, pregnant and living in poverty. Quilty had ended the relationship when she had refused to take part in a child pornography orgy. Humbert murders Quilty and is arrested and jailed. Lolita dies in childbirth. After Humbert's death, his journals and memoir are sent to a publisher, John Ray Jr. PhD. Humbert's manuscript is entitled *Lolita, or the Confession of a White Widowed Male*. In publishing it, Ray states that although Humbert's actions are despicable, he believes that the story will become a favourite in psychiatric circles while encouraging parents to raise better children in a better world.

Lolita has been turned into a play staged on New York's Broadway, and has twice been adapted for film, each time attracting controversy due to its sex scenes and identification with paedophilia. Producer Stanley Kubrick created the first version in 1962, which incorporated a slightly comic element with lots of innuendo compared to the much darker 1997 version which was much closer to the actual text of the novel. Screenwriter Stephen Schiff commented:

> 'Right from the beginning, it was clear to all of us that this movie was not a "remake" of Kubrick's film. Rather, we were out to make a new adaptation of a very great novel. Some of the filmmakers involved actually looked upon the Kubrick version as a kind of "what not to do".'

The 1997 version resulted in considerable controversy due to the sex scenes between an adult male (played by Jeremy Irons) and his underage co-star played by Dominque Swain. Premiered in Europe, it was initially difficult to find an American distributor, while in Australia its controversial nature resulted in the theatrical release being delayed until April 1999. Reviews were mixed. Writing in *RealViews*, reviewer James Berardinelli said:

> '*Lolita* is not a sex film, it's about characters, relationships, and the consequences of imprudent actions. And those who seek to brand the picture as immoral have missed the point. Both Humbert and Lolita are eventually destroyed – what could be more moral? The only real controversy I can see surrounding this film is why there was ever a controversy in the first place.'

While Charles Taylor, writing in *Salon* says

> 'For all their vaunted (and, it turns out, false) fidelity to Nabokov, Lyne and Schiff have made a pretty, gauzy *Lolita* that replaces the book's cruelty and comedy with manufactured lyricism and mopey romanticism.'

Nabokov openly acknowledged that *Lolita* was inspired by the Alice stories commenting, 'I always call him Lewis Carroll Carroll, because he was the first Humbert Humbert'. There are numerous references to the Alice stories throughout Nabokov's *Lolita* such as pig-fig talk on the porch of the Enchanted Hunters Hotel before Humbert Humbert spends his first night with Lolita. Towards the end of the book, Lolita comments, 'Well, everybody knew he liked young girls. He used to film 'em, over in his mansion ... film the whole thing.'

As a result of Nabokov's work and the resultant films, the term 'Lolita' has become assimilated into the English language as a word to describe a sexually precocious young girl. Over the years, there have been numerous pornographic magazines published such as *Randy Lolitas* and *Lollitots*. In the Netherlands, Joop Wilhelmus published a magazine entitled *Lolita* for seventeen years before being closed by the authorities in 1984. The content of the magazine was extremely explicit and included editorial pleas for child pornography to publish. Wilhelmus wrote to his readers, 'This magazine can only exist if you help us! Send us photos from your collection'. It also operated a contact service resulting in adverts such as 'English gentleman ... paedophile ... wishes to meet a mother with Lolita daughter or lady'. As Ian O'Donnell and Clare Milner point out in their 2012 study *Child Pornography, Crime, Computers and Society*, 'Like the *Lolita* film series, Wilhelmus's *Lolita* magazine became an almost universal brand name for child pornography images'. Most recently, financier Jeffrey Epstein hit the headlines when it was discovered that he was a serial rapist and paedophile. His young harem was often taken via his private plane to his private island in the US Virgin Islands or to his New Mexico ranch. Local people seeing the number of young women being transported on the plane eventually nicknamed it the Lolita Express. In the ensuing investigations, many women said they had been assaulted during underage sex parties held on the plush, purpose-built Lolita Express which incorporated deluxe furnishings with queen size bed, padded floors and velvet sofas.

# 64   The Dark Side of Alice in Wonderland

Attention has continued to focus on the concept of Lolita due to the increasing awareness of the issues of child abuse from the latter part of the twentieth century onwards. In 2006, Meenkshi Gigi Durham wrote a book entitled *The Lolita Effect: the Media Sexualisation of Young Girls and What We Can Do About it*. She pointed out that the term Lolita now extends to include young girls who exploring their own sexuality in terms of clothing and makeup, and not just sexual behaviour. The Lolita Effect is used to refer to the blame that young girls can face for any involvement in abuse or harassment.

The presence of this alternative version of the word Lolita horrified and disgusted Japanese Kwaii Lolitas when its existence became known.

Confusion over opposing views of the term have continued ever since. In a world of global media, with manga, anime and cosplay becoming common worldwide, the two viewpoints often conflict. A popular Japanese girl band pop group, Oh My Girl, experienced online criticism because they were filmed wearing Lolita style clothing such as short high-waisted style school skirts and sailor tops with long white socks; Gothic Lolita short plaid skirts, black jackets, bows and white blouses or babydoll style Sweet Lolita. In other cases, such as that of girl group Stellar or the singer Sull, their photographic marketing imagery in which they wore Lolita-style clothing was much more akin a more seductive, sexy approach with hints of a Western usage of the Lolita term.

There are films available worldwide such as Mari Terashima's *Alice in the Underworld: the Dark Märchen Show!!* (2009) based on Tetsua Nakashima's *Kamikaze Girls* manga series. The film takes viewers through a world in which *Alice in Wonderland*-style almost seems to collide with the Goth style Addams family involving the activities of the Osaka based troupe Rosa de Reficul et Guiggles, who create elaborate Victoriana style events within a fashion aesthetic based on the Lolita subculture. The film is an almost macabre trip down the rabbit hole, with lots of living tableaux relating to the *Alice in Wonderland* story together with a cut out technique stressing the darker side of Victorian life and Nabukovian associations of the word Lolita complete with scenes of child abuse and exploitation. At one point in the film, Alice comments, 'I am already an old woman, yet physically I remain a child. Children around me have all grown up, yet I am left alone.'

In 2019, Jim Gamble, a founder of the Child Exploitation and Online Protection Centre, attacked the decision of the Victoria & Albert Museum to focus part of its 2021 *Alice: Curiouser & Curiouser* exhibition on Japanese

Lolita Fashion. He suggested that all visitors should be warned about it, commenting that:

> '... although there was nothing wrong with the fashion itself, which involves dressing up in stylised feminine clothing, people who searched online for the term would find pornographic content. Any paedophile who reads about this, it won't be too long before they say, "I was just reading about Japanese Lolita fashion".'

The term 'Lolita' has clearly become one of the most confused images of the twentieth and twenty first centuries. The potential for confusion and conflict is set to continue unabated.

*Chapter 6*

# X-Rated & Banned Alice

'I'm afraid I can't explain myself, sir. Because I am not myself, you see?'

*Alice in Wonderland*

There are very few children's books that have such a chequered history as *Alice in Wonderland*. Ever since it was published, it has been a story that has attracted criticism for its content and its author. Such criticisms have grown over the years, partly the result of changing social views and norms. At the time of publication, many Victorians felt that the storyline was just too complicated for children and that it was more suited to adults. There were too many puns and there were fears that the content was subversive and inappropriate. Lewis Carroll was even felt to be satirising the political system of the period, with comparisons being made between characters in the book and political and cultural figures. There have been suggestions that Gladstone was the model for the Unicorn, Disraeli as the pathetic lizard Bill, while Tweedledee and Tweedledum were modelled on the poet Tennyson's spoilt children Lionel and Hallam. The chaotic court scenes have been compared to the shambolic legal system of the day.

A key reason why the book has always attracted criticism is the anarchic, topsy-turvy world it portrays. For many Victorian families, it simply created a world at odds with respectability. Film portrayals have picked this up. In Tim Burton's *Alice in Wonderland* film (2010) Alice is shown refusing to adopt conventional norms by rejecting the suitor found for her by her mother and preferring to strike out independently by going off on a boat to China.

More than this, however, the story of *Alice in Wonderland* has been banned from publication in China and in certain states of the USA, as well as proving a mine of stories and images for pornographers.

In 1931, the Imperial authorities in China decided that *Alice in Wonderland* and *Alice Through the Looking Glass* were inappropriate reading matter. The decision was taken by Chinese censors and focused on the way in which animals within the stories were portrayed using human language. The decision was made by General Ho Chien, a government censor located within the Chinese province of Hunan. He believed that such a portrayal was 'disastrous' for children and 'insulting' to humans. Talking animals were seen as an abomination.

By the time General Ho Chien imposed the ban, *Alice in Wonderland* was already a popular story within China, with many readers regarding it as offering satirical and political insights into Chinese life – a factor which may have had some influence on General Ho Chien's decision. In 1922, Zhao Yuanren – a keen participant in the Chinese New Literature movement – published the first vernacular Chinese version. In his preface, he wrote that the main reason why it had not been attempted before was the difficulties of translating Dodgson's play on words as well as his nonsense poems.

The book was a major success, with reviewer Zhou Zuoren stating that the book was essential reading for adults as well as children commenting that 'too many adults, who were once children themselves, lost their child-heart, just as caterpillars have transformed into butterflies, [the former and latter becoming] completely different stages'.

Writing in a Pennsylvania State University doctoral dissertation, 'The Nation's Child: Childhood, Children's Literature and National Identity in Modern China', author Xu Xu asserted that 'Carroll's Alice book … became a national text in the Chinese context. It was intended for the Chinese people, including both children and adults, who were being forged into a modern citizenry'.

Yet another writer, Shen Congwen, created a spin off story entitled *Alice's Adventures in China*. Published in 1928, this story showed Alice and the White Rabbit travelling around China encountering all kinds of scary and strange things such as talking waterwheels, while satirising the superstition and darkness to be found in 1920s Chinese society.

Three years later, one of the most famous of all modern Chinese authors, Chen Bochui, issued a book entitled *Miss Alice*. The book incorporated a dream structure during which Alice has adventures within an animal kingdom. *Miss Alice* contains numerous political overtones highlighting contradictions and conflicts between social groups, as well as political events such as the 18 September incident during which Japan occupied Manchuria, establishing a puppet state headed by the former emperor of China. The 18 September event took place while Chen Bochui was actually writing the final chapters of *Miss Alice*. Bochui later wrote that it made him

68    The Dark Side of Alice in Wonderland

turn Alice from a 'normal and healthy everyday girl' into a 'fearless little soldier resisting violence'. Alice becomes a member of the working class, resisting exploitation in any form.

Chen Bochui's portrayal of Alice marked a major landmark in the transformation of Chinese society and the move towards Maoism. This was quite a notable move, since Bochui is often referred to as 'the Andersen of the East' becoming one of the founding fathers of Chinese children's literature and influencing generations of children.

Over the decades, there have been many other translations of *Alice in Wonderland* into Chinese, such as the version created over a twenty-year period by Taiwan-based writer Zhang Hua. Ren Chao's version became a classic. Ren Chao also translated *Through the Looking Glass*. His first version did hit unexpected problems, as he explained on a postcard to a friend in Shanghai sent on 2 February 1932. Only days before the Shanghai incident had taken place, the Japanese had bombed the city, destroying the headquarters of Ren Chao's publisher, the Commercial Press. He noted, 'I have corrected half of the proofs of my translation of *Through the Looking Glass*. I think the whole thing has been burned up along with everything else at the Paoshan Road office of the Commercial Press.' The completed translation was eventually published in 1969.

*Alice in Wonderland* is a story that has always generated mixed feelings within the USA. Although widely read and recognised as a major piece of literature and the subject of many highly successful films including Walt Disney's iconic animated *Alice in Wonderland*, not everyone has welcomed the story. From a very early point in its history, *Alice in Wonderland* has been greeted with suspicion becoming the subject of various local bans.

In 1900, the governors of Woodsville High School at Haverhill, New Hampshire, decided to ban the book from use within the classroom. Other public schools followed suit. The reasons for the ban were stated to be that the book 'contained expletives, sexual content, derogatory characterisations of teachers and of religious ceremonies'. There were also allegations that it promoted masturbation and sexual fantasies, linking to unease over the author's lifestyle particularly with regard to his child friends and child photography.

Further local bans appeared in the 1960s, when there were suggestions that the story of *Alice in Wonderland* encouraged the use of drugs, with illustrations reflecting images common to psychedelic 'trippy' drugs like LSD and Magic Mushrooms. Opponents to the books referred to the way in which characters were shown using drugs and having hallucinations. This became an oft-heard complaint especially after Walt Disney's animated version appeared in the cinemas. Among the scenes from the story that came under attack was that of the caterpillar smoking a hookah on top of a mushroom. Many American psychiatrists also focused on the character of the Mad Hatter since he had a card in his hat reading 10/6. The problem was that the figure was sometimes written as l/s/d. Although this refers to the English pre-decimal coinage of £/s/d (pounds, shillings and pence), it could easily be misread as LSD.

From the latter part of the twentieth century, *Alice in Wonderland* and *Through the Looking Glass* have been increasingly used for pornographic purposes. As researcher Anna Kérchy points out in her book *Alice in Transmedia Wonderland: Curiouser and Curiouser* (2016), the 'domain gradually gives rise to a whole "Alice Industry" and … a twentieth first century shift in the way Alice is represented to create erotic overtones'. Even the idea of Wonderland has been taken on board by manufacturers of sexual products creating ranges of Wonderland sex toys, illustrating them with Alice related imagery and wording. A typical example taken from the internet reads 'Are you an *Alice in Wonderland* fan? If you are, you NEED the Wonderland Sex Toy Range by Doc Johnson in your life'. The range includes vibrators and massagers with titles such as the White Rabbit Massager Sex Toy and the Kinky Kat Sex Toy. The latter is described in the advertising blurb as 'The Cheshire Cat is a favourite character for many who have read *Alice's Adventures in Wonderland* books or see the magical movies. You'll be grinning like a Cheshire Cat when you get your hands on this the Kinky Kat Silicone Vibrator'.

The reasons for the popularity of *Alice in Wonderland* on a sexual basis are not hard to find. Fantasy forms a key element within pornographic films, making *Alice in Wonderland* an ideal subject choice in view of its instantly recognisable characters and fantastical elements. Wonderland is quite simply a place where rules can be broken. One such movie, *Alice in Bondageland*, actually has Alice specifically stating this saying 'that's the whole point of Wonderland, that all rules must be broken'. As a result, this is a story line with instant appeal for pornographers, providing a vast range of potential ideas which can be delivered at different levels whether it is soft or hard porn.

As Laura Helen Marks points out in her book: *Alice in Pornoland: Hardcore Encounters with the Victorian Gothic* (University of Illinois Press):

'There is a contradiction in the way pornographers have adapted Alice: while hardcore adaptations of the Alice stories claim to

70   The Dark Side of Alice in Wonderland

reveal an inherent sexual quality to the stories, part of the appeal of adapting a children's fairy story is also, as Jason Williams, production manager of *Alice in Wonderland: A XXX Musical*, described the film in *The Rialto Report* as, "I thought it would be a good idea to have the polarity, the contrast. Contrast is interesting and gets your attention. Our job is to entertain, and any time we have a person's attention we are entertaining."'

As a result, *Alice in Wonderland* has formed the basis for numerous pornographic films. It is impossible to say just how many such films have been made, as there are few researchers willing to sift through the mass of pornographic videos that have been produced in order to identify them.

Whatever the film, the traditional storyline is always very loosely interpreted. One such example is *Through the Looking Glass*, which was made in 1976. This film portrayed a middle-aged woman rediscovering herself after being lured for sex by a demon living in a mirror world. While *Miyuki-chan in Wonderland* (1993) was a Japanese anime film adapted from an existing manga novel which comprised an erotic lesbian version of *Alice in Wonderland*.

By far the most popular – and widely distributed – film within this category was the 1976 US porn musical *Alice in Wonderland: A XXX Musical* starring Kristine DeBell (a former Playboy playmate). Other key stars were Gela Nash and Bucky Searles (who also wrote the screenplay under the name B. Anthony Fredericks). Produced during the golden age of US porn, it was elaborately produced with props and costumes to create an interior world even though overall costs were kept to a minimum by shooting almost all scenes outside.

Within the film, Alice is portrayed as a cheerful, outgoing, friendly virginal librarian who dresses younger than her actual age. She refuses her suitor William because he has different ideas as to what is suitable behaviour. Alice is described as a 'prude'. Following her rejection of William, Alice begins to daydream. A White Rabbit taps her on the shoulder and runs off. She immediately begins to follow the White Rabbit and enters the world of Wonderland where animals and people introduce her to previously forbidden pleasures and activities. Eventually she meets the Red Queen and decides that Wonderland is not for her and returns to her own world and William.

Typical scenes within the film included seduction, lesbian sex, sex in the open air and examples of fellatio. At one point, Alice drinks a potion that makes her shrink – but her dress remains the same size. Alice finds herself naked and is given a very revealing dress by the Wonderland characters. Within the script, phrases are often given dual meanings such as the King of Hearts stating, 'may my rod and staff comfort thee'. The Mad Hatter wears a hat with a note saying 9⅞, referring to the size of his 'thingamajig' before he opens his coat and exposes himself to a half-naked Alice sitting in a semi-erotic pose on a toadstool.

It was said that Kristine DeBell didn't have to act too much, 'just be incredulous and open'. DeBell added that the nudity 'didn't bother me a bit. It's like, they're paying me to stand there naked. I'm getting paid.'

Production manager Jason Williams comments:

> 'It was initially going to be hardcore – and the idea was to have the contrast of a film that was hardcore one minute and then funny, light and musical the next. But when we got up to the location and started filming, the vision for the film rapidly started expanding. We had these big sets, elaborate design, and we had this big opportunity. So we had this relatively short shooting schedule and we didn't have much time to go in and do a lot of close-up stuff that you need for hardcore. There was too much work just to film the scenes, so we mostly got wide shots which don't really work in a hardcore film as you can't really see what's going on.'

Sufficient to say that this has been described as one of the most successful pornographic films of all time, grossing nearly $100m at the box office when it was first distributed by 20th Century Fox. Reviewers described it as 'psychosexual terror'. It was marketed as 'the world's favourite bed-time story is finally a bed-time story', using posters showing a half-naked Alice erotically sitting on a toadstool with the Mad Hatter opening his coat, and exposing himself to her, while film trailers stressed that 'this is an X rated musical – but it's not for kids. It's a bedtime story – but it's not for kids'.

The film also aroused considerable controversy. On 21 October 21 1976, the Kingston newspaper in the USA reported:

> 'The producer of an x-rated film has been threatened with a lawsuit for using a state historical site, the Olana mansion, as a backdrop for his movie. Lawyers for the Taconic Park Commission have said that despite a prohibition against filming on the grounds of state

72    The Dark Side of Alice in Wonderland

parks or historical sites without special prior consent, producer Bill Osco used the stately Moorish castle as a background for his film, *Alice in Wonderland*.'

According to Linda McLean, curator of the former home of Hudson Valley artist Frederick Church, only educational companies are given permission to film at the historical site, adding 'certainly not a film like *Alice in Wonderland*'.

There was also a question of money. The film proved extremely profitable, but no-one saw any money. Production manager Jason Williams told *The Rialto Report*:

'Bill ended up hiding everything. He'd tell everybody that the profits were tied up, they were here or there, he had to get it, it was this or that ... but no one could ever get any details. Then Osco just stopped paying anybody anything.

'Meanwhile, he brought a house on Sunset Boulevard that was on four or five acres of land. It was a huge estate ... it had a big enough front-yard to play football on the damn thing. It must be worth $25 or $30 million now.

'He was deeply delusional ... he actually thought that he'd done everything ... In terms of producing anything to do with the films, he delivered nothing. Zero. But he got credit for everything which was pretty incredible.'

As a result of the legal dispute, Osco lost all the rights to the distributors, Kaleidoscope, who placed the negatives in a vault. Some time later, Osco arranged for the negatives to be stolen and released the movie all over again, as a hard core version using extra material that had not been used in the first version using the phrase 'We forgot to add this in'.

For Kristine DeBell it became something of a nightmare. With the arrival of the internet, a child from her son's school Googled the film and subsequently tormented her children. DeBell and her family were forced to move to another state, and she used only her married name in future.

In 2007, Osco expanded his involvement with the *Alice in Wonderland* theme, by writing a book for an Off-Broadway musical version that was staged at the Kirk Theatre, New York City. The show was entitled *Alice in Wonderland: An Adult Musical Comedy* and was set in a trailer park in Weehawken, New Jersey. The posters for the show stressed it was 'For Mature Audiences Only'.

In 2011, filmmaker Ken Russell (best known for his film *A Clockwork Orange*) died while working on an extremely raunchy musical version of *Alice in Wonderland* based on the 1976 adaptation. He had nearly finished what the producers described as a bawdy musical comedy, using a musical score by British composer Simon Boswell. The *Guardian* newspaper reported Simon Boswell as saying, 'it was in many ways a perfect Ken Russell film – raunchy and funny. *Alice in Wonderland* is almost his perfect vehicle, with sexual freakery and religious aspects'. He then went on to say, 'I think that mixture of Catholicism and blasphemy is what tickled Ken'.

Other erotic versions of *Alice in Wonderland* have included a trailer for a later abandoned film *Phantasmagoria: The Visions of Lewis Carroll*. The trailer was made by Marilyn Manson and included a topless female Tweedledum and Tweedledee. In 1977 French director, Claude Chabrol created *Alice or the Last Escapade*, which starred Sylvia Krystal, who had previously starred in the soft porn film series *Emmanuelle*.

The actual characters within *Alice in Wonderland* and *Through the Looking Glass* are equally attractive to pornographers. There are two characters which particularly lend themselves to pornographic interpretations; cute, sweet little girl Alice and the imperious, dominatrix Queen of Hearts, who is also sometimes referred to as the Red Queen by pornographers.

Laura Helen Marks, author of *Alice in Pornoland*, states:

'In the case of Alice, pornographers seem drawn to interrogating a perceived Victorian paternal control of the female protagonist. In response to this perceived paternalism, a handful of hardcore adaptations explicitly Gothicize the tales, such as *Through the Looking Glass* (1976), *Tormented* (2009) and *Malice in Lalaland* (2012). These films situate Alice as an unwilling pawn in a masculine world populated by abusive patriarchs. In the first film, the protagonist, Catherine, is haunted by the incestuous abuse she suffered at the hands of her father and is gradually sucked by a demon (in the shape of her father) into a Looking Glass hell. In *Tormented* and *Malice in Lalaland*, Wonderland is an illusory

74  The Dark Side of Alice in Wonderland

escape from the insane asylum where the female protagonist has been placed due to her inappropriate sexual appetites. Such implicit critiques of the Carroll tales are in the minority, however. Hardcore more commonly rescues Alice from Carroll's controlling grip, either releasing Alice into a joyful Wonderland of sexual development or turning the tables on Carroll and his cast of abusive characters.

'Alice represents light – white, English femininity – and the pleasures of transgressing that chaste boundary. Pornographers take the popular notion of Victorian white femininity as sexually repressed and socially oppressed and recast this feminine character as an active sexual subject.'

It is not just films where erotic elements have been deliberately introduced. Wanting to explore the concepts of pornography, theatre director Mathew Lenton utilised elements of the *Alice in Wonderland* story for his play *Wonderland*, performed by Glasgow based Vanishing Point theatre at the Napoli Teatro Festival in 2012. One reviewer at the time noted that this was a production solely for adults, as 'the company is putting on stage the kind of sexual fantasies that really should stay private'.

The central character is a girl called Heidi who specialises in performing little-girl-lost roles for sadomasochistic movies. Her co-star is John, equally addicted to internet porn. Outwardly respectable in a normal relationship, John uses the anonymity of an online username to develop an appetite for violent sex. The actors perform behind a transparent screen.

According to director Matthew Lenton:

'It's the hardest show I've ever made, because the subject matter is so hard. On a basic level, men and women have different views about it. What one person is a dark and fucked-up fantasy, is for another, very normal and mild. It's also a subject that's hard to find a poetical way of approaching. It's hard to find beauty in it.

'It's about how and why people use the internet, especially pornography on the internet, and pornography that's becoming more and more extreme. It's about how someone can live at home with their family and they can go next door and enter extreme places, then they can come back and sit around that table again, but their mind has been somewhere. That's something that's new that couldn't have happened 20 years ago.

'I'm also interested in what it is that makes someone want to make that kind of pornography – what it is that opens the doors to those places. One really easy answer is money, but the other answer is nobody knows. What I wanted to avoid doing was to explain it by saying it's all to do with a difficult relationship that somebody had with their father when they were a child.'

Books too have been affected by this pornographic version of *Alice in Wonderland*. A typical example is that of a book entitled *Fifty Shades of Alice in Wonderland* written by Melinda Du Champ. The official outline says it all:

'Eighteen-year-old Alice is unhappy. Her boyfriend is nice and polite, but he's also quick and careless in bed, and doesn't give Alice the attention and variety she craves. But he's not entirely to blame, because Alice herself doesn't understand her own needs. She's heard what sex is supposed to be like, but has never felt anything remotely close to what she's read about in runaway bestselling books.

'Then Alice follows a vibrating white rabbit down a deep, dark hole, which leads to a place beyond her wildest imagination. There are no nice boys – or girls – down here. Only those who indulge in secret, forbidden, kinky fantasies.

'Alice is confused and frightened and … Aroused. She is bound. Teased. Spanked. Toyed. Brought to the limits of sexual endurance. And during her trials, she begins to understand her body's needs for the very first time.

'This isn't the fairy tale you grew up reading. This isn't for children at all. This is for those with dark desires, who wish to explore erotic excess beyond the plain vanilla of everyday life. Follow Alice down the rabbit hole, if you dare …'

## 76   The Dark Side of Alice in Wonderland

Adriana Arden wrote a series of three erotic stories focusing on the *Alice in Wonderland* saga entitled *The Obedient Alice, Alice in Chains* and *Abandoned Alice*. The book covers contained a prominent warning – for adults only. Typical images included Alice handcuffed and dressed in corset and suspenders, or half naked set against a spider's web of rope. The basic story lines started with an 18-year-old Alice discovering that the world of Wonderland (renamed Underland) had begun to take young women – or girlings as they were described – from our world as sex slaves. Alice sets out to liberate them, encountering along the way the perverse wiles of the White Rabbit, Hatter and Hare plus a less than regal Duchess and Queen of Hearts. Reviewers described it as, 'A highly original and downright filthy re-imagining of *Alice in Wonderland*.'

Next in the series was *Alice in Chains* with a story line that involved a trip to Underland to solve her personal problems where she becomes used as a pawn by the Red Queen and enslaved by a greedy Tweedledee and Tweedledum involving some very bizarre demands. In the final part of the saga, *Abandoned Alice*, the Cheshire Cat travels from Underland to warn Alice that her friends are threatened by the mad Queen of Hearts and need her to help liberate themselves from sexual slavery. Alice agrees to help – but is accompanied back to Underland by 'an attractive and surprisingly perverse college tutor' enabling her to find her proper place in Underland. Reviewers described it as 'a delightfully perverse retelling of a classic tale'.

Another prominent example of this genre is *Lost Girls*, a graphic novel written by Alan Moore and first published in 1991. It focuses on the sexual adventures of three famous female fairy tale characters: Alice from *Alice's Adventures in Wonderland*, Wendy from *Peter Pan*, and Dorothy from *The Wonderful Wizard of Oz*. Set on the eve of the First World War, the trio are visiting an expensive Austrian mountain resort and begin discussing their erotic adventures. Alice is very much the ringleader, initiating sexual adventures and the storytelling. Wendy Darling talks of her sexual escapades with a homeless boy called Peter who introduces Wendy and her brothers to sexual games. Dorothy has sexual encounters with farm hands described as the Straw Man, the Cowardly Lion and the Tin Man.

Alice herself is seduced by her father's friend, (thus hinting at a portrayal of Lewis Carroll as a pervert and seducer) and later becomes involved in drug-fuelled lesbian sex parties. She comments, 'Desire's a strange land one discovers as a child, where nothing makes the slightest sense.'

Later in the book, while reflecting on the circumstances surrounding her experience of rape, Alice says, 'I fell or floated down a hole inside myself, and its far end all I could see was Mother's mirror … The mirror glass was melting into silver, boiling into mist, and I reached out and felt the young muscle in her shoulder, in her neck, the child-silk at her nape.' Alice's reflection becomes her own abuser and Alice is displaced from the trauma she undergoes saying, 'I no longer felt like me … I had no substance. I was the reflection. From beyond the mirror pane the real me gazed out, lost … I have been there ever since.'

The links into lesbian sex bring *Alice in Wonderland* into the realms of homosexuality. In *Lost Girls*, Alice abuses other girls (the flowers) at her school, fixates upon one of the teachers seen as substitute for the Red Queen, and undertakes non-consensual sex with a variety of partners while under the effect of drugs. All the partners mentioned in the story reflect the traditional characters from *Alice in Wonderland* such as cross-dressing Sapphic host of a hemp-laced tea party who always wears a dramatic hat, while two enormous women toy with Alice while finishing each other's sentences just like Tweedledum and Tweedledee.

*Lost Girls* utilises the concept of Carroll as a child photographer and paedophile. It also plays on Freudian views of the *Alice in Wonderland* story and brings in direct references to Sigmund Freud. When Wendy tells Alice about her childhood encounter with Peter and expresses concern that she may be deranged; Alice responds, saying, 'Fiddlesticks! Why, there is a notable professor of the mind currently practising not far from here, in Vienna. He would find your image of flight perfectly acceptable and indeed appropriate.'

A very different slant on pornographic versions of *Alice in Wonderland* has been taken by sex trafficking survivor Elle Snow, working with playwrights Grace Booth, Erin Johnson and Kate Tobie. Their play, *Jane Doe in Wonderland*, has become one of the most talked about anti-sex trafficking plays in America. The play continuously draws parallels with Alice's Looking Glass world and is based on Elle Snow's own experiences. As a 19-year-old, she met her White Rabbit who took her away on an adventure which although initially was fun, turned into a nightmare. The journey down the rabbit hole resulted in being sold into a brothel and having to encounter all kinds of strange people. Climbing out of that rabbit hole was not easy.

Cross-dressers often find the Alice look irresistible whether via the classical blue and white style costume or a more grungy look complete with

78   The Dark Side of Alice in Wonderland

hearts and stripes. One cross dresser even wrote a memoir entitled *Alice in Genderland*, detailing his transformation, comparing it to the Wonderland stories by falling down a metaphorical rabbit hole, experiencing challenging changes, plus mind opening surprizes which include gritty sex in order to explore the limits of sexuality and gender.

The rise of psychoanalysis during the twentieth century has led to considerable focus on sexual overtones within *Alice in Wonderland*. Writing in 1933, Antony Goldschmidt carried out a Freudian analysis of *Alice in Wonderland*, and concluded that it involved forbidden desires battling with repression in the author's mind. Among the many comparisons that he made was that of falling down the rabbit hole becoming a symbol of coitus, and the little door through which she attempts to pass in the mysterious hall 'symbolises a female child, the curtain before it represents the child's clothes'. Since then, other Freudian writers have made other comparisons especially gynaecological ones, such as the rabbit hole and the curtain that Alice has to push aside. Locks and keys are often used as symbols for coitus, and the caterpillar becomes a phallic symbol of sexual virility, while references to fanning prior to shrinking and the salt water lapping her chin when reduced to just a few inches tall are seen as references to masturbation. Other critics suggest that Alice is a dream child, a sex-kitten teasing Dodgson while some suggest that Alice has to control the properties of the mushroom in order to control her fluctuating size, therefore controlling the bodily frustrations that accompany puberty.

Writing in *Alice in Wonderland: The Child as Swain*, literary critic William Empson stated, 'the books are so frankly about growing up that there is no great discovery in translating them into Freudian terms'. He went on, 'the pool of tears represents both the primeval sea from which life arose and amniotic fluid'. He also suggested that Alice is 'a father in getting down the hole, a foetus at the bottom, and can only be born by becoming a mother and producing her own amniotic fluid'. The Queen of Hearts is a symbol of 'uncontrolled animal passion'.

In the mid-twentieth century, psychoanalyst Paul Schilder even turned Alice into a type of phallic projection. He asked:

'What was [Carroll's] relation to his sex organ anyhow? Fenichel has lately pointed to the possibility that little girls might become symbols for the phallus. Alice changes her form continually; she is continually threatened and continually in danger. There may have been a wish for feminine passivity and a protest against it. He plays the part of the mother to little girls but the little girl is for him also the completion of his own body.'

Speaking at the American Psychoanalytical Association at the Waldorf Astoria in December 1936, he stated that in his view the Alice books were full of fear and 'oral sadistic trends of cannibalism'. Moreover, Carroll himself was 'a warped and fearful creature who really wanted to be doing several other things beside sitting on rolling English lawns spinning yarns to open-mouthed children'. A few days later, the *World Telegraph* newspaper agreed with Schilder, commenting that the 'danger of emotional instability posed by these stories was so powerful that they should be restricted to adults'.

Many critics also read the story as being a reflection of a girl moving from childhood, through puberty and into adulthood. Her body undergoes a number of changes and her sense of self alters, leaving her uncertain as to her exact identity while constantly challenging the authority figures around her. It has also been suggested that Wonderland can be a terrifying, oppressive, violent and controlling space for girls in which Alice is given little room to grow up and is verbally and physically accosted before returning to the real world.

Linked into the concept of a sexual, pornographic Alice are the issues surrounding the Lolita concept as well as the child abuse angles. In 1996, writer A.M. Homes wrote a novel, *The End of Alice*, portraying the central narrator as an unrepentant child abuser who has taken part in the brutal, sexualised murder of a 12- year-old girl. The book depicts Alice as an active sexual participant, testing out her emerging sexuality with an adult whose ability to harm she does not anticipate.

So prevalent are the images and ideas of *Alice in Wonderland* that many people utilise them as a way of exploring their own experiences – the world of pornography is no exception. In 2015, former Playboy Bunny Holly Madison published her memoirs entitled *Down the Rabbit Hole*. Just like Alice, Holly Madison took a momentous step into the dark, seemingly falling through a rabbit hole in an unexpected Wonderland within the extremely bizarre Playboy Mansion. Holly became one of the many girlfriends who lived with Hugh Hefner within the Mansion, experiencing a world that was full of manipulative people, backstabbing bunnies and sexual exploitation. Continuing with the Alice imagery, reviewers commented, 'life inside the Mansion wasn't a dream at all and quickly became her nightmare … But instead of ending her life, Holly chose to take charge of it.'

*Chapter 7*

# Ripper Alice

'The Vorpal blade went snicker-snack!'

*Alice in Wonderland*

Was Charles Lutwidge Dodgson aka Lewis Carroll a murderer? And not just a murderer but one of the most notorious killers in British history, committing a series of very gruesome murders? Such a suggestion might seem far-fetched given that he was a clergyman in minor orders, a respectable Victorian gentleman to whom parents entrusted their children and who mixed in high society. Yet his name was put forward by writer Richard Wallace in *Jack the Ripper: Light-Hearted Friend* as a potential candidate for the position of Jack the Ripper, the murderer responsible for the Whitechapel Murders in 1888.

The Whitechapel murders continue to attract a phenomenal amount of attention with countless books, websites, walking tours and films. There is even a London museum dedicated to Jack the Ripper and the character takes a prominent place in leisure attractions such as the London Dungeon.

Late Victorian London was a place where rich and poor co-existed closely. Areas of extreme poverty could be found very close to wealthy regions. This is clearly seen in the Poverty Maps created during Charles Booth's *Inquiry into Life and Labour in London (1886-1903)*. Booth carried out an exhaustive survey of London streets, identifying each street by the income and social class of its inhabitants. It revealed that wealthy streets like Piccadilly and Regent Street were coexisting with nearby areas of intense deprivation like Seven Dials, while the Royal Courts of Justice in the Strand was close to densely populated slum areas around the Fleet River in which crime was prevalent. Intense poverty and overcrowded housing was all too common across London.

Although murder was a regular occurrence within these overcrowded regions of London, the series of murders which became known as the Jack the Ripper Murders (also known as the Whitechapel murders) attracted attention from a wider public due mainly to the sheer scale of the mutilations committed on the bodies of the murdered women who were described as prostitutes because they had been out on the streets, on their own, at night. It was accepted thinking in police reports that any woman in such an area, at night, on her own had to be a prostitute.

As Hallie Rubenhold shows in her book, *The Five*, the Ripper's victims came originally from places as far afield as Sweden, Wales and Wolverhampton with occupations ranging from a ballad writer to running a coffee house. Just one victim identified herself as a prostitute, while others had been married and had children living in well to do areas like Windsor and Knightsbridge. All that they had in common was their eventual progression away from their families to life in the East End, experiencing the effects of homelessness and alcohol abuse.

These were murders that attracted publicity. People talked about them exhaustively with word spreading quickly around London. Moreover, it was a story that appealed to scandal obsessed newspapers like the *Pall Mall Gazette* and the *East London Advertiser* which devoted considerable editorial coverage to the murders. Such publications were keen to attract new readers and drive up sales, especially when letters – which were probably not written by Jack the Ripper – were sent to the Central News Agency. Many experts believe that these letters were actually written by a journalist, Frederick Best.

This helped to expand awareness of the murders, which soon became a talking point throughout the country. The graphic images within the *Illustrated Police News* (avidly read by people at all levels of society) left little to the imagination. Over in the USA, journalists used phrases such as 'a bloodthirsty beast in human shape' when referring to Jack the Ripper.

Queen Victoria became involved, writing in her diaries on 4 October, 'Dreadful murders of unfortunate women of a bad class in London. There were 6, with horrible mutilations'. She is known to have sent numerous telegrams to ministers and police authorities urging action to solve the case. Following the murder of Mary Kelly, she wrote to the Lord Salisbury, the prime minister saying, 'This new most ghastly murder shows the absolute necessity for some very decided action. All these courts must be lit, and our detectives improved. They are not what they should be. You promised, when the first murder took place to consult with your colleagues about it.'

Even after the murders stopped, people continued to talk about them and discuss them at length, creating theory upon theory as to the identity of the murderer. The police received over 1,000 letters a week on the subject,

82   The Dark Side of Alice in Wonderland

covering potential suspects as well as suggestions on how to catch the killer. In his diary, Charles Dodgson refers to discussing 'his very ingenious theory' about Jack the Ripper with one of his acquaintances, Dr George Dabbs, who lived in Shanklin in the Isle of Wight. This discussion took place on 26 August 1891, some three years after the Whitechapel murders. The sheer extent of interest that has been generated over the years has resulted in more media coverage than any other murders.

The exact number of victims involved in the Ripper murders is uncertain. Some say that there were up to eleven victims covering a period from mid-1888 to 1891, as well as a number of attacks in early 1888, which may have been the early work of Jack the Ripper. Typical of these possible victims was Martha Tabram, who was murdered in the early hours of 7 August 1888. Like the later victims, Martha was a prostitute in her late thirties and had been soliciting on the Whitechapel Road. She eventually went with a client into the dark thoroughfare known as George Yard. Next morning her body was found lying on her back in a pool of blood. She had been savagely attacked, having experienced thirty-nine stab wounds from her neck to her abdomen. Walter Dew, the police constable who found the body, believed that she was an early victim of Jack the Ripper. Many years later, after rising to the rank of Inspector, he wrote in his autobiography 'whatever may be said about the death of Emma Smith, there can be no doubt that the August Bank Holiday murder, which took place in George Yard Buildings … was the handiwork of the dread Ripper.' Since then questions have been raised due to the fact that the mutilations were not identical to those experienced by the Ripper victims, although centred in the same area of the body and the murder location was similar.

The series of murders began on 31 August when Mary Ann Nichols was discovered in Bucks Row, Whitechapel. Savagely mutilated, her stomach had been cut open and her head almost severed from her body. Only a few days later, another homeless woman Annie Chapman was found similarly mutilated. Word had already spread around the area, and feelings were running high. Rumours that the Ripper carried his knives in a black bag led to crowds attacking anyone carrying such a bag. The Central News Agency claims to have received a letter signed Jack the Ripper which threatened more murders exacerbated the situation.

On 30 September, two more murders took place within minutes of each other. The body of Elizabeth Stride was found with blood still pouring from her throat, and it was believed that the Ripper had been disturbed before he could commit further mutilations. Forty-five minutes later, at 1.45 am, Catherine Eddowes was found nearby. Her body had been even more extensively mutilated than previous victims. Her eyelids had been removed, along with parts of her nose and right ear, while the left ear was partially severed.

The Central News Agency received another letter purporting to come from Jack the Ripper, apologising for not being able to send the ears to the police as earlier promised having not had enough time to do so.

On 9 November, Mary Jeannette Kelly was murdered and mutilated in her room in Millers Court. Her body was found by her landlord, collecting the rent, who commented 'I shall be haunted by this for the rest of my life.'

Further murders such as that of Rose Mylett and Frances Coles took place in the area between December 1888 and 1891, which were attributed to Jack the Ripper due to similarities over the method of murder. Newspaper headlines referred to 'The return of the Ripper'. However, questions have since been raised over the attribution and many Ripperologists disagree that they were his victims. That Ripperologists exist and mostly disagree with each other, reflects the way that Jack the Ripper has become a mini industry in itself.

The identity of Jack the Ripper remains unknown. The sheer brutality of the murders and the concept of a serial killer obsessed Victorians at the time, resulting in many theories as to the potential candidates. People across all sectors of society discussed the murders and sought to come up with their own theories. Over the years since the murders came to an end, there have been over 100 names put forward for identification as Jack the Ripper by detectives, researchers and writers. Some of the candidates are regarded as being more likely than others.

McNaughton and Sir Robert Anderson both believed that a Polish born immigrant named Aaron Kosminski was a probable candidate. Kosminski suffered from mental illness and had spent time in a lunatic asylum. His symptoms included delusions, paranoia and schizophrenia. At the time of the murders, Kosminski was living in the East End with his brother, a tailor. Kosminski was subsequently committed to the Colney Hatch Lunatic Asylum.

Also close to the top of the police list was Montague John Druitt, a barrister who supplemented his income by teaching at a boarding school in Blackheath. Macnaghten regarded him as one of the most likely candidates, especially after he committed suicide.

84    The Dark Side of Alice in Wonderland

McNaughton also highlighted Michael Ostrog as a potential murderer. An unsuccessful petty thief and conman, who was also mentally unstable and delusional, Ostrog had spent many years in prison or in hospital and was at large during the period of the murders. His description was published in the *Police Gazette* on 26 October with the words 'Special attention is called to this dangerous man'. Subsequent research has revealed that he was actually living in Paris under an assumed name and had been arrested by French police on 26 July 1888. On 14 November 1888, he was convicted of theft and imprisoned in Paris.

Chief Inspector Littlechild regarded Dr Francis Tumblety as a key suspect. He had been arrested and charged with gross indecency on 7 November 1888. Having been remanded on bail, he subsequently fled from the UK and sailed via Boulogne to the US. His potential involvement in the murders resulted in a lot of publicity within the American media, and he was kept under surveillance by the New York Police Department. The case against him was regarded as fairly weak. He was never arrested or extradited to the UK.

Some years after the Ripper murders, a man named George Chapman – real name Severin Klosowski, of Polish origin – attracted the attention of Inspector Abberline. He had trained as a surgeon but during the period of the murders, was working in the East End as a hairdresser before moving to the USA in 1890. Subsequently returning to the UK, he poisoned three women and was later hanged for murder. During his trial, Inspector Abberline began to suspect him due to the number of 'remarkable coincidences in the two series of murder' such as the surgical skills and the timespan.

There were even suggestions early in the investigation, that the killer might be a woman. Inspector Abberline is said to have discussed this possibility with Dr Thomas Dutton following the murder of Mary Kelly. Dutton believed it was doubtful, but that if it was a woman, then it could only have been a midwife since a midwife would possess the anatomical knowledge required to commit the mutilations. Any blood on her clothing would be simply passed off as being the result of attending a birth.

Although these were regarded as the most likely suspects, there were many famous names already being nominated, including links with the Royal Family, including Prince Albert Victor, the Duke of Clarence was the son of the Prince of Wales and Princess Alexandra. His name appears in at least three major theories relating to the Ripper's identity. Questions have been raised over his mental health, personality and his death. There were unconfirmed reports circulating during his lifetime that he was mildly retarded (due to his deafness) and also suggestions he was suffering from syphilis. Theories connecting him to the murders began in 1962 in *Edward VII*, by Phillipe Jullian. In 1970, Dr Thomas Stowell wrote an article in *The Criminologist* indicating that the Duke of Clarence was the murderer, based on the papers of Sir William Gull, believed to be his doctor. Since then there have been other theories indicating Gull was an accessory, and that there was even a Royal conspiracy designed to cover up a secret marriage between the prince and a poor Catholic girl, Annie Crook.

The name of Lord Randolph Churchill results primarily from suggestions that as a senior Freemason, he was keen to protect the Royal Family and prevent any links to Prince Albert Victor becoming known. One theory postulates that Churchill was part of a group of senior masons who planned to murder five prostitutes led by Mary Kelly, who had been blackmailing the royal family on the basis of Prince Albert Victor's secret marriage.

Artists also came under scrutiny. Walter Sickert was a well-known avant-garde artist, whose work included numerous scenes of nudes, city streets and room interiors. He created sketches and paintings of the Ripper crimes that were said to be quite accurate. In the 1970s, talk of a royal conspiracy led to further consideration of his involvement, and in the 1990s, research by Jean Overton Fuller in *Sickert and the Ripper Crimes*, followed by *Portrait of a Killer: Jack the Ripper Case Closed* by Patricia Cornwell resulted in Sickert being specifically identified as the Ripper. Patricia Cornwell claiming to have discovered DNA evidence linking Sickert to one of the Ripper letters.

It was not until 1996 that the name of Charles Lutwidge Dodgson, author of *Alice in Wonderland,* was added to the list. Richard Wallace, a psychotherapist and a keen Carroll enthusiast, published his book, highlighting the results of research he had been undertaking for some years. His conclusion was that Jack the Ripper was none other than Dodgson himself.

Central to Wallace's thinking is a belief that Dodgson was sexually repressed and had been sexually abused while away at boarding school. This abuse festered and eventually resulted in murder. Wallace pointed to the fact that when Dodgson went to boarding school at the age of 12, he wrote home complaining about night-time activities within his dormitory. Although Carroll never indicates exactly what the problem was, Wallace believed that his letters indicated that older boys were physically abusing him. It is true that such abuse was not unknown in the education system of the period, especially within boarding schools.

Having come to this conclusion, Wallace went on to study Carroll's writing to see if any further evidence existed. In view of the fact that Carroll was renowned for his ability to play with words and enjoyed cryptic anagrams; Wallace believed that there were hidden messages within Carroll's correspondence and published works which highlighted Carroll's mental state. By rearranging letters within Carroll's correspondence, Wallace discovered a plea for help in a letter sent to his brother, Skeffington. Carroll wrote, 'My dear Skeff: Roar not lest thou be abolished.' By rearranging the letters, the line became 'Ask mother about the red lion: safer boys fled.'

Boys at Carroll's boarding school often played a game called Red Lion. Wallace believed that the game had a sexual element and that it upset Carroll to the point that he began to resent his parents who had sent him to the school. According to Wallace, 'he retreated into a world consumed by one goal – revenge on society.'

It was a resentment that eventually affected his views and attitudes towards Victorian society. Living and working at Christ Church, Oxford required Dodgson to take orders and remain celibate, factors which enhanced the feelings of resentment, especially when having to deal with the young men attending the University.

*The Nursery Alice* was published at the same time as the Ripper murders were taking place in 1888. Studying the book, along with another volume, entitled *Sylvie and Bruno*, Wallace came to the conclusion that Carroll was confessing to the gruesome murders that were taking place. Wallace believed that there were hidden messages within the text. By rearranging words in one passage he came up with sentence: 'If I find one street whore, you know what will happen! T'will be off with her head.'

In another passage, Carroll writes:

> 'So we went to the cook, and we got her to make a saucer-ful of nice oatmeal porridge. And then we called Dash [a dog] into the house, and we said, "Now, Dash, your're going to have your birthday treat!" We expected Dash would jump for joy; but it didn't, one bit!'

By rearranging the letters, Wallace created this message:

'Oh, we, Thomas Bayne, Charles Dodgson, coited into the slain, nude body, expected to taste, devour, enjoy a nice meal of a dead whore's uterus. We made do, found it awful – wan and tough like a worn, dirty goat hog. We both threw it out – Jack the Ripper'.

Thomas Bayne was Carroll's lifelong friend and, like Carroll, was an Oxford academic having studied at the same College. An ordained Anglican priest, Bayne was Curator of the Common Room in Christ Church.

In another section within *Nursery Alice*, Carroll writes:

'So she wandered away, through the wood, carrying the ugly little thing with her. And a great job it was to keep hold of it, it wriggled about so. But at last she found out that the proper way was to keep tight hold of its foot and its right ear.'

Wallace turns this into:

'She wriggled about so! But at last Dodgson and Bayne found a way to keep hold of the fat little whore. I got a tight hold of her and slit her throat, left ear to right. It was tough, wet, disgusting, too. So weary of it, they threw up – Jack the Ripper.'

Wallace believed that the key reason Carroll became involved in the murders was a long-held resentment of his parents. As evidence of this, Wallace pointed to the fact that the noses of the victims were mutilated. Since Carroll's mother is believed to have had a large protuberant nose, Wallace jumped to the conclusion that the nose mutilations represented an attack on Carroll's mother. Such a conclusion does ignore the other mutilations experienced by the victims, some of whom had almost every body part attacked. Furthermore, Wallace postulated that since Carroll's personal library contained over 120 books on medicine and anatomy, Carroll had the knowledge of the human body needed to dissect the victims. Such selective evidence does ignore the fact that many educated people of the period possessed such knowledge and had similar books in their homes.

88    The Dark Side of Alice in Wonderland

Wallace claimed to have discovered yet more evidence to support his theory in the poem *Jabberwocky*, written in 1872. Although this poem was written sixteen years before the murders took place, Wallace believes that it indicates the way in which Carroll's mind was working and the latent hatred that was coming to the fore. Wallace points to the verse 'The vorpal blade went snicker-snack!/He left it dead, and with its head;/He went galumphing back,' as being a reference to the eventual murder of the Ripper's third victim, Annie Chapman, whose head was almost completely severed from her body.

Turning to the poem *The Hunting of the Snark*, Wallace discovered various sexual and death themes as well as other anagrams. In the poem, Carroll wrote:

'They sought it with thimbles, they sought it with care;
They pursued it with forks and with hope;
They threatened its life with a railway share;
They charmed it with smiles and with soap.'

Richard Wallace stated that this refers to the fact that all the murder victims had thimbles, forks and soap in their pockets when they died – a belief that had no basis in reality.

Turning to the subject of the Dear Boss letters, Wallace came to the conclusion that the letters were written by Dodgson's friend Thomas Bayne since the handwriting did not match that of Carroll. While admitting that the first 'Dear Boss' letter was received on 29 September while Bayne was in France; Wallace argued, 'A Ripper letter could have been sent by Bayne to Dodgson for forwarding using a domestic post office. He could have used any of a number of enciphering methods he possessed.'

Wallace also looked at what is described as the 'Druitt Connection.' Montague Druitt has long been regarded as one of the key suspects for the Whitechapel murders. He had been educated at New College Oxford and was a teacher in London's Blackheath prior to his death (possibly by suicide) in December 1888.

Wallace believes that there was every possibility that Druitt and Dodgson could have met while in Oxford and that there was no proof to the contrary. Wallace also points to the fact that Dodgson refers to a man named Drewett in his diary, who had stayed with Dodgson on December 12, 1878. Studying

Druitt's final letter before his death, Wallace says that the words 'Since Friday I felt I was going to be like mother, and the best thing for me was to die'.

Using his anagram theory, Wallace turned this into 'I fib, idiots. I – we – are fine faggot killers. C Dodgson, T. Bayne threw me into the Thames.' Again, without any real evidence, both Charles Dodgson and Bayne had again become murderers.

Wallace further points to the fact that Carroll had no alibis for any of the nights on which the Ripper carried out the various murders saying that on the days when those murders took place, Carroll changed his normal purple ink to black when writing his diary. Wallace believes that deleted passages from Dodgson's diaries contained comments on the murders. 'Quite simply, Carroll was a psychopathic killer,' alleged Richard Wallace.

Wallace's theories were quickly attacked and criticised by Ripperologists as well as biographers of Lewis Carroll. There are, quite simply, innumerable flaws in his arguments, some of which are incredibly tenuous and far fetched such as his reliance on coincidence as evidence. One of the strangest pieces of 'evidence' put forward by Wallace was a suggestion that is it a coincidence that DAGGER is an anagram for RAGGED, characteristic of some of the wounds, but more significantly, it becomes RIPPER by Doublet conversion – DAGGER, bagger, bagged, barged, barred, burred, burped, bumped, dumped, damped, damper, dapper, dipper, RIPPER.

Wallace clearly tried to make the number of murders fit his theories. According to the accepted canons of Ripper victims there were five. Wallace opts for eight because there were eight women in Carroll's family, or for nine given that there is an anagram stating, 'I slit nine throats'.

Edward Wakeling, editor of *Dodgson's Diaries*, commented that Wallace's theories as to the timeline involved did not match official dates relating to the activities of Charles Dodgson. On 3 April 1888, when Emma Smith was murdered, Dodgson was in Oxford unable to walk due to 'synovitis' of the knees (an inflammation of the joints). On 31 August 1888, when Polly Nichols was murdered, Dodgson was staying in Eastbourne in the company of his child friend, actress Isa Bowman, who would have noticed if he had disappeared for the long trip to London, returning covered in blood. Dodgson was still in Eastbourne with Isa Bowman when Annie Chapman died on 8 September, likewise on 30 September when the murders of Elizabeth Stride and Catherine Eddowes took place. Throughout this

90   The Dark Side of Alice in Wonderland

period, his friend Thomas Vere Bayne was suffering from severe back pain and unable to move, let alone travel to commit such serious murders.

When *Harper's Magazine* published an excerpt from *Jack the Ripper: Light-hearted Friend*, two anagram aficionados Francis Heaney and Guy Jacobson wrote to the magazine, highlighting the fact that the same anagram technique could give a very different result. They transformed the first three sentences of *Jack the Ripper: Light-Hearted Friend* as follows:

> Wallace's version: 'This is my story of Jack the Ripper, the man behind Britain's worst unsolved murders. It is a story that points to the unlikeliest of suspects: a man who wrote children's stories. That man is Charles Dodgson, better known as Lewis Carroll, author of such beloved books as Alice in Wonderland.'

Heaney & Jacobsen's resultant version reads

> 'The truth is this: I, Richard Wallace, stabbed and killed a muted Nicole Brown in cold blood, severing her throat with my trusty shiv's strokes. I set up Orenthal James Simpson, who is utterly innocent of this murder. P.S. I also wrote Shakespeare's sonnets, and a lot of Francis Bacon's works too.'

One of the most vocal opponents was Karoline Leach, an academic and writer researching the work of Lewis Carroll. She promptly devoted an entire lecture at the 2000 Ripper Conference in the United States to demolishing Wallace's theory, before publishing her lecture as 'Jack Through the Looking-Glass (or Wallace in Wonderland)' in the January 2001 issue of *Ripper Notes*.

So what exactly were her counter-arguments?

Firstly, she queries the use of anagrams. Transforming sentences and paragraphs using anagrams is a technique that can be applied to any written work. She demonstrated her point by reworking sections of A.A. Milne's Winnie the Pooh story to show that A.A. Milne was a murderer. Explaining her argument in her lecture, she stated that the use of anagrams was:

> 'An interesting theory. But it finds a major difficulty in the fact that Wallace cannot seem to discover good anagrams without cheating'.

*Right*: Who am I? The eternal puzzle of the true character of Alice. (*Karis Youngman*)

*Below left*: The original drawing of Alice with playing cards by John Tenniel. (*Mary Evans Picture Library*)

*Below right*: Charles Lutwidge Dodson (Lewis Carroll), pictured here in 1857, was an English mathematician and writer and the creator of *Alice's Adventures in Wonderland*. (*Mary Evans Picture Library*)

"SHE WENT ON GROWING AND GROWING, AND VERY SOON HAD TO KNEEL DOWN ON THE FLOOR: IN ANOTHER MINUTE THERE WAS NOT EVEN ROOM FOR THIS, AND SHE TRIED THE EFFECT OF LYING DOWN."

*Above*: Alice as she appeared in the original manuscript c.1862, as drawn by Lewis Carroll. (*Illustrated London News Ltd/Mary Evans Picture Library*)

*Below left*: Alice Liddell at about 10 years old. (*Mary Evans Picture Library*)

*Below right*: 'Anime Alice' – A representation of the conflicting cultures around Alice in the West and Japan. (*Karis Youngman*)

*Above left*: 'X rated Alice' – Alice has been hijacked by the porn industry and is no longer always seen to be as innocent as Lewis Carroll intended. (*Karis Youngman*)

*Above right*: 'Ripper Alice' – Was Lewis Carroll Jack the Ripper, as has been suggested by some writers? This interpretation shows Alice herself as the Ripper, rather than her creator. (*Karis Youngman*)

*Below*: 'Murder Alice' – Alice is a key player in modern murder mystery culture and is shown here on a stylised Cluedo board. (*Karis Youngman*)

*Above*: 'Alice in Puzzleland' – Alice takes part in a themed locked room EscapeHunt event. (*Escape Hunt*)

*Below left*: A Mad Tea Party. Was the most famous character in the Alice books truly mad? Lewis Carroll never called him so, but most Victorians would have understood the allusion. (*Karis Youngman*)

*Below right*: Alice stretches and grows bigger in this original image from *Alice's Adventures in Wonderland*. (*Mary Evans Picture library*)

*Above left*: 'Drug Alice' – Although it can never be proved that Lewis Carroll took drugs, it was no surprise that Alice became part of the drug-induced counter culture. (*Karis Youngman*)

*Above right*: One of the most iconic events in the Alice story, her fall down the rabbit hole, is intensely surreal. (*Karis Youngman*)

*Below*: Photographer Gary Lindsay-Moore's modern Birmingham-based interpretation of 'Alice in Bad Wonderland'. (*Gary Lindsay-Moore*)

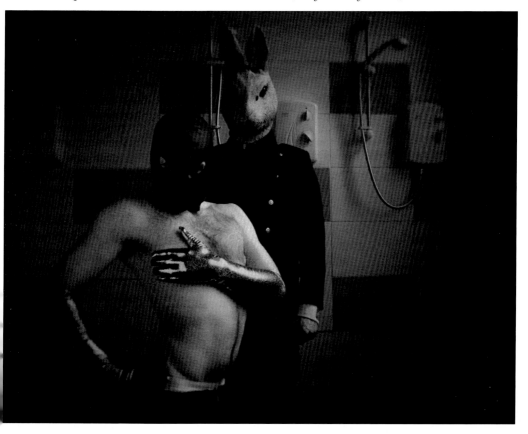

'Horror Alice' – A truly horrific interpretation of Alice in a seriously bad mood. It is typical of the horror genre that has taken Alice to levels that are not found in either book.. (*Karis Youngman*)

The Queen of Hearts in Horrorland – An immersive corporate event staged in the UK. (*Scarlett Entertainment*)

A ghoulish encounter with the Queen of Hearts, Mad Hatter and Alice at the Horrorland event. (*Scarlett Entertainment*)

*Above*: Anyone for Tea? The Mad Hatter and Queen of Hearts at the Alice in Horrorland event – a nightmare of a tea party! (*Scarlett Entertainment*)

*Below left*: At the Halloween Frightmare we encounter the White Rabbit at a truly weird angle. (*Frightmare*)

*Below right*: The Cheshire Cat in female form in another change from the author's original intent. (*Frightmare*)

*Above left*: 'Occult Alice' – An artist's interpretation of characters from the Alice books depicted on Tarot cards. (*Karis Youngman*)

*Above right*: 'Steampunk Alice' – In this interpretation, Alice meets a modern steampunk version of the Caterpillar on a giant mechanical toadstool. (*Karis Youngman*)

*Below left*: Alice and the Dodo – A little girl meets a curious collection. Who is real and who is imaginary? (*Karis Youngman*)

*Below right*: Was the enigmatic Lewis Carroll full of secrets and surprises, or was he just an innocent writer? (*Mary Evans Picture Library*)

She points out that 'when switching letters, or leaving them out, Wallace can produce passages which have words like "ripper" and "whore" in them. For example, a passage from Dodgson's *Nursery Alice* describing how Alice wandered through the wood with a wriggling baby was transformed by dropping a few letters and changing a 'p' into a 'j' resulted in a version relating to Jack the Ripper.

Leach continued her rebuttal of his theories by saying:

'This doesn't make much grammatical sense, but it is at least on message. But when Wallace stoops to saying things like "If we remove eight letters, bringing the fifty letters down to forty-two, we have a manifesto..." or when he doesn't switch letters but tries to work with what is actually there, in Carroll's text, the results are less happy.

'Then d'file noses, lad!'
'Rip no gay peter foreskin.'
'Ah, pants and orgasm hero poet am I'
'I believe the Fathers condemn penile nutrition'
'Urine! Spong't'

'At first glance, they don't look much like an encoded confessional. In fact, they sound more like the kind of conversation employed by lonely and bedraggled people on late-night trains who are having trouble with those voices in their heads. However, Wallace finds in these and similar statements the proof that Carroll was a disordered homosexual psychopath with a mother fixation who vented his hatred of women and his resentment of his own homosexual rape in the murder and mutilation of five (or eight or nine, he seems unsure) women in the autumn of 1888.'

She then goes on to criticise Wallace's views on other work by Dodgson. 'I crave lamb coitus, save up fellatio poison.' This is Wallace's version of the title of Dodgson's anti-vivisection paper *Some Popular Fallacies about Vivisection*.

'Wallace tells us it is a "hidden defense of bestiality;" he doesn't mention what that has to do with Jack the Ripper. But never fear, for Wallace informs us that Dodgson's work is simply bursting

92 The Dark Side of Alice in Wonderland

with encoded confessions to sexual abuse and/or murder. *The Hunt for the Snark: An Agony in Six Fits*, says our man, replete with masturbatory and anal-erotic themes, and the title itself is a thin disguise for three blazing declarations:

'None hunt the King of Hearts in the gay night fits,'
'They, the Uranian kings, often hit on night fags,'
'The king of urnings hateth any Onanite fights.'

Ultimately, the biggest fault in this reliance on anagrams is the simple fact that words and letters can be arranged in almost any fashion as Leach succinctly points out.

'In the final analysis, Wallace's theory is rendered null by the fact that one could rearrange the words in any piece of writing anywhere and make half-connected sentences suggestive of just about anything. The first sentence on the opening page of Winnie the Pooh, for example,

'Here is Edward Bear coming downstairs now'
can be turned into
'Stab red women! CR is downing whores –AA'
'Obviously, the 'CR' is 'Christopher Robin', who is thus revealed as an infant psychopath.'

Turning to the issue of alibis, Leach points out that both Dodgson and Bayne had alibis for the murders of Mary Ann Nichols, Annie Chapman, Elizabeth Stride and Catherine Eddowes. Although both men were in Oxford on the night of Mary Kelly's murder on 9 November, Leach comments that the thought of the two men dashing down to London to commit murder is somewhat implausible.

'Providing we have no problem with the idea of two elderly and slightly infirm gentlemen hobbling painfully around Whitechapel looking for ladies of doubtful virtue, asking them their ages and doing a quick bit of figuring on the back of an envelope before finally escorting Mary Jane off to her lodgings for some slow and creaky dismemberment, then Wallace is okay here.'

Furthermore, on 26 August 1891, an entry in Carroll's diary indicates that he spoke that day to Dr Dabbs regarding 'his very ingenious theory about Jack the Ripper'. No one knows what this theory was, but it reflects the fact that the sheer level of interest being expressed by people throughout England as they followed the story in the newspapers and developed their own theories and ideas.

Leach is equally scathing of the non-anagram 'evidence' Wallace puts forward as 'corroboration' of his theories. She writes:

'He suggests, for example, that the lines from Dodgson's nonsense poem the Mad Gardener's Song, "He thought he saw an Argument, That prove he was the Pope," is a reference to Mitre Square, because popes wear mitres. More obscurely, he asks at one point, "is there a connection between the victim being murdered in Buck's Row, Dodgson's writing on 'sport' and the deerstalker hat seen in the area?"'

According to Wallace, further evidence of Dodgson's culpability as Jack the Ripper can be found in the patterns to be seen within his writing. The number 42 was important to Dodgson as it appears often in his work being mentioned in both *The Hunting of the Snark* and in *Alice in Wonderland* where Rule 42 requires 'All persons more than a mile high to leave the court'. As a result, Wallace believed that the ages of Jack the Ripper's victims were linked to the Rule of 42.

Leach disagrees with this notion saying,

'Emma Smith (whom Wallace claims as the first victim) was forty-five years old. Forty-five, of course, is exactly three more than forty-two.

'Martha Tabram was killed with thirty-nine stab wounds – and she was thirty-nine years old. Thirty-nine – as Wallace points out – is three less than forty-two. And thus, we have a "pattern".

'Elizabeth Stride, of course, was forty-five. Again, three more than forty-two.

'Catherine Eddowes was forty-three, which seems to break the pattern. But Wallace thinks she cannot really count, because having

94   The Dark Side of Alice in Wonderland

just been released from jail, she couldn't have been "selected" in advance. A rush job, in other words – no time for fine details.

'Mary Kelly, the last of the "canonical five" was apparently twenty-five. But, Wallace argues reasonably, Dodgson might have thought she was twenty-four – after all, he had a lot on his mind and several modern authors made the same mistake. Twenty-four, of course, is forty-two backwards.'

So just how much credence can be given to Wallace's theory that Jack the Ripper was Lewis Carroll? When considered among all the various potential suspects put forward over the years, Ripperlogists regard Carroll as being one of the more unlikely suspects. One specialist website – *Casebook: Jack the Ripper* – actually voted Carroll as being the least likely suspect out of twenty-two potential names. When reviewing Richard Wallace's book, a contributor to *Casebook* commented:

'Just when you thought you've heard it all ... Wallace tries to prove that *Alice in Wonderland* author Lewis Carroll was Jack the Ripper. He tries to do this by making anagrams from Carroll's writing which he believes are clues towards his true identity. It's actually quite an amusing book, though I find it hard to believe that even Wallace takes it seriously'.

Part of the problem is that by 1996, after one hundred years of books and articles about Jack the Ripper, new books have to come up with a 'new' Jack in order to gain publicity, and the more famous the name, the better. Charles Dodgson/Lewis Carroll is without doubt one of the more famous names to be branded as a potential candidate for the identity of Jack the Ripper, albeit extremely unlikely.

*Chapter 8*

# Murder Mystery Alice

'The Queen turned crimson with fury, and, after glaring at her for
a moment like a wild beast, began screaming "Off with her head!"'
*Alice in Wonderland*

Murder and mystery are not unknown when it comes to Lewis Carroll
and *Alice in Wonderland*. Even Alice is faced with mysteries ranging from
who stole the tarts to her own identity – 'Who am I?' Quite apart from
any mysteries inherent within the story itself, *Wonderland* has provided
inspiration for countless authors, trails and mystery events. It has even been
caught up in terrorist inspired murder plots. In June 2018, a mother and
daughter team who formed the first all-female Islamic State terrorist cell
were jailed over their *Alice in Wonderland*-inspired plot. Rizlaine Boular
planned to stab random members of the public around the Palace of
Westminster. As part of the coded conversations setting up the plot, they
discussed holding an *Alice in Wonderland* tea party with Rizlaine cast as the
Mad Hatter. The tea party became the code word for the murder attempt,
while the key participant became the Mad Hatter.

The topsy-turvy world of Wonderland and its magnificent characters
has definitely provided considerable inspiration for countless murder
mysteries of all kinds. Typical examples include the *Sherlock Holmes and
the Alice in Wonderland Murders* by Barry Day and *The Wonderland Murders*
by Guillermo Martinez. *The Wonderland Murders* feature a mathematics
student named G, who is trying to resurrect his studies, a task that is proving
hard since he finds himself drawn into investigating a series of mysterious
crimes inspired by the true, strange stories from Dodgson's own life. Not
only does G become embroiled in the Lewis Carroll Brotherhood, he has
to deal with a new discovery by Dodgson's great niece resulting in 'deadly
plots, salacious pictures and murder'.

Best-selling crime novelist Peter Abrahams used *Alice in Wonderland* as
the theme for the first novel in his Echo Falls, *Down the Rabbit Hole* (2012)
mystery series. The story focused on the murder of Katherine Kovac. The

96     The Dark Side of Alice in Wonderland

protagonist, Ingrid Levin Hill, is just 13 years old and a devoted follower of the techniques of Sherlock Holmes. In the story she has taken the lead role in her town's production of *Alice in Wonderland*. When things keep getting curiouser and curiouser, she finds she needs to solve the murder before it is too late.

Turning to the US crime fiction scene, *Alice in Wonderland* is also a constant reference, for example in the Allie Griffin Mysteries by Leslie Leigh, there is a volume entitled *Murder in Wonderland*. The storyline focuses on the 150th anniversary of *Alice's Adventures in Wonderland* at a book club, when a socialite gets murdered. Then a man is murdered at a Lewis Carroll costume party and all the clues point to a guest dressed as the Mad Hatter. Even historical murder mysteries such as the Murdoch mysteries by Maureen Jennings have included *Alice in Wonderland* links. In Season 4 of the TV series, *Murdoch in Wonderland* includes a murder at an *Alice in Wonderland* costume party.

The fantasy sector too has utilised elements of *Alice in Wonderland* concepts to create mysteries set in fantastical or sci-fi locations. Stephen Donaldson is one such writer who incorporated the magic of mirrors, and the ability to move through mirrors into other worlds. In *The Mirror of her Dreams* (1986), the heroine (Terasia) and a Mad Hatter equivalent (Geraden) have to deal with issues of misused power, imagery and what is reality, while coping with treachery, betrayal and murder, even as Terasia has to cope with her own doubts, protests and debilitating passivity. In *The Looking Glass Wars*, the author Frank Reddor pulls together elements of the story of Alice Liddell, alongside that of *Alice in Wonderland* to create a new, updated version. Alyss is destined to become Queen of Wonderland, until her parents are murdered by Redd Queen. Fleeing to safety in our world, she faces the problem of trying to adjust, to understand what is real and what is not, whether the dream she tells Charles Dodgson has any reality. When the Mad Hatter, equipped with all kinds of strange weapons, including a spinning hat, pulls her back into Wonderland, she has to take charge of a war against the Redd Queen, which can only be won by entering the Looking Glass Maze and making the right choices.

The use of *Alice in Wonderland* within the murder mystery genre is not a new thing. In 1933, one of the leading classic detective story writers, John Dickson Carr, wrote The *Mad Hatter Mystery* in which a young newspaperman is gaining notoriety by writing up bizarre crimes involving hats being stolen and returned in unlikely locations. Another classic author,

Nicholas Blake (C. Day Lewis), published *Malice in Wonderland* containing a Mad Hatter Murderer.

It is not just Alice herself or the Wonderland setting that has caught the attention of crime writers. One author, Roberta Rogow, created a series in which Charles Dodgson was one of the investigators. One of the books in the series was *The Problem of the Surly Servant (a Charles Dodgson and Arthur Conan Doyle mystery)*. Set in May 1886, Charles Dodgson is expecting a visit from Dr Arthur Conan Doyle when he hears of some troubling events. Personal items have been disappearing from student's rooms at Christ Church, while at the newly established female college Lady Margaret Hall, one of the students finds herself the subject of blackmail over a photo taken of her by Charles Dodgson when she was a child. Then Dodgson discovers the murdered body of one of the college scouts in the grounds and the only suspect is Dodgson himself.

Alice has even participated in various grisly murder films. *Alice in Murderland* (2011) involved a classic American sorority slaughter style concept combined with characters from Wonderland. The basic storyline focuses on a girl named Alice Lewis who is celebrating her 21st birthday party with her sorority friends. Everyone comes dressed up as sexy Wonderland characters. All goes well until the uninvited Jabberwocky turns up bringing murder and mayhem. The big question is just who can survive the slaughter?

One of the most enduring leisure pursuits over the past thirty or so years has been the rise of murder mystery weekends and activities. It all started when a lady called Joy Swift held a murder mystery weekend in Southport, Merseyside. It was an instant success. The concept was very simple. Groups of people gather at a hotel and seek to solve a murder mystery played out by a group of actors. The story begins during a cocktail reception and continues across various activities throughout the weekend, leading to a denouement late on the Sunday. Participants have the opportunity to question the various characters and discuss their findings with other people within the group. Actors stay in character throughout the weekend, so that participants can question them even if they encounter them in local shops, the surrounding area or the hotel. New plots are released regularly, ensuring that people come back time and time again to take part.

Since then, numerous other companies have set up their own versions using locations as varied as country houses, luxury hotels, National Trust buildings, museums, steam trains, castles and even windmills. Depending

98    The Dark Side of Alice in Wonderland

on the company involved, it can range from a jokey murder dinner to a ghostly murder or a long investigative weekend.

The potential opportunities provided by *Alice's Adventures in Wonderland* were quickly spotted. Such activities are now among the most popular of all the murder mystery events available. Leigh Clements of Shot in the Dark Mysteries says:

> 'It's definitely a favourite. Alice in Wonderland has such a cult following – especially those who appreciate the book over the movie adaptations, and when they discover that there is a way to engage with something they already love by taking on the roles of their favourite characters and dive into the content from the book in a new way, they get really excited.'

Typical of these murder mystery events is Smoke & Mirrors 'Malice in Wonderland'. In this mystery, the King of Hearts is dead, the Queen is missing, and the Duchess rules Wonderland. On the first anniversary of the King's death, the Mad Hatter, the March Hare, Alice and the White Rabbit come together to pay their respects to the great man – and find out what's in his will. This results in a riotous black comedy involving double dealing, dodgy DNA tests and lots of desperate measures. According to Smoke & Mirrors, it portrays Lewis Carroll's best loved characters, as they have never been seen before as it is basically *Alice in Wonderland* meeting the style of *The Rocky Horror Picture Show*, with its musical comedy horror concept.

There is an alternative option at Smoke & Mirrors entitled 'Malice Through the Looking Glass'. This involves a totally different plot and concept. In this event, Alice has been crowned Queen of Wonderland, and all hell has broken loose. The White Queen is on the rampage, Tweedledum is not speaking to Tweedledee and Humpty Dumpty is behaving very strangely. In addition, Alice has discovered a plot to put the Red Queen back on the throne. Alice is portrayed as having established a totalitarian dictatorship and having problems with alcohol.

Alexander Rain from Smoke & Mirrors comments that:

> 'It all started when I was booked to do an event at RAF Benson, which had an Alice theme. Looking at the characters made me think of putting the two concepts together – murder mysteries and Alice. It is an adult version of the story offering gentle comedic

murder. I realised when writing *Malice in Wonderland* that the tea-party is actually a way of putting back the Hatter's execution date, and ensuring that it never happens because they are stuck in a specific time period. This makes it hard for the March Hare who is always in season, and wants to meet another hare so is in perpetual sexual torment. We also have Alice as a slightly naughty character, having an affair with the King of Hearts. Everyone loves the story because it is so over the top.'

Much of the performance involves a classical Carry On film style ethos. Both the Queen of Hearts and the White Queen are played in drag, and at one point the Queen of Hearts loses her dress and is left wearing a leopard-skin sarong. To take another example, Tweedledee and Tweedledum wear striped jackets, tutus and big knuckledusters.

Although Smoke & Mirrors try to be light-hearted throughout, they do bring in some darker aspects. At the beginning of *Malice in Wonderland*, the King of Heart's head is served on a platter, while the Hatter is being poisoned by mercury, which is being administered by some unknown person. In *Malice Through the Looking Glass*, Alice wears vampire dress and heavy Goth makeup, while the Queen of Hearts is a nymphomaniac and her mother, (the White Queen) is even worse. There are political elements too, albeit now a little out of date as Rain admits:

'I wrote it at the time when Corbyn had just been elected leader of the Labour Party so I included some allusions such as Alice bankrupting the country, disbanding the army, removing the nuclear deterrent. Most people don't spot those allusions now, but at the time people did.'

To take another example, Manchester Murder Mysteries offer an opportunity to 'Fall down the rabbit hole into your "Malice in Wonderland" party', creating a dark twist on a classic story. Such events take place all over the world. London-based, event production agency GSP Events highlighted a Murder Mystery birthday event which took at the Fendi Villa in Rome. The Villa was transformed into a Tim Burton-themed murder mystery extravaganza which required guests to fall down a rabbit hole into Alice's world, a treasure hunt among the streets of Rome and the Vatican before culminating in the revelation as to the murderer's identity.

## 100 The Dark Side of Alice in Wonderland

It is now even possible to hold your own personal Alice themed murder mystery within your own home for family and friends. Shot in the Dark mysteries offers a version which you can download from the internet and create your own party. In this murder mystery, Alice is troubled by her memories of Wonderland and wants to know why everyone there had gone mad. Throwing herself down the rabbit hole again, she finds herself at the Knave of Heart's trial (again) and is told by the Cheshire Cat that the Caterpillar has been found dead beneath his mushroom. On investigation, it was discovered that the Caterpillar's hookah had been laced with poison making it homicide. All the residents of Wonderland become suspects not just in the murder of the Caterpillar, but also in a plot to drive the Wonderland residents mad.

Leigh Clements of Shot in the Dark Mysteries says:

'We used our traditional interactive murder mystery format for this mystery – it's the same format as all of our other mysteries, so everyone is sleuthing to find out who had the motive, means and opportunity to both drive everyone in Wonderland mad AND kill the Caterpillar.

'I always loved the story, but I felt like there was a lot lost from the original book to the Disney adaptation. There was always, in the back of my mind, the bigger question of WHY everyone in Wonderland was so mad, and I wanted to explore it a bit more in my writing. I felt there was a mystery there that no one was addressing.

'In creating it we used the book as our template, so the characters come from the original characters – we have taken no liberties on that front. We have two versions of the murder mystery – the non-murder version which just deals with discovering what actually drove everyone in Wonderland mad, and the version that adds a murder onto the mystery. In the version with the murder; the Caterpillar is killed via poison in his hookah. There are many elements, political (i.e. the Red Queen versus the Queen of Hearts), sentimental and of course, good old fashioned revenge. It is all stripped right from the pages of the mystery – and yes, even the inciting incident that drove everyone mad is there, hidden within those pages ... we just took it one step further.'

Such murder mysteries are incredibly popular with the general public. The stories are recognisable, even though they have been altered slightly to fit in with a required murder element. As Alexander Rain comments:

> 'The reactions afterwards are always very positive, recognising how we have extended the original and made something slightly different. It is very much in the Cluedo tradition as we find there is always someone who refers at some point in the proceedings to Professor Plum in the sitting room. Alice is very popular as a concept. It would be hard to do any other child's story like this because this story has all the required elements – the over the top characters, the clearly identifiable baddies, the insanity, madness and the way the Queen of Hearts is always calling "off with her head".'

Alice has also played a major part in the growing popularity of immersive theatre. These are theatre productions in which the audiences move from room to room and are totally caught up in the story. The audience does not just watch, but is expected to participate in some form effectively becoming characters within the play. The episodic nature of the *Alice in Wonderland* story lends itself easily to this concept, since each room used throughout the play can be clearly identified as a specific section within the storyline.

In 2015, London-based theatrical company Les Enfant Terribles & Les Petits Theatre devised an immersive version of *Alice in Wonderland* that took audiences by storm. It adopted a dark mysterious storyline set seventy-five years after Alice had left Wonderland. During that period she had gone missing and no one knew where or why. The story focused on the effect this had on the people of Wonderland. Half the characters were missing her, the other half were glad that she had gone. This meant that Wonderland was now cracking at the edges, and was in a state of crisis. Added to this was the concept that the Queen of Hearts, an overbearing imperious character, had become somewhat fascist and authoritarian in outlook, and was supported by equally authoritarian guards. Her opponents – the supporters of Alice – had formed an underground resistance movement following a prophesy that Alice would return and save Wonderland, returning to glory. Characters were fitted into the different themes such as Bill the Lizard who resembled a French resistance worker fighting against the Queen of Heart's Guards Brigade.

102    The Dark Side of Alice in Wonderland

At the beginning of each show, the audience would enter a dusty, Victorian style room with chandeliers, lots of books, a piano, and a looking glass in which the image of Alice suddenly appeared. She cannot remember her name and keeps asking 'Who am I?' before disappearing. At this point, the audience become Alice as she tries to find her identity. To do so, lots of choices have to be made. The audience enters a tunnel lined with yellowing book pages and are then faced with a choice. Do they choose 'Eat me' or 'Drink Me?'

This allowed the producers to split the audience immediately into two. By choosing 'Eat me', they were given an 'Eat Me' sweet and passed along a corridor. Those choosing 'Drink Me' followed a different path. They were then divided again through the receipt of one of four playing card suits; hearts, diamonds, clubs and spades. Depending on their playing card suit, they then followed yet another different path through Wonderland. This meant that there were twelve audiences entering each night, with different audiences at once, resulting in seventy-eight performances each week. At any one point in the evening, there were twenty-four different *Alice's Adventures in Wonderland* taking place. The production ended with a visit to the Wonderland Bar where themed cocktails were available. Every seventeen minutes, another fifty-six people would enter the bar meaning that speed was of the essence.

For the actors taking part, it involved a continual character rotation in order to ensure that the whole production worked perfectly. For just one episode such as the Mad Hatter's Tea Party, there were no less than 112 potential actor combinations as James Seager, creative director of Les Enfants Terrible explains.

'We realised quickly that if the actors were confined to just one character playing so many performances each week, they would go mad. To give them some variety, we created teams: Team Alice, Team Rabbit, Team Cat, Team Hatter, Team Tweedle, Team Queen, Border Guard. Teams had between 4 to 8 people who would rotate their characters each night.

'When performing, the actors kept to a strict time code. There were signals they recognised such as a beep, a light change or a light flash which was their cue to move the audiences on. With 450 people going through Wonderland each night, timing had to be exact in order to move everyone through otherwise there would be a domino effect causing problems. To get this right, we had to be very mathematical, and had to use a computer to work it all out. Carroll was a mathematician so we thought he would have been proud of that link!

'From an audience perspective, this meant that if they came more than once to see the show, they would always have a different experience.'

The production took place in an underground setting – The Vaults beside Waterloo station, in London. This provided a vast, atmospheric environment perfect for the dark storyline as it used 11 tunnels and 33 rooms totalling 30,000sqft of Victorian underground space. The statistics involved were staggering – the 2015 production resulted in 66,508 jam tarts being eaten, 48,487 eat me sweets swallowed, 92,400 playing cards issued, and 5 miles of cable being inserted in the tunnels along with 203 speakers. This version of *Alice's Adventures Underground* proved immensely popular, resulting in the production being resurrected for a second time at the Vaults in London during 2017. On each occasion, the production attracted 100,000 audience participants.

It has also attracted attention worldwide, resulting in discussions to take it elsewhere such as Spain, UAE, Saudi Arabia, Australia and America. The first such overseas production was licenced to China, where it was performed between 2018 and 2020 in Shanghai. While extremely successful, it did create some difficulties as James Seager indicates:

'The show was exactly the same as in London, just translated into Mandarin. There were a lot of hurdles to jump through with the Chinese government as we did wonder whether they would be OK with the sub text. We were surprised because the Chinese authorities didn't pick up on the political elements with the revolutionary and fascist links. It may be because in China, Alice in Wonderland is perceived as less complex, much more of a children's book when translated into Mandarin.'

In 2004, a new mystery concept emerged in Japan, and has since spread worldwide. Escape Rooms have become one of the fastest growing mystery

## 104   The Dark Side of Alice in Wonderland

entertainments, appealing to people of all ages. Initially conceived as video games, transferring the concept to an actual locked room where you have to solve the mysteries in order to escape has proved extremely popular. Each session has a strict time limit, and it is important for the participants to find all the clues, solve them and discover the final solution before the clock ticks down to zero. In most cases, the time limit is one hour.

Escape rooms are sometimes referred to as quest rooms. Participants in an escape room activity generally have one hour in which to solve the clues that will enable them to find the key to escape. All manner of clues may be utilised, including riddles, puzzles, hunting for specific object, jigsaws, mirror writing, or clues only available to seen with the aid of ultraviolet light. There are numerous props placed within the room and clues may be hidden within those props, for example pieces of paper or jigsaw pieces might be hidden within the pages of a book, within a chest of drawers, in a mirror or even on top of a door. The clues may lead to a key to open a box or door. When one box or door has been opened, the key or number cannot be used again. Some of the doors may well be concealed behind boxes, in wardrobes or fireplaces creating mini tunnels requiring participants to crawl through in order to reach the next room or clue.

With characters like the Queen of Hearts threatening mass executions, the mysterious world of *Alice in Wonderland* has proved fertile ground for escape room operators to create innovative, lively mysteries – and murders. Anything can happen in an escape game.

The complexity of the game depends a great deal on the age-range for which they are destined or whether the game is targeted at people who are new to escape games. It may involve being required to help Alice escape Wonderland, solving a murder or theft such as who stole the tarts; avoiding the threat of execution by the Queen of Hearts or an encounter with a deadly enemy like the Jabberwocky or Bandersnatch. At Escape Hunt, Leeds, participants are encouraged to go down the rabbit hole and follow Alice's footsteps by growing to the size of a giant, attending a mad tea party and exploring the palace grounds. Navigating around Wonderland is not easy since there are countless puzzles that must be solved before the Jabberwocky is let loose.

Escape Hunt is the largest of all the escape room companies and says that:

> '*Alice in Wonderland*, the classic novel by Lewis Carroll, is the perfect setting for an escape game adventure because of its broad

appeal to adults and children alike. The topsy-turvy world of Wonderland inspires us to try new things, meet new people, and embrace pure, unadulterated nonsense. This sense of wonder and excitement is exactly what we want our players to feel as they springboard from reality into the fantastical world of our original game Alice in Puzzleland, making the theme and execution a perfect match.

'Taking this concept and turning it into a mystery escape game is quite simple – there are always more questions to be asked, more characters to interrogate, and an answer to seek at the end of the adventure. With a literary setting as rich and diverse as Alice in Wonderland, we the players cannot help but be intrigued by the who, what, when, where and how. We start with the what – what has happened, and we build backwards from there, paving the way for players to discover their own meaning and adventure in the game.

'The challenge in a project like Alice in Puzzleland is in straying true to a wellknown and loved story, while adding a twist of signature Escape Hunt whimsy and excitement. We wanted the game to feel new and exciting but also like returning home, just as Alice herself felt in the mirrored world of Wonderland.'

Although not outwardly tailored to the *Alice in Wonderland* storyline, many escape rooms stories are influenced by the Alice ideas. At The Dream House for example, Jessica has become trapped inside her dreams and is unable to wake up. Participating teams have to enter the dream, and free Jessica from the dark forces holding her there. Time is of the essence – fail to help her within an hour and participants will find themselves joining her in the dream. An alternative take on the Alice theme is Time Trap Reading's Imaginarium 1863. In this game, participants enter Lewis Carroll's mind in order to restore the memories he used to create his famous book.

The Alice theme has even been used to create mystery mazes. In 2020 Lakeland Maze Farm Park, Cumbria, created a giant maize maze celebrating the 200th anniversary of Sir John Tenniel's work with an elaborate, twisting, turning design focusing on the White Rabbit and his watch. With no dead

106 The Dark Side of Alice in Wonderland

ends, just constantly changing paths, the eight acre puzzle proved extremely challenging.

*Alice in Wonderland* has undoubtedly become one of the most popular murder mystery concepts, appealing to all age groups due to its imaginative content that can be used in so many different ways. There are no indications that this popularity is set to decrease with time. In fact, the opposite is true, *Alice in Wonderland* is proving even more popular and incorporating an ever increasingly imaginative range of murders, mysteries and ideas than ever before.

*Chapter 9*

# Mad Alice

'"But I don't want to go among mad people," Alice remarked. "Oh,
you can't help that," said the Cat: "We're all mad here. I'm mad."'
*Alice in Wonderland*

The fantastical, crazy, upside down topsy-turvy world of *Alice in Wonderland*
has always attracted attention. When created by Dodgson in 1888, it was
a concept that had never been seen before in children's literature. Written
very much from a child's viewpoint, we see Wonderland through a child's
eyes, a child who has the freedom to question everything and everyone. It
is a world far removed from that of the staid Victorian society with which
Dodgson's readers would have been familiar.

Yet it is also a world that reflects some of the concerns and issues that were
becoming apparent. Anyone suffering from any kind of mental problems in
the nineteenth century would simply be regarded as 'mad'. There was no
treatment, with sufferers simply being kept out of the public eye or confined
to an asylum. Public asylums had gained a terrifying reputation. Social
reformer Harriet Martineau wrote 'in pauper asylums we see chains and
strait-waistcoats, three or four half-naked creatures thrust into a chamber
filled with straw, to exasperate each other with their clamour and attempts
at violence; or else gibbering in idleness or moping in solitude'. During
the latter part of the nineteenth century, there was a change from simply
providing custody to treating them like rational people, and actually trying
to cure mentally ill people, with considerable research taking place into
mental illness. It was a world of which Charles Dodgson was very much
aware. His uncle, Robert Skeffington Lutwidge, was secretary of the
Lunacy Commission for ten years, as well as being a member of the Board
of Metropolitan Commissioners in Lunacy. He was regarded as an expert on
the subject. On occasion, Charles Dodgson accompanied his uncle on visits
to asylums and became friends with many of Lutwidge's medical colleagues.
Such visits enabled him to see how the patients were treated in practice, as
well as being able to discuss mental issues with the doctors.

108   The Dark Side of Alice in Wonderland

It was Skeffington Lutwidge who introduced Dodgson to photography and as a result of this new hobby, Dodgson came into contact with one of his uncle's friends – Dr Hugh Welch Diamond, of the Surrey Lunatic Asylum. Victorians believed that a person's state of mind was reflected in their appearance. Dr Diamond took this belief one step further, suggesting that photography could play a major role in diagnosing and recording mental illness. It was a suggestion that Dodgson found interesting, and undoubtedly influenced his development of portrait photography likewise the colourful styling of the Mad Hatter.

Visits to asylums may also have contributed to the portrayal of the Mad Hatter's Tea Party, which is one of the most well-known activities within *Alice in Wonderland*. Similar tea parties were held in asylums as a form of therapy, designed to stimulate and entertain the patients. Typical of these parties is that which was noted at the York Retreat, an institution operated by Samuel Tuke, a pioneer in nineteenth-century mental health care. He wrote:

> 'The female superintendent ... occasionally gives a general invitation to the patients, to a tea party. All who attend, dress in their best clothes, and vie with each other in politeness and propriety. The best fare is provided and the visitors are treated with all the attention of strangers…The patients control, in a wonderful degree, their different propensities; and the scene is at once curious, and affectingly gratifying.'

The constant seat changing and cluttered thoughts expressed by the Mad Hatter, the sleepiness of the Dormouse, and the frantic activity of the March Hare could well reflect some of the actions Dodgson would have observed during those asylum tea parties.

In 1873, Skeffington Lutwidge was killed by an inmate during a visit to an asylum. Charles Dodgson was much affected by his uncle's murder and one year later, wrote *The Hunting of the Snark*. Medical researchers Torrey and Miller have suggested that this poem is a veiled description of the Lunacy Commission inspection team and its work. They point to the fact that the Baker's uncle advises that the Snark be hunted with thimbles, forks and soap – all of which were items checked for safety purposes by the lunatic asylum inspectors during their visits. The poem also provided

Mad Alice   109

inspiration for psychologist Christina Richards to create a caustic take on the poem, highlighting modern attitudes and visits by psychiatrists. Entitled 'The Hunting of the Schizophrenic Snark', it was published in *Psychologist* magazine. Typical verses included:

'There was an elderly psychiatrist, whose life hadn't made him wise
And then a neuroscientist, who had trouble with his eyes.
Several new psychologists wished to come along
And all the undergraduates who said, 'Surely these guys can't be wrong!'

And

'To make lots of money … no! let me start again
It's for a better quality of life – to ease these people's pain,
They don't need work or love or joy with motivation gone
They can "express themselves" at day centres through poetry and song'

Having criticised the motivations of numerous different types of people involved in the mental health industry from psychiatrists to drug companies, she ends:

'You're hunting for a concept which *we* don't recognise
It's a Person in a mirror; not a label meets our eyes
But you can't catch this Snark – it's not a thing: it's just a Boojum
Can you see?'

Over the years, critics have questioned Dodgson's own sanity, raising questions whether he was suffering from some type of psychological problem. Victorians believed that epilepsy was a form of insanity, and Dodgson himself refers to this in an entry in his diary on 6 April 1876.

His diaries reveal an interest in medical issues and the causes of epilepsy. It is possible that he may have had mild epileptic attacks himself. In 1885, Dodgson experienced a severe day-long headache which was diagnosed by his doctor as being an 'epileptiform' – a mild epileptic attack. Having discussed the issue with Dr Yvonne Hart, a consultant neurologist at the

110   The Dark Side of Alice in Wonderland

Radcliffe Hospital, Oxford; Dodgson's biographer, Jenny Woolf, suggests that he may have suffered from migraine, as Victorian doctors believed that there was a link between epilepsy and migraine.

His first biographer, Stuart Collingwood, believed that Dodgson suffered from periods of depression throughout his life. He certainly read widely about the subject and was interested in 'psycho-physiology', dealing with links between the body and mind including elements like hypnotism, delusions, hallucinations and early psychology. Both *Alice in Wonderland* and *Alice Through the Looking Glass* were written during particularly unhappy periods in Dodgson's life. Many observers believe that writing the books may have helped alleviate Carroll's own misery and pain.

In recent years, recognition of eating disorders has led psychologists to question whether this was a problem for Dodgson, who was known to refuse invitations to lunch on the basis that 'he had no appetite for a meal at that time'. It was only when he had his child friends over to visit, that Dodgson ensured there were plenty of sweet treats available. By doing so, he was reflecting desires he could not personally enjoy onto others. Another mental issue portrayed in the story is that of insomnia and irregular sleeping patterns. Dodgson was known to suffer from insomnia and some of his experiences may well be reflected in the Mad Hatter's tea party where the Dormouse is always tired and constantly falling asleep. He highlights the difference between 'I breathe when I sleep' and 'I sleep when I breathe' since some people cannot maintain a regular breathing pattern when sleeping, thus resulting in interrupted sleep. On 9 February 1856, Dodgson wrote about dreams in his diary, commenting that it was 'an inability to distinguish which is the waking and which the sleeping life'. He also commented that, 'We often dream without the least suspicion of reality'.

Dreams are a major theme within the *Alice in Wonderland* stories. The dream is real for Alice, believing that the places she visits and the people she meets should (but don't) obey the logic of her waking world. 'When I used to read fairy tales,' Alice comments when her suddenly gigantic body is crammed tightly in the White Rabbit's house, 'I fancied that kind of thing never happened, and now I am in the middle of one.'

There is madness all around her. She thinks she is not mad, and is horrified when the Cheshire Cat tells her, 'we're all mad here. I'm mad. You're mad ...You must be, Or you wouldn't have come here.'

Dodgson undoubtedly had a deep interest in dreams and mental thought patterns. He owned a copy of *The Literature and Curiosities of Dreams*, which was published the same year as *Alice in Wonderland*. Written by Frank Seafield, *The Literature and Curiosities of Dreams* comprises a history of dreams while attempting to explain their causes, effects and meanings. Psychiatry was in its infancy during Victorian times, and Dodgson's interest reflects the way the Victorians believed there was method in madness. Dreams were seen as a way of illuminating the truth about human consciousness and, as a result, many researchers believed that listening to mad people could shed light on how sane people might think. One of the most famous writers to be influenced by the dream and madness concepts of *Alice in Wonderland* was James Joyce. He was fascinated by Charles Dodgson both as a writer and a person, and Dodgson's writing techniques intrigued him. One of the themes of *Finnegan's Wake* is the way the father figure attempts to tempt the daughter, thus reflecting hints of Dodgson and his child friends. *Finnegan's Wake* is about a dream, and includes references to *Alice in Wonderland* and Dodgson in terms of content, images and the use of nonsensical language such as: 'Alicious, twinstreams twinestraines, through alluring glass or alas in jumboland?' 'knives of hearts' 'from tweedledeedums down to tweedledeedees' 'loose carolleries' and 'Wonderlawn's lost us for ever. Alis, alas, she broke the glass! Liddell lokker through the leafery, ours is mistery of pain'. Elsewhere there are references to 'wonderland's wanderdad', 'Liddel oud oddity', 'Lewd's carol', 'old Dadgerson's dodges' and 'Dodgfather, Dodgson and Coo'.

As a final example, there is the paragraph,

> 'And there many have paused before that exposure of him by old Tom Quad, a flashback in which he sits sated, gowndabout, in clericalease habit, watching bland Sol slithe dodgsomely into the nethermore, a globule of maugdleness about to corrugate his mild dewed cheek and the tata of a tiny victorienne, Alys, pressed by his limper looser.'

During the 1930s, psychoanalysts using Freudian techniques took a look at *Alice in Wonderland* and her creator. Paul Ferdinand Schilder described *Alice* as 'the expression of particularly strong destructive tendencies, of very primitive character,' and labelled its author as being 'a particularly dangerous writer'. In the same decade, biographer Langford Reed diagnosed Dodgson as being the victim of a 'dual personality'. This view was summed up in a chapter entitled 'The Strange Case of Professor Dodgson and Mr Carroll'

## 112    The Dark Side of Alice in Wonderland

postulating that they formed very different personalities since Carroll's cheerful nonsense was totally different to, and continually struggling with, Dodgson's 'frigid' seriousness. In 1960, Martin Gardner wrote in *The Annotated Alice* that the Queen of Hearts constant calls of 'Off with their heads' was 'violence with Freudian overtones' but was quite harmless to children, yet the book 'should not be allowed to circulate indiscriminately among adults who are undergoing analysis'.

On a lighter note, the 2008 issue of the *Journal of Developmental and Behavioural Paediatrics*, contained a letter written by Dublin psychiatrist Brendan D. Kelly, in which he commented that the story was immersed in psychopathology. He suggested that the weeping Mock Turtle was 'clinically depressed' and the Young Crab displayed 'the first case of oppositional defiant disorder ever described in a juvenile crustacean'.

Looking at the characters Alice discovers within Wonderland, some are definitely verging on the insane or display mental disorders of various kinds, for example the White Rabbit's obsession with promptness links to a stress related General Anxiety Disorder, while the Caterpillar's use of riddles and superior manner is characteristic of grandiose delusions. This concept has been taken still further by later renditions of the novel into other print and film versions. Tim Burton's film *Alice in Wonderland* (2010) is one of the darkest versions to be created, with every element from filming techniques to characterisation designed to emphasise a totally crazy, insane world and make it believable. Tim Burton commented:

> 'These characters are all different representations of some kind of madness, and because in terms of past things with Alice, all the characters are just crazy, in their own kind of way; it's not craziness for the sake of it.'

Katherine Miclau, of Harvard Education Mental Health Research, pointed out that:

> 'When looking specifically at adaptions of Lewis Carroll's Alice in Wonderland, the majority of the characters present symptoms of various psychological disorders in some form or another, but without explicitly mentioning mental health. For example, the White Rabbit's obsession about promptness and consequently, his fear and paranoia associated with time, correlates to a stress-related

disorder such as General Anxiety Disorder, the Caterpillar, always seemingly smoking a hookah, speaks in riddles in a slow, prophet-like manner as if he was Alice's superior, which is characteristic of grandiose delusions (DG). In addition, although Alice exhibits symptoms of paranoid schizophrenia, and the Mad Hatter those of both Bipolar Disorder and PTSD ... the audience is not experiencing the characters as diseases, but instead as a plethora of very different individuals with diverse mannerisms. The dialogue between the Mad Hatter and Alice encompasses the perception on mental health in the story: Mad Hatter "Have I gone mad?" Alice: "I'm afraid so. You're entirely bonkers. But I'll tell you a secret. All the best people are.'"

One of the most well-known and instantly recognisable of all the characters in Wonderland is the Mad Hatter yet it is a phrase that Dodgson himself never actually used in the book. The character appears for the first time in *Alice's Adventures in Wonderland*, in a chapter entitled 'A Mad Tea-party'. Alice meets the Cheshire Cat and asks, 'What sort of people live about here?'

The Cheshire Cat responds, 'In that direction lives a Hatter, and in that direction, lives a March Hare. Visit either you like: they're both mad!'

There are two main theories as to the origins of the Mad Hatter. One commonly held suggestion is that the character may have been inspired by an eccentric Victorian furniture retailer who was said to own a shop near Christ Church College in Oxford. His name was Theophilius Carter and become known locally as the 'Mad Hatter' because of his habit of standing in his shop doorway, wearing a top hat. Sir John Tenniel is said to have visited Oxford to sketch him when preparing his illustrations for *Alice in Wonderland*. While an attractive theory, there is unfortunately no evidence in Carroll's letters or diaries to support this.

By far the most popular theory relates to the problems experienced in the manufacture of hats. The phrase 'mad as a hatter' was already common by the early 1800s as it was used to relate to a physical and mental illness found among hatters. Doctors referred to it as an occupational disease known as 'erethism' or 'mad hatter syndrome'. Once a person was affected by the illness, the results were irreversible and the person's condition continued to steadily deteriorate. Hat making was a massive industry as wearing hats was a social requirement. Everyone, no matter what their social standing

114    The Dark Side of Alice in Wonderland

in society, wore a hat. The only difference was the quality and the styling of the hats.

Many versions of *Alice in Wonderland* portray the Mad Hatter wearing a top hat. These hats were first created in 1793, when George Dunnage, a hatter from Middlesex, introduced the style. Within thirty years, top hats had become popular with all social classes and even workmen wore them. When creating the hats, hatters would use a felt base. This felt was made from rabbit fur, which first had to be separated from the animal skin, and then matted together to form a durable fabric. This process involved the use of a toxic substance called mercuric nitrate – a mix of mercury and nitric acid. The process was often described as 'carroting' from the colour of the mercuric nitrate. The long-term effects on hatters were extremely serious. Prolonged exposure to mercuric nitrate led to serious physical and mental diseases including hallucinations, speech problems, emotional instability, psychotic reactions, delirium and tremors (which became known as hatters' shakes). The mercuric nitrate affected the entire nervous system. It also caused skin, nails and hair to become much more orange in shade. Hatters would have experienced very bizarre behaviour and it would have affected all aspects of their daily life.

Such images came very much to the forefront when actor Johnny Depp was researching his characterization of the Mad Hatter in Tim Burton's *Alice in Wonderland*. Talking about his character to a Los Angeles reporter in 2010, he stated that his character had orange hair and 'was poisoned … and it was coming out through his hair, through his fingernails and eyes'.

In order to make this visually apparent, his make-up was designed to reflect the effects of mercury poisoning. In the film, Depp's face was turned matt white, his hair bright orange, eyes bright green and his fingers were tinged with orange. In addition, all the tools of his trade formed part of his costume including his thimbles, while his pincushion was turned into a ring he wore on his finger.

Another key feature of Depp's portrayal of the Hatter's madness was to portray him as a conflicted character, with nervous and mental instability. This is a character which could in turn be funny, sad, intense, angry, and scary with rapid changes of attitude. Depp said:

> 'What is he like? He's mad. It has always seemed to be like he was a beating heart, as if his heart flesh were on the outside. He's like a mood ring, in a sense, impossible to hide anything. His emotions

are very, very close to the surface. It seemed to be that because he would be so hyper sensitive, he would need to travel into another site, as it were, another personality, to be able to survive, which kicks in when he is threatened or when he's in danger.'

He added two accents to the portrayal. A Scottish accent was used whenever the Mad Hatter was thinking about the past, and an English accent whenever he was clearly in the present time.

'The switching between the accents is the safety mechanism that kicks in when he needs to become tough, when he needs to become angry, when he needs to be protected, when he's fearful. I thought it would like experiencing a kinder form of personality disorder in a way. He just kicks into another person at a certain point. I can't remember how many different characters he is. It's one of those things where it's a hit or miss, and you hope it works … You've got to underline the illness.'

Wearing a top hat has become an integral feature of any image of the Mad Hatter. It signifies his profession and would have made him instantly recognisable to Alice when she encounters him at the tea party. His behaviour during the tea party reflects his personality disorders, displaying a wide range of emotional reactions. He is angry with the March Hare for suggesting that butter should be put on his watch, then he pours hot tea on the Dormouse, angry when Alice asks too many questions because it makes the story telling too long, and wants to continually change chairs.

March is the start of the mating season for hares. During that period, they are said to go mad and become very excitable. Hares jump around vertically and generally display abnormal behaviour. There may be madcap chases through the countryside, as well as furious boxing matches. This is the courting behaviour of mating hares. The phrase 'mad as a March hare; has been used for centuries, with examples seen as long ago as the early sixteenth century when the Tudor poet, John Skelton, referred to 'thou madde Marche Hare'. Alice refers to this when musing on various Wonderland characters, saying, 'The Mad March Hare will be much the most interesting, and perhaps as this is May it won't be raving mad – at least not so mad as it was in March.'

Sir John Tenniel also implied this sense of madness by placing straw on the head of the March Hare – a common way to depict madness in Victorian

116    The Dark Side of Alice in Wonderland

times. Twentieth century authors, particularly in Japanese Manga series, frequently exaggerate the madness of the March Hare. A typical example of this is the story *Alice in the Country of Hearts* where the March Hare is portrayed as human with two rabbit ears. He is immediately insulted and angry whenever anyone calls him a rabbit saying that his ears are simply 'just bigger than average'. He is also violent, threatening Alice with a gun.

The Queen of Hearts is one of the most terrifying characters in Wonderland, displaying a typical narcissistic personality. Definitions of Narcissistic Personality Disorder (NPD) point to the presence of 'an inflated sense of their own importance, a deep need for excessive attention … and a lack of empathy for others'. People suffering from NPD often become impatient and angry when they do not receive the special treatment to which they believe they are entitled, and frequently display rage or contempt for others so as to prove they are superior. The Queen of Hearts is depicted as a terrifying creature; very domineering and constantly threatening everyone with decapitation. She is described as 'a blind fury' frequently shouting 'Off with his head' or 'Off with their heads'. Even Alice is threatened with decapitation almost immediately on meeting the Queen. Having just discovered three playing cards painting white roses red, the cards drop to the ground face down when the Queen of Hearts arrives. Alice also falls to the ground. Alice is asked by the Queen for the identities of the cards lying face down. As only the backs of the cards can be seen, Alice has no idea as to the numbers on the cards and says she has no idea. The Queen of Heart's immediate reaction is to order her execution – a sentence which is then mitigated by the King, on the basis that Alice is just a child. The Queen's propensity to order executions can be seen in action throughout the croquet match, with almost every player being hauled away for execution. In the trial of the Knave of Hearts the Queen issues the sentence before any verdict is actually reached.

Despite the frequency of the execution orders, very few are actually carried out. The King of Hearts quietly orders pardons to be granted. The Queen is humoured, but not obeyed in practice. As the Gryphon points out to Alice, 'it's all her fancy: she executes nobody, you know.'

The Queen of Hearts is not the only royal character that Dodgson created, although she is often mistaken for the Red Queen portrayed in *Through the Looking Glass*. The two queens were regarded by the author as being distinctive and different – a fact which is brought out in Tim Burton's film version.

In '*Alice*' *on the Stage*, Dodgson commented:

'I pictured to myself the Queen of Hearts as a sort of embodiment of ungovernable passion – a blind and aimless Fury.

'The Red Queen I pictured as a Fury, but of another type; her passion must be cold and calm – she must be formal and strict, yet not unkindly, pedantic to the 10th degree, the concentrated essence of all governesses.'

Tim Burton's film version makes the Queen of Hearts a much more central character than is usually the case. He divided the character into two – the Red Queen and the White Queen. The setting is some years after Alice's first visit to Wonderland. The Red Queen has assumed control, forcing the White Queen out of power. Alice has to be convinced of her own identity, as the potential saviour of Wonderland who can take on the dreaded Jabberwocky, so as bring the White Queen back into power. It is a story highlighting the differences between the two queens and how mental issues can affect people in different ways.

Playing the White Queen, Anne Hathaway comments:

'She comes from the same gene pool as the Red Queen. She really likes the dark side but she's so scared of going too far into it that she's made everything appear very light and happy. But she's actually living in that place out of fear that she won't be able to control herself.'

Reflecting on her role as the Red Queen, Helena Bonham Carter says:

'She's got emotional problems. She's somebody who doesn't really rule through any kind of justice or fairness, but basically, through terror because she has this Jabberwocky as a pet. So I chop off people's heads. That's my solution to everything. It probably comes from an underlying insecurity in the fact that she has such a big head and everyone else has a normal one.

'According to Linda Woolverton, the screenwriter, there's a tumour in her head and it's pressing on the bit that controls emotions. So it

## 118 The Dark Side of Alice in Wonderland

takes nothing practically for her to lose her temper. She's a bit like a two year old in her tantrums. Basically she's like a spoiled child. Everything's done for her. She has absolutely no compassion for anybody else's feelings, totally oblivious to anybody else's feelings apart from her own. She has no heart even, though she's the Queen of Hearts.'

Turning to the lead character in the Wonderland books, Alice is constantly questioning her own identity. She states, 'I know who I WAS when I got up this morning, but I think I must have been changed several times since then'.

Many neuro-specialists point to Alice's identity crisis as being an example of Depersonalisation Disorder (DPD). This is a mental syndrome involving a lack of ownership of thoughts and memories, feelings of not belonging in your body, numb emotions and that movements are initiated without any conscious decision created a fragmented sense of self identity. These features are often present as a result of stress, tiredness or drug use as well as a result of migraine or epileptic attacks.

Dream Anxiety Disorder (DAD) is another possibility, as it relates to people suffering constant nightmares and night terrors affecting their lives and personal safety as in schizophrenia. Schizophrenics suffer hallucinations, hear voices, experience confused thoughts and exhibit disorganised, unpredictable behaviour. Within the book, Alice is 'very fond of pretending to be two people' and unsure whether she is amounts to a single whole.

In the original story, Alice is close to the onset of puberty with all the emotional confusion that this entails. Other authors have picked up on this aspect. In 2006, a mobile game producer Sunsoft created a game called *Alice's Warped Wonderland* or *Yugami no kuni no Arisu.* It portrays Ariko (Alice) as being constantly depressed due to a traumatic childhood and trying to suppress memories of her earlier life.

In recent years, more and more attention has been focused on eating disorders, and obsessions with food, body, weight and shape. References to food within the Wonderland stories are seen as indicators that Alice was suffering from this problem. Proponents of this theory point to the fact that Alice is constantly experiencing a cycle whereby she overeats, then has to eat or drink more to solve her problem. At the beginning of the story, Alice encounters drink and food labelled 'Eat Me' and 'Drink Me'. Every time she eats or drinks, she dramatically changes size, becoming either too large or too small. Each time, she does not eat a small mouthful, but eats or drinks too much and then regrets her decision. Later in the book, she then drinks too much and grows so rapidly she fills the entire house. When Alice tells the Caterpillar she is unhappy with her size, and wants to be different, the Caterpillar advises moderation, pointing out that she can make her own choice on size by nibbling on different sides of a mushroom.

Neurosurgeons, psychiatrists and psychoanalysts have drawn inspiration from the *Alice in Wonderland* stories, pointing out that the stories explore numerous facets of the human personality such as to whether there is a continuous self, identity, how events from the past are remembered and how the future is envisaged. Given that the story itself is set in a dream, it contains many elements of a dream world – objects that change into new identities, mixed images and Alice's belief that time is playing tricks. According to neuroscientists such impressions reflect the way in which the sleeping brain consolidates memories, creating links which enable people to process information and observe a bigger story. Alice's memories of a pig are combined with a memory of a baby.

In 1938, Paul Schilder set out to undertake a psychological study of *Alice in Wonderland* and Lewis Carroll which was published in the *Journal of Nervous and Mental Disease*. His aim was to explore the value of the Alice books to children by using the stories to psychoanalyse Lewis Carroll and Charles Dodgson on the basis that 'Carroll himself has pointed this way by choosing a pseudonym and holding Charles Lutwidge Dodgson strictly separated from Lewis Carroll'. He concluded that Wonderland offers an extreme aggressiveness, which was a manifestation of repressed sentiments and extensions of the author's psyche into the story. Alice is full of anxiety especially over her body image and experiences:

> 'It is either "too small" or "too big" … She feels "separated from her feet", "Animals pass remarks about her", "the food is taken away from her" and the banquiet scene ends in an uproar in which she is "threatened by the candles, by the ladle and by the bottles which have become birds" These are indeed nightmares full of anxiety. We are accustomed to find such dreams in persons with strong repressions which prevent final satisfactions.'

Psychiatrist and psychoanalyst Carl Jung took a different approach, focusing on the conscious mind and the ego as it comprises thoughts, memories and emotions. Jung wrote, 'A typical infantile motif is the

## 120   The Dark Side of Alice in Wonderland

dream of growing infinitely small or infinitely big or being transformed from one to another – as you find it, for instance, in Lewis Carroll's *Alice in Wonderland*.' Unlike Freud, he believed that such symbols should be considered in the context of the dream, rather than as self-explanatory ciphers. The theme of transformation continues throughout the books, with elements such as the Caterpillar and the Pool of Tears and even Alice herself, given her power to be destructive as seen in her attempts to escape the White Rabbit's house.

Jung went on to write that 'the child motif represents the preconscious, childhood aspect of the collective psyche … a symbol which unites the opposites; a mediator, bringer of healing.' Alice becomes a symbol of unity, linking together opposites such as white and red roses, black and white kittens, Red Queen and White Queen. It is a unity from which adults can benefit by becoming more child-like.

In 1955, psychiatrist John Todd identified the Alice in Wonderland syndrome. This has become a term used by doctors to refer to altered bizarre perceptions and shapes of a person's body, along with the illusions of changes taking place in the forms, dimensions and motions of objects that may be experienced during a partial seizure, migraine headache, or when intoxicated. Todd highlighted examples of patients in his care who had experienced sensations similar to those of Alice when shrinking and growing. Among the examples he quoted were:

'A single woman, aged 39 … Complained of recurrent attacks during which she feels that her body is growing larger and larger until it seems to occupy the whole room …

'A single man, aged 40 … recurrent feeling that he was much taller or shorter than was actually the case. Sometimes he felt he was eight feet tall, but at other times he felt as though he had shrunk to a mere three feet.

'A housewife, aged 24 … Periodically she felt that her stature had altered – "the ground comes up and I go down or vice versa, so that sometimes I feel myself to be six inches tall and sometimes twelve feet".'

\*\*\*

> "'T'was brilig,
> And the slithy toves,
> Did gyre and gimble in the wabe …'

is the start to the fantastical poem about the Jabberwocky in *Alice in Through the Looking Glass*. Neuroscientists now use 'Jabberwocky sentences' during brain scans to show that the brain processes meaning and grammar separately. Other studies of language development highlight the way in which Alice's conversations with Humpty Dumpty deal with the nature and sound of words.

> 'My name is Alice, but –'
> 'It's a stupid enough name!' Humpty Dumpty interrupted impatiently. 'What does it mean?'
> 'MUST a name mean something?' Alice asked doubtfully.
> 'Of course it must,' Humpty Dumpty said with a short laugh: 'My name means the shape I am – and a good handsome shape it is, too. With a name like yours, you might be any shape, almost.'

For centuries, it has been assumed that there is no inherent meaning in sounds. Researchers are now questioning that assumption suggesting that the Humpty Dumpty may well be correct. Nicknames can reflect appearances.

In 1968, British physician Eric Bywaters identified a Cheshire Cat syndrome relating to 'innate commonsense untrammelled by the rigorous laws of proof' citing the Cheshire Cat's suggestions to Alice as to where to go next. While in recent years, a neurological condition has been diagnosed as Prosopagnosia referring to 'the selective inability to recognise faces' and is usually the result of head trauma as highlighted in *Alice in Wonderland*.

Humpty Dumpty tells Alice:

> "'I shouldn't know you again if we did meet. Your face is the same as everybody else has – the two eyes, so –" (marking their places in the air with his thumb) 'nose in the middle, mouth under. It's always the same. Now if you had two eyes in the same side of the nose, for instance – or the mouth at the top – that would be some help.'"

122    The Dark Side of Alice in Wonderland

This is now regarded as being possibly the earliest description of prosopagnosia in literature. Sufferers find it hard to distinguish family members or friends from total strangers, and quite often cannot identify people whom they know well. In severe cases, this can totally disrupt their lives, resulting in people seeking solitary lifestyles with minimal social interaction.

The connotations of madness inherent within *Alice in Wonderland* have appealed to many writers, creating a useful hook on which to create stories especially within the young adult sector. Typical of these stories is the series created by A.G. Howard dealing with issues of sanity and the extent to which it can be inherited. *Splintered* is the first book in the series and involves Alyssa Gardner, whose great-great-grandmother was Alice Liddell. Alyssa's family suffers from a curse, which stretches back to Alice Liddell – they can hear the whispers of bugs and flowers. Alyssa's mother was already in a mental hospital as a result. Now Alyssa is beginning to hear those whispers too. When her mother's mental health becomes worse, Alyssa discovers that what she thought was fiction is a terrifying reality and it is her task to go down the rabbit hole to break the curse by passing a series of tasks, including draining an ocean of Alice's tears, waking the slumbering tea party and subduing a vicious Bandersnatch. In the second volume, *Unhinged*, Alyssa faces yet another dangerous quest in the dark, challenging Wonderland at the request of the mysterious Morpheus. In the concluding volume, *Ensnared*, Alyssa has embraced her madness and gained a perspective on the subject. She is determined to rescue the two linked worlds in which she inhabits, and the netherlings she loves even though it means challenging Queen Red. This time the only way into Wonderland is through a looking glass world parallel dimension filled with mutated and violent netherling outcasts. Together with her father, Alyssa travels into the heart of the magic to find her mother, convince her she is not mad, and set right all that has gone wrong, salvaging Wonderland from the decay and destruction that has ensnared it.

Scriptwriters have been equally keen on the subject. One of the most recent films was in 2016, when Disney released a live action sequel to the earlier Tim Burton film. In *Alice through the Looking Glass* (also produced by Tim Burton), Alice discovers a magical looking glass which takes her back to Wonderland. The Mad Hatter is acting madder than ever, and Alice uses the Chronosphere to travel through time in a race to save the Hatter before time runs out. The Chronosphere helps her visit friends and enemies at different points in time seeing how their personalities change. At one point, Alice runs into a mirror which returns her to her own world, only to wake up in a mental hospital, diagnosed with female hysteria. This was an all too common diagnosis involving an array of symptoms ranging from anxiety, fainting, nervousness, sexual desire, loss of appetite and even a 'tendency to cause trouble for others'. In some circumstances, such a diagnosis could result in the unfortunate woman being forced into an insane asylum or undergoing a forced hysterectomy.

Scenes in a mental hospital could also be found in an American ABC miniseries, *Once Upon a Time in Wonderland* (2013). Alice is locked in an asylum and is believed to be insane after telling people about Wonderland. Her doctors plan to cure her with a treatment that makes her forget everything about Wonderland and the boyfriend she lost there. Saved in the nick of time from the treatment, she is whisked back to Wonderland by the Knave of Hearts and the White Rabbit. Her task is to find her boyfriend, evading the Red Queen's plots while dealing with the many dangers Wonderland poses, including the mysterious Jabberwocky.

*Warehouse 13* was another TV series created by the Syfy Channel featured an extremely evil version of Alice. The series works on the premise that Lewis Carroll's books were actually true and were chronicles of Alice's adventures in Wonderland just pretending to be fiction. Using the mirror to enter into Wonderland eventually makes Alice 'mad as a hatter' and she becomes a sociopathic killer. Forcibly trapped in the mirror, she is accidentally released when the mirror is dropped. Her attempts to destroy the mirror eventually fail and she is returned to her imprisonment.

Another good example is that of American McGee's *Alice* video game series. This has become one of the premier Alice themed video games experiencing worldwide popularity. The first game follows the basic traditional storyline, but with tweaks. It begins with a house fire in which her parents are killed, but Alice is left with serious burns and psychological damage. She taken to an asylum in a catatonic state. Treatment has no effect. Her toy rabbit calls for help, she mentally retreats into Wonderland where she meets the Cheshire Cat. Discovering that the Queen of Wonderland has put Wonderland into a state of decline and despondency, Alice is given the task of being Wonderland's champion. Subsequent events take her through places like the Vale of Tears, the Fortress of Doors, meeting characters like the Mad Hatter and the Red King and undertakes a fight with the Jabberwocky. By overcoming the Jabberwocky, and the Queen of Hearts,

**124** The Dark Side of Alice in Wonderland

Wonderland is restored, and Alice regains her sanity, allowing her to leave the Asylum.

In *Alice: Madness Returns*, Alice is living in a Victorian orphanage known as the Houndsditch Home for Wayward Youth, but still experiences hallucinations of Wonderland. A more complex storyline than in the original *Alice* computer game, *Alice: Madness Returns* involves frequent shifts between Victorian London and Wonderland. An entity called the Dollmaker has taken over the Infernal Train and is corrupting Wonderland. While in Victorian London, she discovers that the orphanage's psychiatrist Dr Bumby was involved in the fire that destroyed her home, and is trying to erase her memories (along with the memories of other children in the home) so as to leave them as 'blank toys' to be sold to molesters and abusive masters. Some of the scenes take place in a very creepy lunatic asylum in which she is strapped in a straitjacket, fastened to an operating table surrounded by white coated people. There are captions such as 'Madness is not a state of mind', 'Madness is a place', 'Let's go There Shall We' and Alice asking tremulously, 'Is it mad to pray for better hallucinations? She also comments that 'the destruction of Wonderland is the destruction of me' and that 'I'm in hell'. The resulting images of Wonderland are terrifying and nightmarish, with a blood-stained Alice fighting playing card soldiers, an almost skeletal Cheshire cat, and evil minotaurs with scythes.

The next instalment of the series focuses on *Alice Asylum* in which a young Alice is shown fighting through the trauma of losing her family. With phrases such as 'Denial is the Ultimate Asylum', it involves a psychological escape from reality through regression – going back to a happier time in her mental state, before seeking an escape by diverting her thoughts into creating an alternate reality. This alternate reality includes a denial circus zone, run by Tweedledee and Tweedledum.

Numerous computer games invoke the ambiance or characters of *Alice in Wonderland*, often as the games come towards an end. *Call of Duty: Modern Warfare* includes Down the Rabbit Hole as its second to last mission, while *Deeper into Madness* is the second to last game in *NaissanceE*. A key reason for this use of Alice imagery and concepts is the fact that it involves universally familiar images, adding to their marketing quality.

Goth actor and film maker Marilyn Manson (aka Brian Warner) was fascinated by the Alice/Lewis Carroll concept creating songs such as *Eat Me, Drink Me* and *Are You the Rabbit?*. He took on the role of Queen of Hearts in a Carroll related film *Living in Neon Dreams* which was later abandoned before production, and later was determined to create his own film. He commented that:

> 'I identified with him so much because I wanted to write a story about a fractured personality like Jekyll and Hyde, which is what I think *Alice in Wonderland* is about ... It's about someone not knowing who they are supposed to be.'

As a result, in 2006 he released a trailer for a horror version of an *Alice in Wonderland*/Lewis Carroll orientated film which proved so unacceptable to the public that it died a rapid death. Known as *Phantasmagoria: The Visions of Lewis Carroll,* the trailer included a topless teen-girl Tweedledee and Tweedledum, a bloodied and tortured Alice, clashing industrial style music and an overall gothic, fetish sexuality. In 2014, Manson released a Twitter message commenting, 'Happy that my PHANTASMAGORIA screenplay, with me portraying Lewis Carroll, is in production. His diaries inspired the best horror film ever'. Despite such comments, the film was never made, and the following year, Manson said, 'I made a joke to my manager that I wanted to self-induce schizophrenia and I think I may have done that while writing it.'

*Chapter 10*

# Drug Alice

'The Caterpillar and Alice looked at each other for some time in silence: at last the Caterpillar took the hookah out of its mouth, and addressed her in a languid, sleepy voice.'

*Alice in Wonderland*

The 1960s was a decade of transformation and change. It marked the rise of feminism, of pop culture, sit-ins and protests, of vast music festivals such as Woodstock, and psychedelic drugs. It was the era of LSD, mescaline, DMT, marijuana and heroin – drugs that were designed to bring out changes in thought, sight, hearing and an altered state of consciousness due to mind expanding properties. American psychiatrist Humphrey Osmond coined the phrase psychedelic to describe the effects hallucinogenic drugs had on the senses, comparing it to a trip into the world of the imagination like that seen in *Alice in Wonderland*.

Alongside the impact of these drugs, there was a growth in psychedelic art especially posters involving densely packed, vivid (often fluorescent) kaleidoscopic patterns and spirals sometimes linked to giant images of suns, moons or even flowers. As the decade wore on, the stories of *Alice in Wonderland* and *Through the Looking Glass* became associated with this psychedelic culture. In 1963, US pop artist John Wesley created images directly inspired by the Alice story entitled *Falling Alice* and *Humpty Dumpty*.

In 1968, the Avalon Ballroom issued a poster promoting a concert by Iron Butterfly, Indian Head Band, The Collectors and Electroluminescence which incorporated flower bedecked borders together with Tenniel's illustration of Alice meeting the Gryphon.

The images of Alice falling through space and time, of talking flowers, Mad Hatters, playing card soldiers and above all, the grinning Cheshire Cat that disappears leaving just an enigmatic grin behind provided instant psychedelic & hallucinogenic qualities. The Caterpillar smoking a hookah and indulging in a very confusing conversation with Alice contained implication of drug usage:

'The Caterpillar and Alice looked at each other for some time in silence: at last the Caterpillar took the hookah out of its mouth, and addressed her in a languid, sleepy voice.

"Who are YOU?" said the Caterpillar.

This was not an encouraging opening for a conversation. Alice replied, rather shyly, "I—I hardly know, sir, just at present—at least I know who I WAS when I got up this morning, but I think I must have been changed several times since then."

"What do you mean by that?" said the Caterpillar sternly. "Explain yourself!"

"I can't explain MYSELF, I'm afraid, sir" said Alice, "because I'm not myself, you see."

"I don't see," said the Caterpillar.

"I'm afraid I can't put it more clearly," Alice replied very politely, "for I can't understand it myself to begin with; and being so many different sizes in a day is very confusing."

"It isn't," said the Caterpillar.

"Well, perhaps you haven't found it so yet," said Alice; "but when you have to turn into a chrysalis—you will some day, you know—and then after that into a butterfly, I should think you'll feel it a little queer."

"Not a bit," said the Caterpillar.

"Well, perhaps your feelings may be different," said Alice; "all I know is, it would feel very queer to ME."

"You!" said the Caterpillar contemptuously. "Who are YOU?"

Which brought them back again to the beginning of the conversation.'

## 128   The Dark Side of Alice in Wonderland

'Chasing the white rabbit' became a popular slogan within the drug culture of the 1960s. It was used to describe the taking of hallucinogenic drugs, in which the altered state of consciousness experienced during LSD trips was linked to Alice's emergence in a strangely altered world. As the Tate Liverpool pointed out in its 2011 *Alice in Wonderland* exhibition, 'Alice became the poster-child for the psychedelic generation.' Typical of the resultant art works were the swirling, vividly psychedelic kaleidoscope triptych of paintings entitled *Alice Down the Rabbit Hole, The Mad Hatter's Tea Party, Alice and the Pack of Cards* created by Adrian Piper in 1965. He even created a specifically LSD Alice – a *Study for Alice down the Rabbit Hole*.

Among the sensations experienced by drug users, similar to those recounted in *Alice in Wonderland* were mushrooms that alter perceptions of height and size. In 1968, writer Thomas Fensch described Lewis Carroll with his Eat Me cake as being 'the first acidhead' commenting:

> 'When you take something that tastes like cherry tarts, roast turkey, toffee, and toast at the same time and makes you grow and shrink – baby, that's tripping out.'

*Alice in Wonderland* even crept into the drug culture music. In 1967, pop band Jefferson Airplane released the *White Rabbit* song, which became an icon for the 1960s drug culture. The lyrics had been written by singer/songwriter Grace Slick, who acknowledged that the stories by Lewis Carroll had been a major influence on her work. She claimed that it was designed to hide lyrics dealing with drug usage past the censors, as well as acting as a cautionary tale to parents who would read *Alice in Wonderland* to their children. Grace Slick believed that Alice's consumption of substances making her feel larger and smaller by turns would encourage children to eventually experiment with drugs. The song became the anthem for the drug culture with lyrics such as:

> 'When the men on the chessboard get up
> And tell you where to go
> And you've just had some kind of mushroom
> And your mind is moving low
> Go ask Alice
> I think she'll know.'

It was a song which become enormously popular. Other artists and musicians began to explore the imagery of Alice to such an extent that researcher Scott Parker in his study 'How deep does the Rabbit-Hole Go? Drugs and Dreams, Perception and Reality' pointed out:

'Many of us also associate drugs, especially hallucinogenic drugs, with Alice. Indeed Alice's journey can be read as an allegory for an intense drug experience. Rephrasing the plot only slightly, Alice gets lost and tries to find her way back to normal reality. Within the story are specific allusions: the caterpillar smokes a hookah, Alice drinks mysterious liquids and eats mushrooms, Alice's interpretations of time and space are altered and the impossible is everyday. The association of drugs with Alice is so established that Alice is now a slang term for LSD.'

Another popular 1960s song linking Alice with the drug culture of the period was The Beatles' hit, *I Am the Walrus*. The song includes lines like 'I am the egg man', 'I am the walrus', 'see how they run like pigs from a gun See how they fly,' 'see how they fly like Lucy in the sky', 'I'm crying', 'Sitting on a corn flake'. When *Playboy* magazine asked the Beatles about the lyrics, John Lennon stated:

'The first line was written on one acid trip one weekend. The second line was written on the next acid trip the next weekend, and it was filled in after I met Yoko … I'd seen Allen Ginsberg and some other people … It was Ginsberg, in particular that I was referring to. [Ginsberg's facial appearance has been compared to illustrations of Humpty Dumpty]'

'It never dawned on me that Lewis Carroll was commenting on the capitalist system. I never went into that bit about what he really meant, like people are doing with the Beatles' work. Later, I went back and looked at it and realised that the walrus was the bad guy in the story and the carpenter was the good guy.'

Lennon was referring to the poem of *The Walrus & the Carpenter* recited by Tweedledee and Tweedledum in *Through the Looking Glass*. Just as the

130    The Dark Side of Alice in Wonderland

song *I am a Walrus* contains meaningless sentences, *The Walrus and the Carpenter* states:

> '"The time has come," the Walrus said,
> To talk of many things:
> Of shoes – and ships – and sealing wax –
> Of cabbages – and kings –
> And why the sea is boiling hot –
> And whether pigs have wings.'

Prior to the release of The Beatles' hit song *Lucy in the Sky with Diamonds* on their 1967 album *Sgt Pepper's Lonely Hearts Club Band*, there was a lot of speculation that the first letter of each noun deliberately spelt the words LSD – used to describe the hallucinogenic drug Lysergic acid diethylamide. John Lennon denied this, saying that he had not intended it to be seen as a drug song, but rather that the fantastical imagery was due to reading *Alice in Wonderland*. Seeing a drawing made by his young son of a girl with diamonds reminded him of the 'Which Dreamed it' chapter contained in *Through the Looking Glass*. In that chapter, Alice floats in a boat beneath a sunny sky. Recalling the sources of song writing inspiration in 1980, Lennon commented:

> 'It was Alice in the boat. She is buying an egg and it turns into Humpty-Dumpty. The woman serving in the shop turns into a sheep and the next minute they are rowing in a rowing boat somewhere and I was visualising that.'

His co-writer Paul McCartney agreed, commenting:

> 'We did the whole thing like an Alice in Wonderland idea, being in a boat on the river … Every so often it broke off and you saw Lucy in the sky with diamonds all over the sky. This Lucy was God, the Big Figure, the White Rabbit.

> 'I showed up at John's house and he had a drawing Julian had done at school with the title "Lucy in the Sky with Diamonds" above it. Then we went up to his music room and wrote the song, swapping psychedelic suggestions as we went. I remember coming up with

'"cellophane flowers" and "newspaper taxis" and John answered with things like "kaleidoscope eyes" and "looking glass ties". We never noticed the LSD initial until it was pointed out later – by which point people didn't believe us.'

In 2004, McCartney admitted that the band had used drugs. He told the *Daily Mirror*:

'"Day Tripper", that's one about acid. "Lucy In The Sky", that's pretty obvious. There are others that make subtle hints about drugs, but it's easy to overestimate the influence of drugs on The Beatles music. Just about everyone was doing drugs in one form or another, and we were no different, but the writing was too important for us to mess it up by getting off with our heads all the time.'

*Lucy in the Sky with Diamonds* and the *Sgt Pepper's Lonely Hearts Club Band* is usually regarded as forming a key moment within British surrealistic psychedelia especially when linked to the drug culture. In 2013, *Ultimate Classic Rock* commented that although Lennon had insisted that the title did not hold any drugs references, the track was 'Three-and-a-half minutes of pure lysergic bliss, full of pictures and surreal lyrics set to one of the Beatles' most trippy songs'.

Similar psychedelic features have continued to re-emerge frequently in art. Having experimented with hallucinogenic drugs in the 1970s, German artist Sigmar Polke created abstract paintings showing red and white mushrooms complete with the caterpillar from *Alice in Wonderland*. More recently, Japanese artist Yayo Kusama took psychedelia to a new level by creating versions of Alice using lots of disorientating dots, infinite spaces, swirly mushrooms and neon flowers.

Films too have included drug inspired references to Alice. In *The Matrix*, Neo is told to 'follow the white rabbit'. Elsewhere in the film are the words, 'You take the blue pill, the story ends, you wake up in your bed and believe whatever you want to believe. You take the red pill, you stay in Wonderland, and I show you how deep the rabbit hole goes.'

The sheer number of similarities between psychedelic and hallucinogenic drug experiences the images in *Alice in Wonderland* has led many critics and researchers to explore the question as to whether Dodgson had used

132    The Dark Side of Alice in Wonderland

drugs himself. The nineteenth century had witnessed the growth of a drug culture focusing primarily on opium and laudanum. Opium users gained their fix by smoking special pipes, similar to that used by the Caterpillar. At the Harry Ransom Centre at the University of Texas, there is a short, undated document in Dodgson's handwriting containing a recipe for grams of opium and camphor divided into pills, but there is no indication as to the reason for this recipe or for whom it was designed. It is known that one of Dodgson's favourite authors was Thomas De Quincy, author of *Confessions of an Opium Eater* but however hard researchers have looked, it has proved impossible to prove that Dodgson was a recreational drug user.

Another frequent argument rebutting the links with hallucinogens points out that people were simply reading their own experiences into the story since in the 1960s, hallucinogenic drugs and psychedelic references were part of the culture.

Interestingly, Alice has also been used to create an alternative psychedelic rendition against drug use. In 1971, there was a US government sponsored educational film entitled *Curious Alice* designed specifically to rally against drug use and abuse among young people. It set drugs, narcotics, psychedelics, alcohol, amphetamines and barbiturate abuse within the context of the story. Intended for 8-10-year-olds, it involves Alice falling asleep while reading a book. During her journey she meets cigarettes, alcohol, medicines and stronger drugs. Drinking from the Drink Me bottle immediately takes her into a fantasy world known as Drug Wonderland. The Mad Hatter introduces her to LSD, the March Hare amphetamines, the Dormouse barbiturates, and the King of Hearts has a hypodermic needle full of heroin. The March Hare for example says, 'You oughta have some pep pills! Uppers! Amphetamines! Speed! You feel super good.' Throughout the film, there is continuous use of psychedelic animation and mesmerizing images – which explains why the film was heavily criticised. Children watching were more interested in the pretty images than in listening to the hidden message, while the drug using cartoon characters had no connection to real life or real drug problems. Even the way the drugs were portrayed meant that the message was easily overlooked since it involved features such as LSD laced sugar lumps at the Mad Hatter's Tea Party, or the King of Hearts carrying a hypodermic needle like a sceptre. The Dormouse is seen comatose on barbiturates, and the Caterpillar puffing a weed-filled pipe. Accompanying the film was a colouring book and comprehension test. Children were required to answer multiple choice questions such as 'the

Cheshire Cat was (a) scary, (b) Alice's friend, (c) took drugs too, (d) gave Alice bad advice'. A crossword enabled children to test their knowledge of heroin, LSD and speed.

Within one year of the film's release, the US National Coordinating Council on Drug Education (NCCDE) had attacked *Curious Alice* for being confusing and counterproductive. It stated that children watching the film 'may be intrigued by the fantasy world of drugs' and that it should only be presented with a 'very skilled facilitator' in order to 'probe for the drug attitudes' of the class. This was a film that, quite simply, was making drugs look like fun!

John Donne's 1969 film *Alice in Acidland* was positioned as an anti-drugs production complete with a moralising voice over. In reality, this film was effectively softcore porn. Alice falls into a rabbit hole of pool parties, naked people, smoking weed, dropping acid and engaging in lesbian sex. Eventually she loses her mind completely and has to be confined in a straitjacket. It becomes a journey of sexual liberation in which all danger signs such as talk of a friend's suicide whilst under the influence of LSD are ignored.

The drug link and drug images have continued ever since with film producers recognising the potential story ideas and concepts provided by the haphazard, unstructured mix of images presented within the Alice stories. For example, drugs of an emotional kind formed a key element in an Alice themed TV series broadcast in 2009. The Mad Hatter becomes a drug peddling revolutionary, and Alice has to experience an outlandish, Salvador Dali style dreamscape involving underground cities comprising twisted towers and a deadly casino in order to escape back to her own world. Images of Alice have never been the same again. In the series, the rulers are harvesting people from our world, regarding them as oysters. The oysters are kidnapped in order to take them to Wonderland through a mysterious door so as to harvest their emotions in order to create mind controlling drugs to keep the populace under control.

Although drugs and drug taking were not unknown in Victorian times, these drugs were very different to the mind bending psychedelic drugs which became fashionable in the 1960s. *Alice in Wonderland* is very much the result of a fantastic imagination rather than the use of chemical substances and one which modern writers are continually attempting to emulate.

*Chapter 11*

# Surreal Alice

'Down, down, down. Would the fall never come to an end! "I wonder how many miles I've fallen by this time?" she said aloud.'
*Alice in Wonderland*

The fantastical, imaginative images and the links with the dream state evoked within the *Alice in Wonderland* stories struck a chord with an artistic movement which began in the early years of the twentieth century. Known as surrealism, it focused on strange, dreamlike, unconventional images. David Haycock, curator of the 2020 British Surrealism exhibition at the Dulwich Picture Gallery believes that:

'Carroll was one of the most important "ancestors of surrealism" and the British surrealists looked to his ludicrous and wildly imaginative writing as inspiration for their movement. It's a perfect example of "the surreal" having roots in Britain long before the international movement's official beginnings in the 1920s.'

Just like the Scottish National Gallery of Modern Art's 2015 exhibition entitled 'Surreal Roots: From William Blake to André Breton', the 2020 British Surrealism exhibition pointed to *Alice in Wonderland* as having a key role in the movement's development with early editions of the *Alice in Wonderland* story and *The Hunting of the Snark* placed prominently on display.

In 1924, André Breton's Surrealist Manifesto defined surrealism as being:

'Pure psychic automatism, by which one proposes to express, either verbally, in writing, or by any other manner, the real functioning of thought. Dictation of thought in the absence of all control exercised by reason, outside of all aesthetic and moral preoccupation.' It was quite simply a movement which set out to explore the workings of the mind, highlighting all that is irrational, poetic, revolutionary and different within a society that was structure and rigid.

Although the Alice books were not themselves surrealist, they have proved extremely influential with many surrealists. Some of Tenniel's classic images such as the Cheshire Cat's head floating above the Queen's croquet ground are regarded as having anticipated surrealistic preoccupation with the juxtaposition of objects. The Surrealists saw Dodgson as being a Surrealist '*avant la lettre*', an artistic predecessor and found his stories and poems irresistible.

There are many references to *Alice in Wonderland* within surrealist art and literature. In Breton's book *Surrealism and Painting* (1928), he described Picasso's cubist paintings as demonstrating how 'the mind talks stubbornly to us of a future continent, and that everyone has the power to accompany an ever more beautiful *Alice in Wonderland*'. The following year, Louis Aragon translated *The Hunting of the Snark* into French, while exploring how nonsense poetry rebelled against tendencies to subvert children's literature. In 1933, French painter Balthus created *Alice dans le mirroir*, portraying an ambiguous image of Alice which could be read either as Alice contemplating herself in the mirror, or Alice gazing out of a world behind the mirror.

In 1935, Carroll's drawing of the Gryphon and the Mock Turtle formed part of the Fantastic Art, Dada and Surrealism exhibition held at the Museum of Modern Art in New York. This exhibition placed *Alice in Wonderland* and her creator into a lineage of art stretching back to the sixteenth century Flemish artists Bosch and Brueghel. André Breton and Paul Eluard's *Dictionnaire abrégée du Surréalisme* included the poem *The Hunting of the Snark*, while the Lobster Quadrille appears in Breton's *Anthologie de L'humour Noir*. In 1941, Eluard quoted from both *The Hunting of the Snark* and *Through the Looking Glass* in his book, *Poésie involontaire et poésie intentionelle*. In 1943, Alice formed one of a series of Surrealistic characters such as Freud and Sade in a mock Tarot series known as the *Jeu de Marseille* reproduced in a surrealistic magazine *VVV*.

In 1935, literary academic William Empson and a supporter of Freudian concepts wrote, 'Alice has, I understand, become a patron saint of the Surrealists'. One of the key interests of the surrealists involved the

## 136   The Dark Side of Alice in Wonderland

psychoanalytic ideas of Sigmund Freud, especially regarding the concept of sexual repression taking the form of dreams and delusions. Surrealists like artist Salvador Dali sought to capture dreams whether derived by lucid dreaming, hypnotic dreaming or memories of dreams in paint – and the stories of *Alice in Wonderland* were perfected suited to this concept. Dali set out to use dreams as a way of probing the mind and analysing it, exploring the deeper realms of ideas.

Magritte, another Surrealist, painted an image of a disappearing person; on one side is the back of a bowler hatted man staring out towards the horizon, beside him there is a brown curtain in from which the man's image has been cut allowing the viewer to see the coastal image beyond. It acts as a play on positive and negative images – just like the disappearing cat in *Alice in Wonderland* who disappears into thin air, leaving Alice saying, 'Well, I've often seen a cat without a grin, but a grin without a cat! It's the most curious thing!'

The British Surrealists such as Dorothea Tanning, Paul Nash, Roland Penrose, Conroy Maddox and F.E. McWilliam were often referred to as 'the children of Alice' due to the way in which they were influenced by the Alice stories. Many of the British Surrealists referenced Carroll and *Alice in Wonderland* either through direct references or by implication. Dorothea Tanning's *Eine Kleine Nachtmusik* (1943) is often described as an *Alice in Wonderland* visual narrative, being reminiscent of scenes in *Through the Looking Glass* in which Alice meets talking flowers. Tanning takes this further by using overgrown, menacing flowers offering erotic, nocturnal knowledge. One year later, Tanning created a painting entitled *Endgame* in which a giant girl's shoe tramples a bishop in a setting very similar to that of Tenniel's chessboard images. In *Birthday*, Alice is shown at the start of a hallway of doors, albeit as an adult rather than a child with a model gryphon close by.

David Haycock, curator of the 2020 British Surrealism exhibition highlights other examples saying:

> 'Leonora Carrington references Carroll at various points in her work, and Susan Aberth's book on her has references to her reading Alice as a child, and to the work she made (including a sculpture later in life) called *How Doth the Little Crocodile*. I feel Leonora Carrington's painting in the exhibition "The Old Maids" (1947) references Alice in the figure of the tall girl in blue.'

One of Leonora's lovers was Max Ernst, who identified his partners with Alice, for example the painting *Alice in 1941* sets her as a partially clad, grown up erotic woman within a fantastical landscape. He wrote:

'It is as if Alice were to grow up in Wonderland ... and you were to meet her one day, to re-discover her enchantment, now filled with love and terror. Max Ernst became her guardian when you had forgotten her.'

Ernst was very keen to engage with Dodgson's work, and created numerous works referring directly to Alice or relating to it. Quite apart from the numerous paintings bearing the name Alice, he exhibited a painting *The Imagery of Chess*, plus a sculpture entitled *The King Playing with the Queen* at the Julian Levy Gallery, New York in 1944. He also produced illustrated books such as *La Chasse Au Snark*, and *Lewis Carroll's Wunderhorn*.

Another Surrealist, Eileen Agar, created a painting of Lewis Carroll with Alice presenting them as geometrical characters composed of lots of triangles set within a fantastical landscape. She also wrote:

'Lewis Carroll is a mysterious master of time and imagination, the Herald of Sur-Realism and Freedom, a prophet of the Future and an uprooter of the Past, with a literary and visual sense of the Present and inwards into scientific questions which are alarmingly couched in fairy-tale accounts of a small girl child who believes everything she is told. All is well with Alice, she is untouchable and eternal with a Mammalian Brain – and a sense of the wonderful world we live in.'

Jorges Luis Borges is another surrealist who acknowledged his debt to the *Alice in Wonderland* stories and focused particularly on the darker aspects of the plots. He read the books as a child, and they inspired many of his own reflections and literary works involving games with time and space. This can be seen clearly in books like *The Garden of Forking Paths, Death and the Compass, An Examination of the Work of Herbert Quain*. Such books involves a game in which the protagonists do not know what they are playing, nor are they aware of any rules, or in fact what exactly they are supposed to be doing; for example, a writer might be trying to include all of literature in his work, while a detective is shown trying to unravel a murder, not knowing

## 138    The Dark Side of Alice in Wonderland

that it is actually his own murder. Readers of Jorges Luis Borges novels have to wait to discover why such things happen, whereas in *Wonderland,* Alice takes charge and insists on knowing everything. The characters in Borges' novels have nightmares and become their victims, while Alice accepts that it is a dream and challenges it. Writing in an introduction to *The Complete Works of Lewis Carroll* in Spanish, Borges commented that:

> 'Both of Alice's dreams continually border the nightmare. Tenniel's illustrations (now inherent in the work, and which Carroll disliked) accentuate the menace. At first sight or in our recollection, the adventures seem arbitrary and almost irresponsible, then we see that they hold the secret rigour of chess and card-games, which are also adventures of the imagination.'

For Jorges Luis Borges, the most memorable section of the book is Alice's farewell to the White Knight. He comments:

> 'Perhaps the Knight is moved, because he knows that he is Alice's dream, just as Alice was a dream of the Red King, and that he is about to vanish. The Knight is also Lewis Carroll, bidding farewell to the dear dreams that inhabited his loneliness.'

In 1961, Marcel Duchamp gave a lecture entitled 'Where do We Go From Here' and suggested that artists 'like *Alice in Wonderland* … will be led to pass through the looking-glass of the retina, to reach a more profound expression.'

Eight years later, Random House Publishers commissioned Salvador Dali to illustrate *Alice in Wonderland* for a small, exclusive edition of their Book of the Month series. Only 2,7000 were ever printed. Introducing the story, Mark Burstein, president of the Lewis Carroll Society of North America, wrote:

> 'For both Carroll and the surrealists, what some call madness could be perceived by others as wisdom. Even the creative processes of Carroll and the surrealists were similar. The surrealists practised automatism in their writing and drawing; Carroll called the initial telling of the tale … "effortless", saying that "every such idea and nearly every word of the dialogue, came of itself … when fancies

Surreal Alice    139

unsought came crowding thick upon [me], or at times when the jaded Muse was goaded into action more because she had to say something than that she had something to say."

'In addition, collages were a serious apparatus in the surrealists' arsenal. Carroll invented the term portmanteau – combining words – and produced *Jabberwocky*, the most famous example of pure neologistic nonsense in the English language … His bestiary of mome, raths, toves, and Bread-and butter-flies, also from *Through the Looking-Glass*, could easily have been products of the surrealists' game of Exquisite Corpse.'

Dali's work was regarded as the perfect match. To illustrate the book, Dali created twelve heliogravures – a method involving etching an image onto a special gel-covered copper plate that had already been exposed to film. There was a frontispiece – which he signed personally in every copy, together with one illustration for each chapter. The illustrations contained many of the popular images he had long been experimenting with such as a girl with a skipping rope (found in his *Landscape with Girl Skipping Rope*) while the melting clock seen in the depiction of the Mad Hatter's Tea Party is sourced from his painting *The Persistence of Memory*. Every illustration contained the image of a girl with a skipping rope, turning it into an icon representing not just her presence in the story, but the words of Carroll in the story 'the rest next time –' 'it is next time!'

The image of Alice as a girl with a skipping rope had been a feature of his work since the late 1930s. She had appeared in his painting *Morphological Echo* (1935) and was one of his popular images. The idea of Alice was the eternal girl child, permanently naïve and innocent. For Dali, the concept of the skipping rope provided perpetual motion, mirroring femininity and youthfulness suspended between reality and fantasy. Among his most well-known works is the sculpture *Alice in Wonderland*, initially conceived in 1977 and first cast in bronze in 1984. It is a sculpture which captures a combination of ages, youth and old age, with Dali seeking to combine multiple meanings. It portrays a young Alice with a skipping rope above her head, leaning towards a crutch in front of her, linking the surreal and the real world. This combination of youth and age constituted what Dali described as a 'unique togetherness' since 'in my mind desire and science were but one single and unique thing and I already knew that only the

140    The Dark Side of Alice in Wonderland

prosperity and then the wear and decline of the flesh could bring me illuminations or resurrection'.

The links between *Alice in Wonderland* and surrealism have continued to influence artists in all types of media. Merely googling surreal art and Alice reveals countless surrealistic images taken directly from the world of *Alice in Wonderland*. One of the most surreal film versions of *Alice* was the 2007 stop motion version from Brothers Quay. A monochrome film, it was set to a Prokofiev score which pitches to a wailing kettle crescendo when Alice falls beyond the looking glass. As to the storyline, the producers were said to have a 'mystifying ability to turn the "degraded reality" of discarded doll parts, screws, string and metal filings into profoundly expressive characters within playful, perplexing, life-and-death scenarios within wonderous, handmade sets and across dreamlike landscapes.'

Illustrator Mervyn Peake created highly surrealistic dark depictions of *Alice in Wonderland* which were heavily influenced by his experiences as a war correspondent travelling through the bombed out landscape of Germany at the end of the Second World war. He reported from a series of destroyed, deserted cities, the horrors of the Bergen-Belsen concentration camp as well as reporting on a war crimes trial. Peake believed that illustrations had to create an extra dimension into the text, not just act as a picturesque accompaniment. As a result, his illustrations are far removed from those of Tenniel. Peake's use of a black, cross hatching technique along with terrifying images like that of the Jabberwocky resulted in the creation of very dark, eerie, gloomy and dramatic illustrations.

This surreal Alice has even crept into the realms of modern tattoo art thus resulting in the creation of a unique literary art project. A US company, Lithographs, used *Alice in Wonderland* as a way of promoting their new temporary literary tattoos. They aimed to create the world's largest tattoo chain across 5,258 bodies. Participants were asked to back a Kickstarter campaign by pledging $1 or more for a temporary Alice tattoo. Using the 55,668 words written by Lewis Carroll for the book *Alice in Wonderland*, they created 5,268 unique tattoos, which were sent out to all the backers. Each supporter in the campaign received a selection of the text as a tattoo and were encouraged to upload the images of themselves wearing their specific tattoo so that viewers could read the entire novel in tattoo format. Many of the participants added props and surrealistic devices to their image to further explore its meaning. Since then the company has gone on to create a variety of Alice themed images and text superimposed on textiles and blankets.

Jazz musician Tom Waits worked with scriptwriter Paul Schmidt and avant-garde director Robert Wilson to create a surrealist musical opera, premiered in Hamburg in 1992, which played for eighteen months. It was a melancholy production, in which sorrow and reverie, insanity and resignation all combine to create a lyrical modern version loosely based on the Alice story. According to Tom Waits:

> 'Alice is adult songs for children, or children's songs for adults. It's a maelstrom or fever-dream, a lone poem, with torch songs and waltzes – an odyssey in dream logic and nonsense.'

They wanted to explore all the aspects of the relationship between Dodgson/Carroll and the historical Alice within the context of the well-known story, including psycho-sexual child molestation implications linked across decades. Their storyline was based on the idea that Lewis Carroll was obsessed with Alice Liddell, confusions between dream and reality, and looking back across their lives. It moves between a fantasy world and the real-life relationship, which at times takes on a frightening, surrealistic aspect. There is, for example, a scene in which a slightly intoxicated Alice is portrayed in a blood red gown, imprisoned within blood red walls and recalling the loss of her virginity. Apart from Alice, all the characters have chalk white faces. The final scene shows an elderly Alice in her seventies or eighties reflecting back on her life and the eternal partnership that has developed with Dodgson/Carroll as a result of the book.

Commenting on the portrayal, scriptwriter Paul Schmidt said:

> 'One of the things we were trying to do was to balance the character of Dodgson and portray him first as the photographer as this slightly un-innocent figure, and then the second part is the White Knight from the second Alice book, from *The Looking Glass*, which is clearly, which Dodgson means as a portrait of himself, and is one of the most wonderfully gentle old people in literature. So it was trying to show that relationship of how a world of grown ups can scare children and threaten children, at the same time that's its love and it means to be love.'

142    The Dark Side of Alice in Wonderland

'A lot of fun fairs that I know of in America are called Wonderland. You get that all the time. It seemed to me it was kind of a natural connection. And the other interesting thing that Tom really found, was sort of the underside of Victorian life, I mean we think of proper Victorian England, but you look at some of the freak shows and things that grew up in the nineteenth century, it was a sort of darker underside of it. And that's were a lot of Tom's images plug in beautifully. I think they really reflect terrifically, there was a tension between some of those images and the surface innocence of the Alice story.'

Schmidt had been keen to explore the relationship between Carroll and the Liddell family and how an innocent relationship could easily result in unexpected meanings and links:

'Scenes four and eleven would be monologues by Alice Liddell and Charles Dodgson, presumably spoken later in life, recalling their relationship. I thought it would be interesting to have each of them remember the period quite differently: Dodgson with a sense of wonder and fulfilment, Alice with an element of fear and regret. For the other scenes I wanted to show Alice as determined, sassy even, not merely the passive onlooker she is in the books. ... the White Rabbit in Act One, a threatening character, and the White Knight in Act Two, a protective character, who saves Alice at the trail and leads her gently through the dark forest. That seemed to me an interesting comment on the ambiguities involved.'

Tom Waits went on to release an album entitled *Alice*, with songs such as *We're All Mad Here, Alice, Watch her disappear,* and *Fish and Bird*. The lyrics include many references to the Alice story with surrealistic images such as 'I disappear in our name', 'Arithmetic arithmetock, Turn the hands back on the clock, How does the ocean rock the boat' 'You can hang me in a bottle like a cat'. Other songs highlight the strained relationship that developed between Dodgson & Alice Liddell as portrayed in the musical. *Fish and Bird* focuses on forbidden love, a Romeo & Juliet style relationship in which two people from different worlds are forced to go their separate ways using lyrics like:

'he said, "you cannot live in the ocean"
and She said to him
"you never can live in the sky"
but the ocean is filled with tears
and the sea turns into a mirror….

I'll always pretend that you're mine
Though I know we must part
You can live in my heart.'

The Royal Opera House, London, has staged two variations of the *Alice in Wonderland* story – a ballet and an opera. Both highlight the surrealistic nature of the story, combining and creating unusual images. In Gerald Barry's opera, *Alice's Adventures Underground,* characters are transformed with rapidity such as the all-male chorus of four Drink Me bottles that change into Eat Me Cakes. Tweedledee and Tweedledum wear giant ice cream headdresses, there are giant baby bottles, fluffy coffee pots, a king of hearts looking like an eighteenth century aristocrat, giant masked babies and an animated Cheshire Cat. Music from all traditions is involved including classical soprano roles, to a version of *It's A Long Way to Tipperary* and Beethoven's *Ode to Joy.*

Christopher Wheeldon's ballet version of *Alice's Adventures in Wonderland* combined surrealistic images with comedy, stage magic and an explosion of colour. The Queen of Hearts is an outrageous character, at one point seen confined within a giant wooden heart dress and on another occasion giving a comedy send up of the renowned Rose Adagio from The Sleeping Beauty ballet in which the suitors present her with jam tarts, and get kicked or lift her in zany positions. There is a tap-dancing Mad Hatter, a nightmarish kitchen, panoramic boat ride, shape shifting video projections and a disembodied Cheshire Cat.

An equally surrealistic experience was provided by the immersive theatre experience created at The Vaults in London referred to in Murder mystery Alice. Even watching the promotional online video film involved a trip into a surrealistic universe falling down ladders with grotesque masked white rabbits, a macabre almost gothic style white faced Alice and border guards with face masks. For participants, whether online viewers or actually attending the event, *Alice's Adventures Underground* proved to be totally

144    The Dark Side of Alice in Wonderland

disorientating and bizarre at every point as the adventures of Alice became a very personal experience.

In 2020, Swedish singer songwriter Robin Lundbäck turned to the Alice books as inspiration for a song entitled *Caroline*, with a YouTube video incorporating surreal Alice themed images. He told *Billboard* magazine:

> 'For this video I wanted to create this trippy wonderland where your brain kinda takes you when you can't get a specific person out of your mind. It envelopes everything around you and can be magical but also really dark at the same time.'

The resulting video involves the singer lying flat on the floor, then appearing to sink through it as if going down a rabbit hole into a world of lush vegetation, with surreal combinations of images and flashing words, neon lights, gardens, the spectre of a girl just out of reach before finally rising upwards towards reality.

To take another example of modern Alice interpretations, photographer Gary Lindsay-Moore developed a Bad Wonderland concept set within the backstreets of Birmingham:

> 'It was based on my love of *Alice in Wonderland*. I wanted to do something different, so I took the angle of Alice going down the rabbit hole again but this with a drink problem. I created images of dirty, drunken glamour, meeting unsavoury people such as a man in a rabbit mask who live in Bad Wonderland. Alice had tattoos and a drunken 1950's glamour within the gritty streets of run down Birmingham. There were bits of broken dolls and mannequins, very ragged and creepy with hints of insanity.'

Over in America, lyricist Steven Sater created an unusual adaptation of *Alice in Wonderland* under the title *Alice By Heart*, which has since become a book. *Alice by Heart* is set amid the London Blitz of the Second World War. A group of children from a children's home are taking refuge in the tunnels within a London Tube Station. Alice Spencer wants to help her friend Alfred, who is in quarantine with tuberculosis, but is being prevented by an officious Red Cross nurse constantly ordering that Alice must get BACK. TO. HER. BED. Alice has been told that Alfred might not survive the night, but she believes that if she can get to him and keep the pages turning, allowing them to enter the world of *Alice in Wonderland* together, he might just survive. As the film progresses, the borders between the two worlds blur and eventually Alice has to decide whether to stay in Wonderland forever, or to grow up, thus accepting reality. The music and setting evokes many surrealistic elements. In the song *Down the Hole*, Alice transforms into the Storybook Alice, turning Alfred into the White Rabbit, while many of the young people within the underground station become other traditional Wonderland characters. Meeting two cool kid, seductive Caterpillars smoking from a hookah, Alice is offered a puff on the basis that it can 'stop time'. It is a recommendation that Alice takes to Alfred, saying that 'all he has to do is take a puff, The Key to Wonderland is right here at hand'. When singing *Manage Your Flamingo*, a cross-dressing, body shaming Duchess scolds Alice for altering the traditional story saying that 'the bigger Alice grows, the older she makes the Duchess feel'. The nonsense style of speech found through Alice in Wonderland is utilised in creating weird medical language when the Doctor is discussing Alfred's circumstances. Alice wants to avoid her trial, and her identity is constantly questioned because she wants to rewrite the traditional story.

Kate Bailey, curator of the V&A's *Alice Curiouser & Curiouser* exhibition, refers to Carroll's 'distorted environment' incorporating a 'diverse range of imaginations, dreams and transformations'. Responding to the strange, topsy turvy world of 2020 lockdowns, Gyre & Gimble could find no better images than those of *Alice in Wonderland* to give gins names such as Queen of Hearts and Calloh Callay. Alice has become the perfect inspiration for surrealists in every way.

*Chapter 12*

# Horror Alice

"'I wish I hadn't cried so much," said Alice, as she swam about, trying to find her way out. "I shall be punished for it now, I suppose by being drowned in my own tears!"'

*Alice in Wonderland*

Horror, cruelty and fear are all too common within the *Alice in Wonderland* stories which, if written today, would be frowned upon. The Dormouse has hot tea poured on him, he is punched awake and forced into a teapot. Guinea pigs are tied into bags and sat upon, an inkstand is thrown at the lizard, Alice kicks the lizard, threatens to silence the daisies by picking them and shakes the Red Queen into a kitten. In the White Knight's song, the old man is kicked until he is calm, punched and has his hair tweaked. Alice herself is threatened in various ways including drowning in tears, trampled by a puppy, attacked by a pack of cards and having her head cut off.

To Victorian children this would not have been too unusual. Fairy tales often involved quite grim punishments such as feet being cut off or being forced to walk over hot coals. Alice herself comments that she 'had read several nice little stories about children who had got burned and eaten up by wild beasts'.

In his letters to his child friends, Charles Dodgson included many fearsome suggestions such as how to inflict pain on others by using tiny pen knives and pins; how to make a little girl's railway journey more exciting by ensuring she arrived in London without a ticket, had a pistol fired at her through the carriage window, or giving her a rattlesnake disguised as a Banbury cake. He also suggested that a trip to the zoo could be enlivened by feeding a little girl to the big cats, beating her with a big stick and confining her in the coal hole.

Many people have found *Alice in Wonderland* to be just too scary for words. In 1939, writer Virginia Woolf commented:

Horror Alice   147

'Down, down we fall into that terrifying, wildly inconsequent, yet
perfectly logical world ... the two Alices are not books for children:
they are the only books in which we become children.'

In 1966, journalist and editor of the satirical *Punch* magazine Malcolm
Muggeridge wrote, 'From a child's point of view, the story is full of
indefinable and incomprehensible horror ... Alice is a very sick book
indeed.' While an American writer, Flannery O'Connor said quite simply,
'I could never stand *Alice in Wonderland*. It was a terrifying book.'

Over the past century or so, there has been an ever-growing interest in
horror and the darker side of life with tales of zombies, spooky graveyards,
deserted churches, of vampires and infernal creatures. The traditional
images have been brought up to date with modern concepts of worlds being
taken over by robots, being attacked by artificial intelligence and the horror
inducing concept of being trapped and unable to escape. Although *Alice in
Wonderland* is a children's novel, this does not mean that it is all light. As
with other children's novels, there are darker elements present and some
interpretations have focused on the darker side of the story.

As the Australian Centre for the Moving Image pointed out in its
Wonderland exhibition:

'Alice has come to embody some of our darker fantasies. Alice
is now commonly reoriented within stories for adults. She can
embody innocent discovery of the enchanting and unfamiliar.
Yet at a time of cultural upheaval Alice can now be represented
as mentally disturbed or murderous. This contrasts with her
traditional role as a bastion of sanity among 'all mad' characters.
These dark visual manifestations reconfigure Alice in ways that
Carroll never imagined.'

Many observers now see elements of horror to be found throughout the
story. Alice's encounter with Humpty Dumpty and the fast change of topic
she initiates has been regarded as being almost hinting at the possibilities
of murder and death:

'"Seven years and six months!" Humpty Dumpty repeated
thoughtfully. "An uncomfortable sort of age. Now if you'd asked
my advice, I'd have said, 'Leave off at seven' but it's too late now."

148   The Dark Side of Alice in Wonderland

"I never ask advice about growing," Alice said indignantly.

"Two proud?" the other enquired.

Alice felt even more indignant at this suggestion. "I mean," she said, "that one can't help growing older".

"One can't perhaps," said Humpty Dumpty "but *two* can. With proper assistance, you might have left off at seven."

"What a beautiful belt you've got on!" Alice suddenly remarked.'

As a horror concept, *Alice in Wonderland* undoubtedly has a lot of offer – and it has been recognised as such by numerous film makers, event organisers, Halloween horror companies to name but a few. These are stories with a distinctly nightmarish quality, with episodic scenes containing mixed images of falling through space, of imperious demands for heads to be chopped off, of growing and shrinking, being submerged in lakes. There are transformations and shapeshifters, babies turning into pigs, playing cards, while a Mad Hatter and the Queen of Hearts are never what they seem at first. Nor is it confined to the story itself since horror stories have also referred to Lewis Carroll for example in the steampunk horror novel *Anno Dracula* sees Lewis Carroll being taken prisoner by vampires.

Even the natural world is not exempt from these horror references. In Australia and New Zealand, the caterpillar of the Uraba Lugens moth (gum-leaf skeletoniser) is nicknamed the 'mad hatterpillar' due to its habit of wearing its old moulted skulls as a type of hat. As the caterpillar grows and creates a new head, it sheds its skin leaving it on top of its body. Each empty skin is larger than the previous one. Although it seems like a gruesome fashion style, naturalists say that it enables the moth to bat predators away.

Film makers have been quick to recognise the potential of *Alice in Wonderland*. One of the earliest known Alice horror themed movies was filmed in 1933. This was a black & white version of the story produced by Norman McLeod involved a distorted, claustrophobic Wonderland with bizarre, menacing costumed figures. Since then there have been many other adaptations.

One of the most horror inducing films was Czech animator Jan Svankmajer's version of Alice made in 1988. It was described by the

British Film Institute as being 'full of sly allusions to authoritarianism and brilliantly inventive in its characterisation and use of props, this is the most audacious interpretation of the story's darker aspects'.

It certainly was. In the prologue, Kristyna Kohoutava, playing Alice, says, 'Now you will see a film. Made for Children. Perhaps.' The ensuing scenes are far removed from the Walt Disney adaptation or Tenniel's classic drawings. There is a close up of Alice's mouth as she states they should close their eyes 'otherwise you won't see anything'. The first shows a stuffed rabbit tearing its stomach open to escape a glass display case, and then continues to leak sawdust throughout the remainder of the film. Alice follows the rabbit through a desk drawer into a world that is wondrous rather than wonderful. She transforms into a china doll and is trapped in a rabbit cage like house. When a skull head lizard is thrown through the window to scare her out, she kicks him away, causing him to burst and spill his sawdust filling everywhere. She is then imprisoned in a pot of milk, trapped in a white Alice-shaped shell, locked in a storage room filled with specimen jars. A sock-like caterpillar is encountered near a room swarming with sock-like worms, while the Mad Hatter's tea party contains a taxidermic ferret, hare and wooden-puppet Hatter. Within the Queen of Heart's garden, the White Rabbit decapitates playing cards using scissors. Sentenced to death, a card-playing Hatter and Hare exchange their heads and continue playing. During Alice's trial before the Queen of Hearts, she eats the tarts causing her head to shapeshift into the heads of other characters. When the Queen demands that all her heads be cut, the White Rabbit confronts Alice with a pair of scissors. The story ends with Alice standing in front of a broken glass case, before taking out a pair of scissors from a drawer while commenting, 'He's late, as usual. I think I'll cut his head off.'

Horror fans regard *Resident Evil* (1999) as being among the most terrifying films ever made, grossing over $100m worldwide. *Alice in Wonderland* and *Alice through the Looking Glass* were major influences on the creators of *Resident Evil*. Set in an underground research facility involved in the outbreak of a deadly virus, the Hive's artificial intelligence – the Red Queen – has sealed off the research area and killed everyone inside. Alice and a group of commandos have to enter the Red Queen's lair and contain the virus. The actors were told to study the Wonderland characters in order to understand their roles in *Resident Evil* and throughout the film there are constant hints of the *Alice in Wonderland* ideas for example, the first victim is beheaded within the Red Queen's laser corridor.

*Red Kingdom Rising* (2014) is another modern variation on the Alice theme, involving some very graphic horror elements complete with blood and gore. Within minutes of entering Wonderland, creatures are punching fists into stomachs to yank out monsters with occult paraphernalia and demonic creations lurking around every corner. The central character is Mary Ann, a troubled young woman with an abusive mother who is secretly involved in black magic. Forced by her mother to go back in time to when her father dies, Mary Ann is never sure what is a dream or reality within the terrifying Red Kingdom where a Red King lies sleeping. She encounters a mysterious little girl named Alice, dressed in typical Alice clothing, yet wearing a horrific Cheshire Cat mask Mary Ann has to discover whether this is her own dream or that of the Red King, in order to deal with a final confrontation with her own childhood fears.

There are many examples to be found of horror films that have incorporated or been clearly influenced by *Alice in Wonderland*. *Alice or the Last Escapade* (1977) takes various elements of the story into a twentieth century setting. Driving away from her husband, Alice has an accident forcing her to seek sanctuary in a strange mansion where an elderly man tells her that the next day her 'spirit will be free to roam'. The following scenes are pure psychological terror involving parallel dimensions, and a paradox defying reality within a deserted estate. As with *Alice in Wonderland*, sights and sounds disorient, there are screeching kettles, corkscrew stairs, vine covered pillars and a disembodied voice telling her 'You have to live in the dark for a while. Make the most of it.'

In *Marx Reloaded* (2011), a film about Marx and Trotsky takes on a horrific aspect by interspersing animation with a cartoon character parodying *Alice in Wonderland*. In *Alice in Midsommar* (2019), filmmaker Ari Aster commented that his 'psychedelic horror film is a "fairytale" not a million miles away from something like Alice in Wonderland'. Reviewers agreed, noting the links with Victorian fantasy styles. Writing in *Prospect Magazine*, Caspar Salmon commented:

'The film, centring as it does on Dani, a young American woman accompanying her anthropologist boyfriend to a Nordic festival that turns steadily more sinister, brings to mind Lewis Carroll's *Alice's Adventures in Wonderland*. In both, whimsy and horror collide. In Midsommar's presentation of a vulnerable, virginal femininity rubbing up against cruelty and unreason, the movie creates a familiar sense of disturbance which it then takes a wicked pleasure in subverting. Just as Alice experiences a blurring of the line between the real and the fantastical, between normality and nightmare, so the beginning of Midsommar flips between America and the trip to Sweden, prefiguring the descent into chaos of its heroine.'

Other scenes in the film include familiar Alice elements such as constantly apologising for her behaviour and spending a lot of time crying. Her body stretches and distorts under the effect of various biscuits and medicines while drug fuelled hallucinations allow Dani to perceive her hands as being overgrown with moss and grass.

Salmon goes on to say:

'Although *Alice's Adventures in Wonderland* is a creepy, unsettling story that inflicts kink, shame and physical suffering upon its young heroine, she still manages to fight back. In an evolution of this idea, Dani not only challenges her wayward boyfriend but also learns to control the horror of her deranged environment. Alice is only ever a guest in Wonderland, whereas Dani effectively acclimates to her new setting. In the unhinged Midsommar cult where she finds herself, Dani makes herself at home and learns to fashion the world in her own way. In the "other" world, this upside down land with its own codes – its gender segregation, its strange feasts and death rituals, Dani is a queen.'

The rise of computer gaming has proved fertile ground for the use of *Alice in Wonderland* themes in horror situations. By far the most scary of all these games is Alexander McGee's Alice Madness returns series of games which focus on psychological horror with lots of blood and gore . Throughout the games, there is a constant use of strong language, sexual themes and graphic violence. The world of Alice is turned into an adult nightmare, with its focus on death, violence, rage, madness and aggression. Even the traditional childlike image of Alice is transformed, with her blue dress and white pinafore adorned with astrological symbols and constantly splattered with blood. Her traditional Mary Jane style strapped shoes are replaced with black boots.

In 2018, a science fiction game anthology *Black Mirror* released an interactive film on Netflix. *Black Mirror: Bandersnatch* was deliberately

## 152    The Dark Side of Alice in Wonderland

named after the Bandersnatch in *Alice Through the Looking Glass*. The film is based on the activities of a computer programmer who is adapting a fantasy choose-your-own-adventure novel into a video game. It combines both elements of the Alice stories with a science fiction setting. Among the many Alice links present in the film are an option to find the programmer's stuffed toy rabbit which leads him along pathways resulting in even deeper secrets – just like Alice's quest to find the White Rabbit. Another episode involves the programmer experiencing a psychedelic, hallucinogenic event similar to that of the Mad Hatter's Tea Party, complete with an equivalent Mad Hatter. In another story option, the programmer travels through a mirror.

Participants have to choose their own route through the narrative and there are millions of unique story permutations. Among the possible versions include references to a stuffed rabbit and alternate realities which may include taking hallucinogens, jumping off balconies, branching pathways involving crossing through a mirror to meet the programmer's 5-year-old self, or killing his father. Although there are five main endings, there are actually multiple endings available depending on player choices. According to the creator of the game, Charlie Brooker, 'We genuinely haven't sat down and chatted about how many we think there are! We haven't actually sat down to count them.' One such ending can result in moving to the present day where the programmer's daughter is now a programmer herself, attempting to adapt a story into an interactive film which leads into the same 'branching path' imagery experienced by her father. Just like *Alice in Wonderland*, the film focuses on issues of free will and control.

Special events and unusual party concepts are extremely popular ways of providing entertainment for groups. Not surprisingly, *Alice in Wonderland* has been targeted as being perfect for horror related events. In 2019, the O2 Arena held a special 'Trapped in Wonderland' Halloween party. Participants were welcomed with a Mad Hatter cocktail before entering a nightmarish world of deranged personalities, spooky surprises and spectacular music. The basic theme is simple – trapped in Wonderland for too long, Alice has gone crazy and evil.

Scarlett Entertainment is one of the leading UK entertainment agencies, with topics focusing on traditional subjects celebrating the rich history of the British Isles ranging from magic acts to swinging 1920s jazz bands along with fairy tales and circus. Not surprisingly, *Alice in Wonderland* forms an

Horror Alice 153

important element within their mix – in the form of *Alice in Horrorland*. Juliana Rodriguez of Scarlett Entertainment comments:

> 'We are huge fans of Alice in Wonderland and so are many of our clients. It's a story with many variants and that leaves lots of room to be creative because of the complexity of its characters and the story itself. The horror characters were created with Halloween events and adult audiences in mind, because we saw a market demand for this type of entertainment and because we're fascinated by the dark aspects of the original *Alice in Wonderland* story.'

> 'Lewis Carroll was quite a complex and dark writer, and Carroll created a very fascinating and chaotic world that was not only dreamlike and surrealistic, but dark and gloomy, even terrifying. That's how we interpreted it to create our horror characters, that's the base of our concept and costume designs.'

> 'When training the actors, we focus a lot on facial expressions and try to ask our actors/performers to put themselves in the shoes of each character (by embracing their personality, their mannerism etc) but imagining how they'd like or how they'd act if they were zombies or if they had gone mad. In the case of the Mad Hatter (as he's already mad), we try to push our actors to go a step further by adding a touch of true psychopathy to their acting with a creepy smile, eyes wide open and a fixed gaze....'

During an *Alice in Horrorland* themed event, the characters of Alice, the Mad Hatter and the Queen of Hearts interact with the guests including sneaking up and scaring them, playing pranks on them and telling scary stories or dark jokes. They may offer the guests cups of tea in the Mad Hatter Tea party area – that guests accept at their own risk since no one quite knows what might be inside that cup. The trio also entertain the guests by performing choreographed routines. According to Juliana, 'the Mad Hatter or the Red Queen performing Michael Jackson's 'Thriller' is unique to watch!'

Demand for the *Alice in Horrorland* events is not confined to the UK, with many countries worldwide especially in Europe and North America

154    The Dark Side of Alice in Wonderland

expressing interest. There has also been a growth in interest from the Middle East such as the UAE.

> 'Halloween is one of our busiest times of the year. *Alice in Wonderland* is a story that is in the public domain and so is a great way of giving clients entertainment with a big name that will draw footfall and create a buzz at the event. Combining our stunning Alice characters with the Halloween theme seemed a perfect choice.'

Although Halloween has always been celebrated in the UK and Western Europe due to its Celtic origins; in the USA it is a major festival. American children have long taken part in Trick or Treating on October 31, dressing up in scary costumes. Halloween has become big business in the States, attracting vast numbers of people to extremely frightening scare attractions and haunted houses. In recent years, these concepts have spread to the UK creating a major commercial and entertainment opportunity in mid-autumn, at a time when previously little was happening. As a result, Halloween festivities are no longer confined to children dressing up in costumes and visiting local houses. British companies have taken on board the US scare attraction concept to create some very stunning, and spectacular attractions which take place in all kinds of locations.

Theme parks such as Adventure Wonderland complete with Alice related characters in Dorset turn their activities into moderately scary family friendly centres, with added scares in the evenings, while at Thorpe Park, visitors face the challenge each day all year round of the Black Mirror Maze: Bandersnatch. A digital maze attraction, it invites visitors to:

> 'Get lost as you enter a hypnotic maze using cutting-edge visual technology or will you lose yourself in the digital mainframe as this unpredictable digitised dimension reveals an uneasy truth that manipulates and displaces your very existence, leaving you questioning how well you really know yourself?'

There are also specially created Halloween events such as Frightmare near Gloucester, one of the most popular Halloween attractions in the west of England. It initially began with a Haunted Hay Ride event back in 2002, which steadily grew and expanded over the years. By 2013, it was attracting around 600 people each night. The decision was taken to expand the concept and Frightmare was born. The 2019 event comprised six scare attractions: Carnival: The Killing Booth, Haunted Hayride, Offering: Cataclysm, Caged, Séance 666, Wonderland along with a Vintage Fairground. Visitor numbers have grown rapidly, with the 2019 event attracting over 2,000 people per night – and that doesn't include the people who pay for a ticket, encounter the first few scary characters and decide that it is just too scary for words and leave. Wonderland is regarded as being one of the scariest of all areas within Frightmare, terrifying everyone who enters it.

Owner Matt Keane explains what attracted his company to this theme. While looking for a new attraction for their annual Frightmare, he watched the Tim Burton film version of *Alice in Wonderland*. He immediately recognised that *Alice in Wonderland* was ideal for a scare attraction due to the range of potentially scary characters, the disorientation and psychological topsy-turvy world experienced by Alice.

> 'There is a great array of scary characters. The movie came at the same time as UV attractions were appearing in the UK. By combining the Tim Burton styling with the twist of UV, it could lead into a really psychological scare which is very distinctive.'

Wonderland initially joined the line-up of scare attractions at Frightmare in 2016. One year later, the use of UV spray paint with 3D glasses enabled the organisers to develop a disorientating attraction which was truly terrifying since it allowed them to create the impression of things coming out of walls.

Matt explains the basic outline of the scare:

> 'Wonderland begins with people donning 3D glasses and entering a large rotating tunnel giving the impressing you are walking through a vortex. This leads into Claustrophobia where you have push your way through the walls and you meet the Mad Hatter. Entering a mirror maze, you encounter Tweedledee and Tweedledum. It is very creepy as they are talking at people constantly. There is a card section where the walls are filled with cards and playing card characters appearing. The playing card tunnel gets smaller and smaller as you walk down it, and then suddenly opens out into a huge jungle scene complete with Cheshire cats appearing and disappearing. A blacked out room has people appearing out

## 156    The Dark Side of Alice in Wonderland

of nowhere, and a castle corridor with lots of characters popping out, whispering. This leads to a meeting with the Queen of Hearts who is wielding a chainsaw and shouting off with their heads – it gets people running out!'

It is never the same two years running – or indeed from day to day. The actors constantly change what they are doing and how they respond to the people coming through the attraction, so that everyone has a very different experience. Some people find the screaming most scary, while others may be more freaked out by constant whispering or being disorientated.

Familiar costumes such as Alice's traditional blue & white styling are made more scary, with elements often being exaggerated especially using stage makeup. The actors work with the key characteristics of well-known characters like the Mad Hatter to make them even more terrifying. Adding to the disorientation is the fact that some of the Alices are male. Throughout Wonderland, the actors have total freedom to amend and change their interaction with people passing through. The aim is always to terrify every person within the vicinity. If screaming or sudden appearances are not proving sufficiently scary with a group of visitors, the actors will suddenly start whispering.

'Tweedledee and Tweedledum see immediately who is terrified, who is enjoying it and those in the middle who are freaked out. They stress the fear and almost mentally torture them making them the last to leave the section. We aim to leave people very disorientated.'

Wonderland is now one of the most popular attractions within Frightmare simply because it is so different. Even those visitors who come every year never find themselves bored, simply because it is never the same two years running; for example, the direction of paths through the mazes are changed every year. In addition, around 30 per cent of the area is altered, for example in 2018, Tweedledee and Tweedledum occupied an upside down room.

Interestingly, it is not just adults who enjoy the night-time Frightmare experience. It is advertised as being suitable for 12-year-olds and above, and anyone under 16 has to be accompanied by an adult. 'We have had adults bringing younger children – we have even had five year olds through the evening event. They love it!' says Matt.

During the day, a far less scary SpookOut Festival is held for families, which is slightly toned down.

It is not just in the UK that *Alice in Wonderland* has been turned into a scare attraction. In 2015, Universal Studios introduced a 3D haunted house based on an evil version of *Alice in Wonderland* and the notorious tea party for its Halloween event. Visitors to the attraction entered through a small doorway within a giant comic book entitled 'Asylum in Wonderland'.

The doorway led into a room where the White Rabbit jumped out at visitors with his pocket watch. Passing through a revolving tunnel symbolising the rabbit hole brought visitors into a room resembling a garden with Dodo birds jumping about. On entering the next room, visitors were greeted with flashing lights lining the walls, and an image of the caterpillar sitting on a mushroom appearing slowly on the ceiling. Further on there are the Tweedle Tweaks hidden behind the lights, Alice popping out of giant book pages and plant monsters with mouths for hands. At the Mad Hatter's tea party, the Mad Hatters walks on the table amid the corpse of the March Hare while, not far away, a man is electrocuted. There are Queen of Hearts' guards dressed in chessboard outfits, some are statues while others suddenly reveal themselves to be people. After meeting the Queen of Hearts on her throne, there are encounters with disembodied heads flying around, an asylum and an eventual murder scene with Alice being killed by the Queen of Hearts.

There have also been horror-based escape rooms, requiring participants to solve puzzles in order to escape from an Alice themed nightmare. Alice in Nightmareland was operated by Claustrophobia in Moscow. Even colouring books based on the Alice theme have been given a horror slant. *Alice's Nightmare in Wonderland* colouring books are set a few years after the events in the original stories. Alice finds herself back in Wonderland and has the task of saving the world from an increasingly deranged Queen of Hearts. But that's not all – she soon finds herself battling to save herself from the nightmare and people using the book are able to not only decide whether the characters are good or bad, how they should appear but what might have happened if Alice hadn't drunk from the bottle labelled 'Drink Me' or joined the Mad Hatter's tea party.

*Chapter 13*

# Occult Alice

'It would have made a dreadfully ugly child; but it makes rather a handsome pig.'

*Alice in Wonderland*

During the mid-nineteenth century, there was an explosion of interest regarding spiritualism, paranormal activity and even occultism within Victorian society. Stories about mediums and ghosts were common and attending séances was a fashionable activity. 1843 had witnessed the publication one of the most successful ghost stories of all time – *A Christmas Carol* by Charles Dickens. There was widespread belief in ghosts, possibly assisted by the increasing use of gas lamps, since hallucinations could result from the carbon monoxide they emitted. In 1848, the Fox sisters of New York claimed to be communicating with spirits via tappings. Seances became ever more popular and included ever more dramatic phenomena such as floating tables, floating musical instruments, and the materialisation of ghosts, dressed in white. Spirit photographers charged high fees to create photos of people with ghostly images. Many people believed in mesmerism, said to offer miraculous medical cures by manipulating invisible flows of energy during a trance. The onset of the First World War led to another upsurge in interest in occult topics due to the huge death rate experienced in all areas of combat.

Spiritualism was extremely popular, with numerous societies being formed, particularly in London. There were several widely circulated magazines and newspapers such as *The British Spiritualist Telegraph, The Spiritualist, Medium* and *Daybreak*. Even Queen Victoria and Prince Albert took part in séances as early as 1846, when clairvoyant Georgiana Eagle gave a demonstration of her powers at Osborne House. In 1861, the same year that Prince Albert died of typhoid, a thirteen year old boy named Robert James Lees is said to have taken part in a séance during which he had a message from Albert to the Queen involving a pet name which was known only to them. As a result of this message, Lees was invited to undertake séances at Windsor Castle during which Prince Albert was called. Following her death, Queen Victoria is said to have sent messages to her last surviving daughter, Princess Louise, using the medium Lesley Flint.

In 1882, the Society for Psychical Research (SPR) was founded in London and among its early members was Charles Dodgson. He is listed as a member in all the *Publications of the Society for Psychical Research* between 1882 and 1897. Other famous members have included John Ruskin, Charles Dickens, physicist Sir Oliver Lodge, Edmund Gurney, Sigmund Freud, Carl Jung, Aldous Huxley, and J.B. Priestley.

A non-profit making enterprise, the SPR was set up to investigate 'that large group of debateable phenomena designated by such terms as mesmeric, psychical and Spiritualistic'. Membership of the society did not imply 'the acceptance of any particular explanation of the phenomena investigated nor any belief in forces other than those recognised by physical science'. All observations and views would be considered, but any articles would be the responsibility of the author, not the society. Anyone could join the society, and just had to have an interest in the subject. Subscribers were not allowed to use their membership as evidence of any expertise as it was purely for personal interest. Meetings of the SPR included explorations of a variety of phenomena. They conducted séances and were known to debunk mediums and even some of the claims of people like Helena Blavatsky, a Russian occultist who was a co-founder of the Theosophical Society.

Dodgson is known to have possessed an extensive library of books relating to the supernatural and paranormal. Among the volumes listed in his estate catalogue following his death were titles like *Shadows of Spiritualism, Thomson's Philosophy of Magic*, and *Christmas' Phantom World*. One of his books was *The Literature and Curiosities of Dreams*, which sought to explain the causes, effects and meanings of dreams – a book which would have encouraged his interest in psychology. There may well have been many others. No one knows exactly what was contained within Dodgson's library since his family went through his possessions after his death, removing books, giving some away and keeping others. The identities of such books were never released.

Dodgson undoubtedly had a keen interest in the subject and believed that the mind could break through into the supernatural realms. He wrote:

'All seems to point to the existence of a natural force, allied to electricity and nerve-force, by which brain can act on brain. I think

160   The Dark Side of Alice in Wonderland

we close on the day when this shall be classed among the known natural forces, and its laws tabulated, and when the scientific sceptics, who always shut their eyes till the last moment to any evidence that seems to point beyond materialism, will have to accept it as a proved fact in nature.'

He believed too that he had practical experience of the supernatural. Dodgson believed that Tuesday was his lucky day – but no one knows why he believed this. There are also hints within his letters and diaries that he had experienced supernatural events and was sure that he had received answers to a prayer.

Turning to his books, the final scenes in *Through the Looking Glass* contain examples of supernatural phenomena. There are the bizarre queens who fall into a dead sleep on either side of Alice, references to zombie-like servants and food that comes to life. As Alice prepares to cut up a chunk of cooked meat, it suddenly reanimates. The diners change places with their food, and the cooked meat leaves her plate and turns up beside her, laughing hoarsely. The table rises, and food flies around just like it did in the much-publicised séances held by the Victorian medium, Mrs Guppy who used conjuring tricks to dupe people into believing she was communicating with spirits.

One of his poems – *Phantasmagoria* – is a satire on ghosts. It tells the story of an annoying ghost assigned to haunt a new house. The owner tells the ghost to leave. The ghost then tells him about all the other types of ghost and their duties who might replace him such as spectres focusing on scaring people, making them ill or causing mysterious disturbances.

Writing in *The Annotated Alice*, Martin Gardner used this comment to suggest that Dodgson was a proponent of extra sensory perception (ESP) and psychokinesis. As further support for such a view, he points to the fact that in *Alice in Wonderland*, the caterpillar is suddenly able to read Alice's mind. While in *Through the Looking Glass*, Alice unexpectedly takes out a pencil and starts to write lots of unintelligible words in a book. Gardner claims that this scene reflects Dodgson's support for automatic writing, in which a spirit passes messages through the hand of a psychic. Likewise, the famous riddle – Why is a Raven like a Writing Desk? – might reflect the fact that ravens are symbolic messengers of the dead and automatic writing performed on a desk is also communication with the dead. Many people

Occult Alice 161

believe that his interest in the occult was reflected in the story of *Alice in Wonderland*, resulting in a search for hidden meanings.

Followers of Gnosticism have highlighted the fact that *Alice in Wonderland* contains parallels with the myth of the fall of Sophia. Both Sophia and Alice fall into another dimension as a result of their boredom, curiosity and disobedience. They frequently lose direction and need aid from trickster beings while both discover they are part of the living dream of an ultra-supreme being; Alice – the Red King, and Sophia – the Virgin Spirit. The two characters represent the soul's quest for self-knowledge required to bring about release from corrupted matter: Alice has to solve riddles and reflect on her true nature, while Sophia has to discover the correct prayers to understand her place in the world. Another comparison has been made with the fact that both create bizarre creatures that must be overcome in order to return home. Alice has to overcome the Jabberwocky, while Sophia is faced with the dragon-like form of Jehovah. Finally, there is the question of their names. Sophia means wisdom and Alice means truth.

Turning to other occult interpretations, many practitioners point to the fact that throughout late nineteenth century fiction, one figure constantly appears – the occult mother. This may be Ayesha in Rider Haggard's *She* (1887), Arabella Donne in Thomas Hardy's *Jude the Obscure* (1892) or the Queen of Hearts in *Alice in Wonderland*, who possesses a transformative power. Further links with occult include the way in which the power of divination is highlighted by the comments of the White Queen who states she can remember future events.

Other writers have pointed to similarities with occult based initiation practices noting that the original title of the book was *Alice's Adventures Under Ground*. Initiates into secret societies and ancient religions such as that of Mithras underwent rituals requiring them to consider their own death, and entry into the underworld by physically going underground. Alternatively, they would use drugs to enter an altered state of mind during which their spirit was believed to traverse the universe coming back to reality as a new person. Alice of course, enters the underworld by falling through a rabbit hole and has to undergo a variety of tests. This represents her initiation process incorporating a variety of symbols.

The use of the chessboard as an important aspect of *Through the Looking Glass* is said to reflect occult and Freemasonry beliefs regarding the rise to high ranks. In the story, the Red Queen shows Alice the countryside set out

162    The Dark Side of Alice in Wonderland

in squares resembling a gigantic chessboard. Alice is told that she can gain the status of a queen if only she can move all the way to the eighth rank/row during a chess match. Taken from an occult point of view, this means that Alice can become a high degree initiate just like the Red Queen if she makes the right moves. Similarly, within Freemasonry, worthy participants are required to progress steadily through a sequence of degrees during which they acquire additional levels of secret knowledge. When Alice successfully reaches the eighth rank, a crown appears magically on her head. Followers of the Kabbalah point out that this marks the topmost point of the Kabbalah Tree of Life, and the goal towards which all initiates strive to reach.

The use of red/black and white representing opposing forces can be found throughout the stories. Alice has the task of restoring balance just like any initiate.

*Alice in Wonderland* has been described as being one of the most mystical and surreal works in occult literature, having influenced numerous practitioners. Occultist and ceremonial magician Aleister Crowley, who called himself the Beast 666 and was described as the 'wickedest man in the world' due to his links with black magic and sacrilegious rituals, is said to have ordered his followers to read both *Alice in Wonderland* and *Through the Looking Glass*. There have also been suggestions that the stories about Alice support the ideas of alternative religions such as Theosophy (which inspired the occult beliefs of the Nazis).

In her book *Behind the Looking Glass*, researcher Sherry Ackerman suggests that Dodgson was exploring the world of Neo-Platonism. She writes:

> 'Carroll's personal epistemology took on a counter-cultural flavour as he battled to come to grips with the scope and limits of material existence. His intellectual journey, intentionally or otherwise, carried him deep into the waters of mysticism. Nineteenth century currents of spiritualism, theosophy and occult philosophy co-mingled with Carroll's interest in revived Platonism and Neoplatonism.'

Turning to the Tarot, *Alice in Wonderland* is proving to be a very popular design option for Tarot cards. Tarot is a divination system descended from ancient divination methods like Viking Runes and Vedic text, as well as gambling and games of chance. The cards are used to gain insight into the past, present and future depending on the choice of cards and their

Occult Alice    163

placement, plus their interpretation during a reading. The major arcana cards are the most important as they represent large turning points, whereas the minor arcana deal with day to day insights. Although the cards do not suggest a specific action to be taken, they shine a light on individual choices and possible outcomes. There are two main types of Tarot cards – a full 78 card deck containing both major and minor arcana which are used for detailed tarot readings, whereas a smaller Oracular deck usually around 22 cards comprising the major arcana is used to provide inspiration. All kinds of designs can be found on Tarot cards from trees to fairy tales, cats and ferrets to Victorian steampunk. There is no particular reason for the choice of a design, just personal preferences. Likewise, the placing of any particular scene or character within the card deck depends on the choice of the card illustrator as to what they felt fitted any specific card. Tarot readers choose whatever pack designs that appeal to them, or to their clients. Often they provide clients with a choice of different packs, and leave them to choose whichever feels most appropriate to their circumstances or inclinations.

Consequently, there is considerable variety of cards and images from one deck to another. In some decks, the high priestess represents the goddess Isis, the river on which Alice was travelling when the stories began; while the Priestess card uses the concepts of black and white twin pillars, guarding hidden knowledge. Yet another deck portrays the characters and words from Tim Burton's *Alice* film. Often the same design idea can be used in different ways depending on the artist's preference; for example the Wonderland card deck uses an image of Alice's hand dropping the White Rabbit onto a window for the Tower card; whereas in Tarot Card Alice it is used on the Death card.

The sheer range of variations can be clearly seen when comparing different decks. The Wonderland Tarot created by Morgana Abbey incorporates four suites – flamingos (clubs), peppermills (spades), oysters (diamonds) and hats (hearts). Card design choices include:

The Chariot – a railway carriage with Alice inside
Magician – the Hatter pulling a white rabbit out of a hat
Judgement – the white rabbit blowing a trumpet (reflecting the idea
of a trumpet being blown on Judgement Day in the Bible)
The World card – Alice on a chessboard
The Queen of Hearts – red queen with flamingos
Nine of Hearts – Alice wearing a white crown knocking at a door
surrounded by nine oysters

164    The Dark Side of Alice in Wonderland

The Wonderland Tarot created by Barbara Moore uses cups, swords, wands, pentacles for its suits while the designs include:

The Fool - Alice jumping down a rabbit hole
The Hierophant – the Cheshire Cat talking to Alice
The Wheel of Fortune – Alice chasing the white rabbit on a clock
The Moon – the Walrus and the Carpenter with the oysters
Two of Swords – Alice holding two swords while sitting beside a signpost
Nine of Cups – the caterpillar with a hookhah linked to nine goblets.

As a final example, the Korean Tarot Card Alice has just 22 cards relating to the major Arcana. It is based on the illustrations by Sir John Tenniel and include:

The Magician – Cheshire Cat
The Lovers – Tweedledee and Tweedledum
The Hermit – Mad Hatter
Justice – Alice
The Devil – the Cheshire cat sitting in a tree.

Within the fantasy/occult genre, shapeshifting is a common element. Not surprisingly, it is very much to the forefront of the Alice stories, whether it be a physical transformation from one type of creature or another or a personal experience within Alice's own body. Drinking a bottle of unknown liquid, she comments, 'What a curious feeling! I must be shutting up like a telescope.' By the time she is just ten inches high, Alice becomes a little nervous, wondering if she is going to shrink any further and says, 'for it might end, you know, in my going out altogether, like a candle. I would what should I be like then?'

In a bid to become large enough to reach the key, she then chooses to eat a piece of cake. Uncertain about the possible consequences, she weighs them up saying, 'Well, I'll eat it, and if it makes me grow larger, I can reach the key; and if it makes me grow smaller, I can creep under the door: so either way I'll get into the garden, and I don't care which happens.' The process of eating brings about another instant shapeshifting transformation which makes her think about practicalities.

Occult Alice 165

'Now I'm opening out like the largest telescope that ever was. Good-bye, feet! (for when she looked down at her feet, they seemed to be almost out of sight, they were getting so far off) 'Oh, my poor little feet, I wonder who will put on your shoes and stockings for you now dears? I'm sure *I* sha'n't be able! I shall be in a great deal too far off to trouble myself about you, you must manage the best way you can – but I must be kind to them,' thought Alice,' or perhaps they won't walk the way I want to go. I'll give them a new pair of boots every Christmas.'

And she went on planning to herself how she would manage it:

'They must go by the carrier,' she thought: 'and how funny it'll seem, sending presents to one's own feet! And how odd the directions will look!
Alice's Right Foot, Esq
Hearthrug,
Near the Fender,
(with Alice's love).

Elsewhere in the story, Alice experiences other problems caused by varying sizes. She becomes small enough to lean against a buttercup, dodging behind a thistle and trying to deal with a puppy that seems like a giant. Even the process of trying to reach a normal size becomes something of a puzzling nightmare:

'Alice crouched down among the trees as well as she could, for her neck kept getting entangled among the branches, and every now and then she had to stop and untwist it. After a while she remembered that she still held the pieces of mushroom in her hands, and she set to work very carefully, nibbling first at one and then at the other, and growing sometimes taller, and sometimes shorter, until she had succeeded in bringing herself down to her usual height.

It felt so long since she had been anything near the right size, that it felt quite strange at first: but she got used to it in a few minutes and began talking to herself as usual.'

166    The Dark Side of Alice in Wonderland

Shapeshifting from one type of creature to another is equally disconcerting. Given the Duchess's baby to hold, Alice finds it is a queer shaped creature and compares it to a starfish, 'snorting like a steam engine … and kept doubling itself up and straightening itself out again'. Telling it not to grunt, 'Alice looked very anxiously into its face … it had a *very* turned up nose, much more like a snout than a real noise, also its eyes were getting extremely small for a baby … "If you're going to turn into a pig, my dear," said Alice, seriously, "I'll have nothing more to do with you." … it grunted again, so violently, that she looked down into its face in some alarm. This time there could be *no* mistake about; it was neither more nor less than a pig.'

The shape shifting concept popularised in *Alice in Wonderland* has influenced many writers, song writers and artists for example Hatcham Social's debut album *You Dig the Tunnel, I'll Hide the Soil* used typical Alice references such as Alice's size transformations and almost drowning in tears; while Japanese band Buck-Tick 's song *Alice in Wonder-Underground* includes a macabre depiction of the story with the band periodically becoming rabbits.

When considering the influence of the occult and magic within *Alice in Wonderland*, it must also be remembered that at the time of writing these novels, Victorian society was becoming very much aware of the seemingly magical properties of lantern shows and the beginning of the film industry. Charles Dodgson was very much aware of the effects such technology could create on the imagination. He frequently took children to magic lantern shows, or visiting such shows on his own.

In 1860, he attended a show of dissolving views and wrote:

'The pictures dissolved rather suddenly into each other, and one of the gentlest of the dissolutions rather lost its effect by coming back by mistake in the same picture. Such little incidents, interspersed with periods of total darkness, when everything seems to have gone out at once, and periods of bright light, where the doors of the lantern were thrown open, and the gas lights in the room turned on to enable the lecturer to see what to do next, left nothing to complain of on the score of variety.'

The impact of experiencing these effects can be seen in his writing. Depending on the way the shutters on dissolving lanterns were used, images could be changed quickly or slowly – just like the scenes involving the Cheshire Cat. Alice complains at one point that the Cheshire Cat's sudden appearances and disappearances made her quite giddy, and then the Cheshire Cat vanished quite slowly, beginning with the end of his tail and ending with the grin. Likewise, in *Through the Looking Glass*, Alice catches the Goat's beard, only to find it melting away – just like a dissolve technique. Similar transformations were created by 'slipping slide' mechanisms which relied on the concept of persistence of vision to give the illusion of movement thus resulting in lengthening noses, necks, vanishing bodies, moving limbs and mouths. There was also a special wheeled lantern possessing an automatic focusing device, which could be withdrawn from or moved towards the transparent screen between it and the audience. When this lantern was in use, images seemed to grow and diminish just like the effects described in the *Looking Glass* world. Alice notes that the 'egg seems to get further away' the more she goes towards it. Dodgson put this effect to further use in his creation of the Wonderland postage stamp case with pockets for different types of stamps due to his frustration in 'constantly wanting Stamps of other values, for foreign Letters, Parcel Post, &c.., and finding it very bothersome to get at the kind I wanted in a hurry'. The design was carefully chosen to include what he described as 'Pictorial Surprises' When using the case, the viewer would be watching the image of the Cheshire Cat on the case, while withdrawing the inner case revealing Tenniel's second picture of the Cat below, creating the feeling that the Cat was fading away and just leaving its grin behind. On the other side of the case, an image of Alice holding the Duchess's baby has the same effect when the inner case is drawn out as it shows the baby turning into a pig.

Equally effective were the spectral effects that could be created by the use of magic lanterns. Lanterns with multiple grooves allowed slides to be inserted from above and below, reflecting the *Looking Glass* scene where Alice's railway carriage rises 'straight up into the air'. All kinds of phantasmagorical effects could be created using lanterns including growing and shrinking. Lanterns were used to create figures rising on a cloud of smoke above a chafing dish, while candles simply went out. There can be little doubt that in a world where talk of ghosts and hauntings, of magic and shapeshifters, such illusions would have been very impressive.

*Chapter 14*

# Bizarre Alice

'Curiouser and curiouser.'

*Alice in Wonderland*

Are there any boundaries as to how far *Alice in Wonderland* can be re-interpreted? It seems as though there are none. New interpretations, new ideas are constantly emerging. Even politics has been brought into the mix. Researchers have suggested that there are distinct undertones of political satire present especially with regard to the chaotic legal system that existed in Victorian times. Dickens portrayed that chaos surrounding the legal rights involved in the inheritance laws within his novel Bleak House. The final scenes of *Alice's Adventures in Wonderland* are equally satirical. 'Sentence first – verdict afterwards,' states the Queen of Hearts, reflecting the fact that Victorian trials were sometimes only a semblance of justice, with foregone conclusions and sentences already prepared. There is a presumption of guilt before the trial takes place or any witnesses heard. Other researchers such as Daniel Bivona have compared Alice to an allegory for colonisation, in which Alice is unable to understand the native culture and values. Such interpretations stress Dodgson's love of wordplay and hidden meanings which would have been recognised by adults reading the book to children. Typical of such events are the pointing to the political events in taking place in France when the book was written. The February Revolution in France involved corrupted court systems used by the French king to subdue rebellions, using his power as king to act as judge. In *Alice in Wonderland*, the court asks:

> '"Are they in the prisoner's handwriting?" asked another of the jurymen. "No, they're not" said the White Rabbit, "and that's the queerest thing about it." (The jury all looked puzzled.) "He must have imitated somebody else's hand," said the King. (The jury all brightened up again.) "Please your Majesty", said the Knave, "I didn't write it, and they can't prove I did: there's no name signed at the end."

> "If you didn't sign it," said the King, "that only makes the matter worse. You MUST have meant some mischief, or else you'd have signed your name like a honest man." There was general clapping of hands at this: it was the first really clever thing the King had said that day. "That PROVES his guilt," said the Queen.'

The political allusions and links continued through the work of Sir John Tenniel, creator of the iconic Alice illustrations. Tenniel frequently provided cartoons making fun of politicians and political situations to the satirical magazine *Punch*. There was considerable crossover between ideas that he created for *Punch*, and those of the *Alice in Wonderland* illustrations, and vice versa. Disraeli possessed distinctly goatlike features, and these were highlighted in Tenniel's cartoons as well as in scenes involving the Goat in the Train featured in *Through the Looking Glass*. It has been suggested that Gladstone was one of the sources of inspiration for Tenniel's drawings of the Mad Hatter – although most people believe that the main inspiration was provided by an eccentric Oxford inventor and furniture dealer named Theophilus Carter who always wore a top hat and invented items like an alarm clock bed that woke sleepers by throwing them out of bed.

The legal system was a frequent target for Tenniel's caricatures and the paper's mascot – Mr Punch – was portrayed as the Lord Chancellor on several occasions. While working on the illustrations for *Alice in Wonderland*, he created a political cartoon commenting on a bill to make bankruptcy proceedings less costly. In *Reversing the Proverb*, he utilised a popular fable The Oyster and the Litigants in which the judge swallows the oyster and hands the shell to each of the litigants. In Tenniel's drawing, the suitor gets the oyster, the lawyers the shells. The *Alice in Wonderland* links continued through to the *Looking Glass* story in which Dodgson wrote that Hatter 'is only just out of prison and he hadn't finished his tea when he was sent in … And they only give them oyster shells in there – so you see he's very hungry and thirsty.'

Following the success of *Alice in Wonderland*, Tenniel's colleagues at *Punch* persuaded him to adapt Alice themes to political themes. He continued doing this for many years. The most well-known Alice-themed political cartoons he created include the Pope & doctrine of papal infallibility (1869), in which Tenniel linked Dodgson's ideas of the White Queen with Pope Pius IX. Dodgson described the White Queen as being 'gentle, stupid, fat and pale, helpless as an infant, and with a slow, maundering, bewildered air

170   The Dark Side of Alice in Wonderland

about her, just suggesting imbecility, but never quite passing into it'. Tenniel linked his caricatures of Pope Pius IX to the images he subsequently created of the White Queen in *Through the Looking Glass*. In the cartoon, he showed the Pope sliding on thin ice towards the dangerous area of Infallibility, with his papal crown falling over his eyes, wearing rosette slippers followed by various clerics. A few months later, he created the image of the White Queen showing her as pudgy, flat footed, trailing a shawl, with a crinoline hoop showing beneath her dress and her hands clutching ineffectively at a sceptre with Alice following closely behind.

Is 'The Monster Slain' the Jabberwocky? On 16 March 1872, this cartoon commented on the lengthy Tichborne Case, which had occupied inheritance lawyers for nearly twenty years. Roger Tichborne had been lost at sea in 1854, and there were several claimants to his fortune including Arthur Orton, a butcher from Wagga Wagga in Australia. The resultant caption read: 'And has thou slain the Wagga-Wock? Come to my arms, my beamish boy.'

'Alice in Blunderland' (30 October 1880) was a comment on traffic congestion outside the church of St Clement Dane at the entry point to the City of London due to the installation of a gryphon statue. The cartoon showed Alice with the Gryphon and Mock Turtle – images that he frequently used to represent City of London officials.

'April Showers: or a Spoilt Easter Holiday' (April 1892) involved a triple version of Tweedledee and Tweedledum to reflect the activities of triplet Members of Parliament Goschen, Salisbury and Balfour who are portrayed gathering primroses (the late Benjamin Disraeli's favourite flower) sheltering from the rain of a threatened parliamentary dissolution and no umbrella in sight.

'Father William' (March 1887) is turned into the 80-year-old German Kaiser and in 1893, he is turned into a parody of Gladstone making fun of his adherence to the Irish Home Rule issue.

'Alice in Bumbleland' (8 March 1899) shows Alice reading from a sheet of paper accompanied by a Mock Turtle and a Gryphon. This was a reference to the conservative politicians such as Arthur Balfour bumbling through a reading of the London Government Bill accompanied by the words 'It's by far the most confusing thing I ever heard!'

Perhaps one of the most bizarre and chilling ways in which *Alice in Wonderland* has been utilised for political reasons was by Michael Fry in 1934. He wrote a book entitled *Hitler's Wonderland* which was effectively hero-worshipping Adolf Hitler as a model political leader. The book focused on Nazi foreign and domestic policy describing Hitler as having a 'voice charged with the electricity of enthusiasm and unshakeable sincerity – his heart bent on revitalising the Fatherland'. One year earlier, Hitler's ideas and activities had been satirized in a special issue of the *Jewish Chronicle* under the title 'Alice in Naziland', highlighting the Silent Voices in Germany dealing with religious persecution and the plight of refugees seeking sanctuary in Poland.

The twenty-first century has witnessed ever more bizarre methods of re-imagining the world of *Alice in Wonderland.*

Celebrity chef Heston Blumenthal pioneered the idea of multi-sensory cooking, food pairing and food encapsulation. His vivid imagination has led him to create some extremely strange concepts. Writing in the *Telegraph*, Jason Gerard described him as being 'the Lewis Carroll of cooking, whose snail porridge and egg and bacon ice-cream lured a sceptical public through a door into a Wonderland of fantasy food'.

It was in 2009 that Blumenthal began investigating *Alice in Wonderland* related food resulting in a special Mad Hatter's Tea Party event held at his restaurant, the Fat Duck at Bray. The eleven-course tasting menu combined food texture, food experience, aroma and magical theatre all of which were designed to play with the diners' senses and evoke memory and emotion. There were sorbets that ignited by the click of fingers, mock turtle pocket watches, snail porridge, sound of the seashells, lamb with cucumber. The mock turtle watch together with truffles, vegetables, calf's cheek and tongue was served in a jewellery box fitted with a machine making a ticking sound.

One year later, he continued the theme via a TV series entitled *Heston's Feasts*. He commented, 'I want my guests to go through the rabbit hole like Alice and enter Wonderland.' A group of celebrity diners encountered a "Drink Me" Potion, Mock Turtle Soup, an edible garden and hallucinogenic Absinthe Jelly. While paying homage to Alice, the meal incorporated a distinctively Victorian base complete with Victorian inventions such as helium, while being dark and adventurous.

Blumenthal found the idea of creating a 'Drink Me' potion irresistible, saying, 'Toffee, hot buttered toast, turkey, cherry tart, pineapple & custard all in one glass – a magical drink that never existed was a red rag to a bull to me. I cannot resist the challenge of turning a fictional drink into reality,'

To create the drink, he turned actual solid food items, such a cherry tart or turkey into liquid form, by using a process of extraction; for example,

## 172    The Dark Side of Alice in Wonderland

the cherry tart was added to milk, heated and the solids extracted. Having created distinctive flavours, a gelling agent was added to each of the strawberry coloured liquids. To ensure that the liquids were kept separate, a special test tube style glass was created possessing an integral straw allowing the liquids to drunk from the bottom of the glass. Each gel was carefully layered in, so as to create a sense of total surprise on drinking, such as turkey between cherry and pineapple. This resulted in a 'slightly drug like experience'.

Guests were then served with a soup plate containing a Mock Turtle egg created out of ingredients like swede juice, turnip juice, and a toast sandwich involving bone marrow salad, tomato ketchup, egg yolk mustard, truffles, cubed ox tongue, plus a teacup with a Mad Hatter's pocket watch style teabag containing concentrated beef stock with Madeira, and covered in gold leaf. This was infused in hot water, to make a consommé to be poured over the food items in the soup plate. This was followed by a totally edible garden served on a platter, including soil made from eels, potato pebbles, baby carrots, flowers, greens, black olives and nuts plus crispy insects like wasps, maggots and crickets.

For dessert, Blumenthal and his team created a three-fold sensation to appeal to all the senses. First came a Victorian decorative centrepiece in the form of a giant, luminous, wobbling, absinthe jelly. Green absinthe flavoured drinks contained within helium balloons accompanied the centrepiece. Diners were given ice cream containing liquid nitrogen and Earl Grey Tea (both Victorian inventions). There was also strawberry and elderflower absinthe jelly containing frozen cream that ran out when diners cut into the jelly.

Guests commented that they felt they had 'fallen through a hole and eaten a biscuit and grown up and woken up the on the other side.' 'This was the Victorian era with magic mushrooms and turbo boosting.'

Another equally bizarre pop up event has been occurring at periodic intervals in locations like Hollywood, Los Angeles and London. Held in 2019 in London, it involved the creation of an Alice Inspired Gin Palace offering immersive entertainment, an innovative food menu and the provision of four strange cocktails: jaBOEwocky, Alice's BOE, Drink Me BOE and the Cheshire Cat Gin. After knocking on a doorknob in the shape of a rabbit's head, guests entered Mr Mercurial's Hat Emporium where they were required to choose an elaborate, flamboyant hat. The White Rabbit appeared with instructions to be followed, along with the Queen of

Hearts ordering 'off with their heads'. Upon going down the rabbit hole, they entered a psychedelic tea party with numerous strange characters appearing, lots of entertainment and party games such as passing round the baby. Strange canapés were provided including ones involving liquid nitrogen, an InHale-able Victorian sponge, and a sweet meringue dessert which had to be smashed to pieces before eating in order to find the key to save Dave the Knave from the Queen of Hearts. Gin makers Boe taught guests how to make the various Alice themed cocktails within The Cheshire Cat cocktails and culinary contentment area.

And it is not just organisations and restaurants that have highlighted the food opportunities presented by *Alice in Wonderland*. Faced with problems trying to encourage her daughter to eat during school lunchtimes, an Australian mother began creating edible portraits of celebrities – with one of the first being Johnny Depp as the Mad Hatter, complete with pitta bread face, and facial features, hat and clothes made from vegetables.

Such a focus on food reflects both the fun and darker sides of food within *Alice in Wonderland*. In Victorian times, following rules was an extremely important part of mealtimes. Books such as *Hints on Etiquette and the Usages of Society* were widely read, offering advice such as 'you cannot use your knife, or fork, or teeth too quietly', 'ladies should never dine with their gloves on – unless their hands are not fit to be seen'. In 1855, using his Lewis Carroll nom de plume, Charles Dodgson had even written his own satirical guide to dining entitled *Hints for Etiquette; Or, Dining Out Made Easy*. Typical recommendations included: 'On meat being placed before you, there is no possible objection to your eating it…' and 'As a general rule, do not kick the shins of the opposite gentleman under the table, if personally unacquainted with him; your pleasantry is liable to be misunderstood a circumstance at all times unpleasant.' In the Mad Hatter's Tea Party, conventional etiquette was replaced by chaos and rule breaking. In addition, the Tea Party reflected concerns about the issues of food adulteration and its health concerns – it was not unknown for tulip bulbs to be sold as onions, lead used in mustard, mercury and arsenic in confectionery, or alum in bread.

In the 1980s, a new fantasy genre took hold in the form of steampunk. A science fiction writer, K.W. Jeter, created this word in order to describe an alternative world of Victorian fantasy combined with high tech steam technology. Numerous versions of this world have since been developed blending ideas of fantastical realms with Victorian society and variations

## 174  The Dark Side of Alice in Wonderland

on technology. A typical example is that of Gail Carriger's steampunk stories involving a Victorian lady named Alexia Tarabotti with a Scottish werewolf aristocrat, a battle parasol and airships. Novelist George Mann created a series of steampunk stories involving a gentleman 'investigator to the crown' (reminiscent of Mycroft Holmes in the Sherlock Holmes stories). Steampunk is varied – from mad scientists travelling the world in airships to metal robots, Victorian high society to werewolves. *The League of Extraordinary Gentlemen* and Guy Ritchie's 2010 Sherlock Holmes films are imbued with the steampunk style.

Steampunk fans not only read or watch appropriate films and books but dress steampunk style, attend conventions and events. Steampunk clothing involves typical Victorian dress such as long frilled dresses, corsets, hats and fascinators, goggles, suit jackets embellished with a variety of chains plus all kinds of scientific often futuristic looking gadgets and accessories.

With its mad Victorian style combined with steam related gadgetry, steampunk has become a leading fantasy genre based very much around the strange worlds portrayed within the stories of Jules Verne, H.G. Wells, H.P. Lovecraft – and *Alice in Wonderland,* especially the Tim Burton film. Charles Dodgson was renowned for his love of wordplay and logic games, reflecting the Victorian fascination with the inner working of the human mind, especially when it was at its most nonsensical. The idea of a Victorian girl going crazy among ever madder creatures, her body constantly growing and shrinking, has become an essential part of the steampunk tradition, along with the concept of an adventurer with a rational machine such as hot air balloons and airships. Part of the appeal to steampunk fans is the way in which *Alice in Wonderland* suggests there is method in madness, especially within her dreamlike experiences and her uncontrollable mass of growing and shrinking limbs. It is a marriage of escapism, protest and imagination.

Leading Cyberpunk Sci-Fi writer Jeff Noon has been highly influenced by the Alice stories. Interviewed by American book retailers, Barnes & Noble, he stated that:

> 'I was introduced to the works of Lewis Carroll at an early age … later, in my teenage years, I rediscovered the books in the college library. Actually, it wasn't the Carroll novels that I found that day, but a book about them – Martin Gardner's *The Annotated Alice* … In *The Annotated Alice* he teases out and elaborates on many of the

Bizarre Alice   175

ideas and coded messages that Carroll wove through the two Alice books. It's not so much an explanation, more an X-Ray of a mystery.'

He went to say that later while working as a playwright, he stared at Gardner's book and in his mind's eye, the title changed to *The Automated Alice*. His fascination with Alice remained, and ultimately provided many of the themes for his best-selling novels.

> 'In fact, the central story structure that I return to again and again could well be taken from the two Alice books: the lonely child, the difficult family life, the descent into a fantasy land, the trial and rigors of a journey through a strange and barely understandable region: it's all there in Vurt, Pollen, Need in the Groove, Channel SK1N and so on.'

> 'In *Falling Out of Cars*, I imagined the broken pieces of Alice's magical looking glass and the various people who were looking for them in a transformed England. For my third novel I went back to *the Automated Alice* idea and found myself writing an imagined sequel to the first two Carroll books. Many times during the process I felt myself taken over by the man's creative spirit. Indeed, when I glance at *Automated Alice's* pages now, it seems impossible that I actually wrote those words and made up all those puns and philosophical jokes!'

The Alice theme continues into his *Man of Shadows* novel which is a mix of science fiction and detective genres. The central character is a private eye who is able to travel through three distinct regions of a city – Dayzone where the lights never go out and the sky lies hidden behind lamps; Nocturna is the eternally darkened area to which people go when they want darkness. Between these two regions is a mysterious region called Dusk, an area where dreams and nightmares reside. As Jeff Noon explains:

> 'The private eye's journey through this fog-bound, surreal twilight realm mirrors in many ways Alice's journeys through her own regions of the inner mind: they both encounter people and creatures evil and benign, surprisingly everyday and outrageously bizarre. Indeed the fiction writing process itself can very much

176    The Dark Side of Alice in Wonderland

seem like just such an undertaking, a walk through strange lands in search of imagined, hoped for treasure. Over the years, I've found Lewis Carroll to be a fine travelling companion.'

In 2015, the Hard Rock Hotel & Casino hosted ALICE, A Steampunk Concert Fantasy, which attracted numerous repeat visits by steampunk enthusiasts. It began with an original song called *Rabbits for Alice*, followed by a mix of lively and melancholy songs like renditions of *Call Me When You're Sober, and Mad World*. Dressed in steampunk style costumes, the singers took the roles of characters as the Caterpillar, Red Knight, The Duchess and Alice. Not content with just dressing up and singing, the characters were also brought vividly to life by emphasising key characteristics from the books such as a twitchy White Rabbit, mysterious Cheshire Cat and an intimidating Duchess. According to Anne Martinez who played Alice, she felt it was important to incorporate a sense of fun and adventure along with the darker aspects of *Alice in Wonderland*.

Equally important within the steampunk realms are the frequently imitated Alice-themed illustrations created by Tenniel. The image of Alice with the caterpillar symbolises the concept of Victorian madness, and clothing inspired by the Tenniel drawings are very popular among steampunks and steamgoths. For steampunks, *Alice in Wonderland* is very much at the heart of the steampunk tradition due to the way it combines both escapism and protest.

Alice has become a popular theme at steampunk weddings. There has even been an attempt to raise funds for a very special steampunk *Alice in Wonderland* themed wedding on Kickstarter with the aim of having cake, atmosphere and accessories along with wedding dress suit reflecting Alice's world. This is not an unusual concept – there have been many steampunk brides. One couple getting married in a garden, created an *Alice in Wonderland* rabbit hole walkway through which guests entered the wedding. The garden was filled with Alice-themed props such as little furniture, a table containing glasses marked Drink Me, fire jugglers, fancy dress costumes for guests to wear, images of a skull wearing a Mad Hatter style top hat complete with playing cards, and distorted photos of the bride and groom printed with the words 'Everyone's mad here'.

The steampunk Alice theme has continued through to the world of novels, with numerous steampunk Alice-themed books being published. Typical of these stories are ones by Melanie Karsak who created a series of steampunk fairy tales such as *Curiouser and Curiouser*: which dealt with Alice's attempts to save the Hatter who is in trouble. In this steampunk wonderland, Alice has turned over a new leaf and is no longer working for the Jabberwocky. This means she does not have to spend time at the Mushroom with tinkers, prostitutes, scoundrels and thieves operating within London's criminal underworld. She doesn't even have to make any deals with the ruthless Queen of Hearts. Unfortunately, the Hatter gets into trouble and needs help. To help him, Alice has to seek the assistance of the Caterpillar – whose help comes at a price. Alice has to steal a diamond from a very royal lady. To take another example in *Dirty Deeds and Bloody Knaves*, the focus is on the activities of the Knave and Rabbit. The Countess requires them to board a pirate ship and take everything stolen by the pirates. While on board, the Knave becomes close to a young girl named Mei.

The nature of human imagination means as time goes on, ever more bizarre and unusual interpretations of *Alice in Wonderland* are going to surface – a fitting tribute to the topsy-turvy, chaotic world that Charles Lutwidge Dodgson invented over 150 years ago.

*Chapter 15*

# The Last Mystery

Charles Lutwidge Dodgson aka Lewis Carroll will forever remain something of an enigma, with many unanswered questions. Unless someone invents a time machine or finds concrete evidence in historical documents, many of these mysteries will always remain unanswered. In many ways, Dodgson is himself a mystery. His family remained silent on the subject, never discussing his life and work with anyone outside the family. Likewise, his friends never shared any details of his private life.

When looking at the mysteries surrounding Dodgson himself, one mystery can be discounted. The idea that he was the notorious Victorian murder Jack the Ripper is highly unlikely, with every Ripper specialist regarding his name as being by far the most outlandish of all.

To what extent were his relationships with little girls innocent ones? Was he a child abuser? Was he involved in child pornography? What was his exact relationship with young girls and young women? There was unease expressed even during his lifetime concerning his relationships with little girls, an unease that become even more predominant in the past few decades as awareness of issues of child abuse and child pornography have become more dominant. It is always difficult to judge someone when looking back across the mist of time because our views are always coloured by our own experiences and events that have taken place around us.

What happened to cause the Liddell family to break off the relationship with Charles Dodgson so abruptly in 1863? There are theories, but no specific answers. Even his diaries contain no relevant information. Whatever happened, even though Henry Liddell was Dean of the college in which Charles Dodgson was a lecturer, it was not sufficiently severe to make Liddell seek a way to remove him from his position. Charles Dodgson remained a lecturer at Christ Church for many more years. His rooms continued to overlook the Liddells' garden and he would undoubtedly have come into occasional contact with members of the Liddell family. Mrs Liddell even arrived unexpectedly at his studio accompanied by Lorina and

The Last Mystery    179

Alice requesting him to make some portrait photographs to celebrate Alice's coming out into society.

Why did he give up photography so suddenly in 1880? For twenty-four years, photography formed a central part of his life and interests. Then, suddenly he stopped. Was it due to changing tastes, new styles of printing methods that he disliked or was it due to problems relating to the situation with Mrs Sidney Owen?

Why did his family remove pages from Charles Dodgson's diary after his death? What did those pages reveal?

A similar mystery exists regarding the years 1858–1862, when he wrote no diaries at all, nor are there any records of any letters and correspondence. During those years, all that is known of his life is that he was a lecturer at Christ Church. There are hints that he may have been in some kind of relationship, but nothing has been confirmed. He was clearly very upset when he resumed writing his diary in early 1862. This period also covers part of the time when he was involved with the Liddell children – a relationship that came to an end abruptly a year later.

Linked with this is a mystery that has arisen from a study of his accounts by biographer Jenny Woolf. Discovering that all his bank account details existed within the archives of the Oxford Old Bank, Jenny Woolf became the first person to research those archives. Charles Dodgson opened the account in 1856 when he was 24 years old and continues until 1900 when his brother and executor Wilfred closed the account when he wound up Dodgson's estate. As Woolf points out, these accounts are useful in that:

> 'It is the only major document about him which is both factual and completely unaltered … nobody ever went through Carroll's bank account snipping out the names they did not like, or rubbing out transactions they thought ought not to be there. So these rows of figures and names are a treasure trove of private fact against which to measure other information.'

Dodgson never made a massive income from his work as a lecturer, photographer or writer and certainly not from *Alice in Wonderland*. His overall income never approached that of Alice's father, Dean Liddell. Dodgson paid all the publication costs of the book himself – for example commissioning Sir John Tenniel to do the pictures for *Alice's Adventures*

180    The Dark Side of Alice in Wonderland

*in Wonderland* cost £138 in 1865 – a figure that was almost a quarter of Dodgson's entire annual income. He never expected make much money on the books. He wrote:

> 'The loss on the first 2000 will probably be £100 leaving me £200 out of pocket. But if a second 2000 could be sold it would cost £300, and bring in £500, thus squaring accounts: and any further sale would be a gain: but that I can hardly hope for.'

Payments from his publishers Macmillan were rarely more than a few hundred a year and were simply labelled as Cash. Apart from some profits on the books, he did gain some cash from limited merchandising such as an Alice postage-stamp case, and an Alice biscuit tin.

What makes these accounts particularly interesting – and where the mystery arises – is the fact that they do provide some information about those missing years in his diaries such as where he spent Christmas in 1861. The fact that he drew cash out in Darlington at that time shows that he was staying at Croft-on-Tees with his parents and siblings. It was a time when he was under strain and appears to be trying to come to decisions about his future, for example the issues regarding ordination in order to comply with University and College requirements.

By 1861, he was earning around £450 a year from his teaching responsibilities at Christ Church College. The mysterious payment for which there is no explanation took place in November 1861 during a period when he was making several major demands on his income. He paid the sum of £94 4s 0d to someone called Forster living in the Oxford area. This was a massive sum representing roughly a quarter of his annual income at that time. This is the only payment Dodgson ever made to someone called Forster. There were at this time, no tradespeople in Oxford bearing this name. Shortly after the payment was made, Dodgson reluctantly took partial Holy Orders as a deacon as required by Christ Church College.

The identity of this person known as Forster remains unknown. Although there was a Revd Thomas Forster at another Oxford College, there is no record of a corresponding sum entering his account, nor does he appear have been acquainted with Dodgson. The only Forster with whom Dodgson ever corresponded was John Forster, the biographer and friend of Charles Dickens, who – like Dodgson's uncle Skeffington Lutwidge – had been a Commissioner for Lunacy. The two men were on friendly terms, as can be seen by a letter written to John Forster in 1872. However, John Forster did not live in Oxford. No payments were made by the Oxford Old Bank for an out of town charge, which means the mysterious payment is unlikely to have been for John Forster. Likewise, there is no evidence that has appeared so far to link Dodgson with William Forster, steward of Jesus College around the period in question.

So who was the mysterious Forster? And why did Dodgson make this payment? No one knows. Equally unknown is the reason for the payment. There is no indication as to why the payment was being made, whether he was buying a very expensive product or service. The mystery remains. Was it an innocent payment for some item? Did it relate to family concerns perhaps in relation to the welfare of one his siblings? Did it relate to his own personal life? Was it blackmail? Was he paying someone off? Did it have something to do with a disastrous relationship? There is no information available. All we know is that this period in his life was extremely traumatic and involved considerable despair. A few months later, in 1862, when he resumed writing his diaries, the first entry began with a prayer seeking help to 'overcome temptation' and describing himself as being 'utterly weak, and vile and selfish'.

Even his most famous book poses a mystery in the form a riddle that has never been fully answered. The Mad Hatter asked Alice 'Why is a Raven like a Writing desk?':

> '"Have you guessed the riddle yet?" the Hatter said, turning to Alice again.
> "No, I give it up," Alice replied. "What's the answer?"
> "I haven't the slightest idea," said the Hatter.'

When undertaking a revision of *Alice's Adventures in Wonderland* in 1897, Dodgson suggested that it might be, 'Because it can produce a few notes, though they are very flat; and it is never put with the wrong end in front!' Early versions of the revised edition spelt 'never' as in 'nevar' i.e. Raven with the wrong end in front. No one, even Dodgson himself, has ever been totally convinced of this solution. Other suggestions made since 1897 have included: because the cause (caws) comes before the pause (paws); because in French all the letters in bureau are contained in corbeau; the answer lies in the quill: both may be penned, but they can never truly be captive. The truth is – no one really knows. Dodgson was a mathematician and loved

## 182    The Dark Side of Alice in Wonderland

puzzles, so may well have deliberately created puzzles to which there is no answer!

Given the years that have passed, no one will ever be able to know the entire truth concerning the lives of Charles Dodgson and Alice Liddell, although there is every chance that new information will surface in due course, hidden in documents and manuscripts located in archives and record offices. Dodgson himself stated, 'my constant aim is to remain, personally, unknown to the world'.

Other mysteries continue to surface – although now these are created by modern ideas. For a book that began life as a simple children's story, it has aroused a vast array of concepts, ideas and mysteries. There can be little doubt that over the past decades, authors, film producers, artists, event organisations have taken the *Alice in Wonderland* stories in directions that he would never have anticipated often creating new mystery angles. Anyone attending an Alice-themed escape room, mystery event, reading or watching an Alice themed book or film are often being taken into something new and different. Human ingenuity ensures that new ways of exploring and investigating Alice with all its fantastical imagery and concepts will continue to expand, with the Dark side providing just as much entertainment, interest and controversy as the books themselves.

Fittingly, for a book centred around an enigma, a permanent mystery full of riddles and word games; Alice remains a riddle. The historical Alice, the real Alice has been named and her story told. Yet Alice is now much more than a person. Ultimately, the Alice of *Alice in Wonderland* has come to stand for many things including purity, innocence, madness, and horror. She has become the Universal Alice, a character with whom everyone can relate in some way. She is a mystery, an enigma. Exactly what she stands for at any one point, only you can decide. As Alice points out:

'Who in the world am I? Ah, that's the great puzzle.'

# Resources

ACKERMAN, Sherry, *Behind the Looking Glass*, Cambridge Scholars Publications, 2008

CARROLL, Lewis, *'Alice' on the Stage,* Carson and Comerford, 1887

CARROLL, Lewis, *Collected Works* Various publishers.

CLARK, Anne, *The Real Alice*, Michael Joseph 1981

COHEN, Morton (ed), *The Selected Letters of Lewis Carroll*, Palgrave Macmillan 1982

CORNWELL, Patricia, *Portrait of a Killer: Jack the Ripper Case Closed*, Little Brown, 2002

DOUGLAS-FAIRHURST, Robert, *The Story of Alice: Lewis Carroll and the Secret History of Wonderland* Harvill Secker 2015

ENGEN, Rodney, *Sir John Tenniel Alice's White Knight*, Scolar Press 1991

FULLER, Jean Overton, *Sickert and the Ripper Crimes*, KDP, 2012

GERNSHEIM, Helmut, *Lewis Carroll Photographer*

LEACH, Katherine, *In the Shadow of the Dream Child*, Peter Owen 1999

MORRIS, Frankie, *Artist of Wonderland: The Life, Political Cartoons, and Illustrations of Tenniel*, Lutterworth Press 2005

ROUSMANIERE, Nicola Coolidge and RYOKO, Matusba, (eds) *The Citi Exhibition Manga*, Thames & Hudson The British Museum 2019

RUBENHOLD, Hallie, *The Five The Untold Lives of the Women Killed by Jack the Ripper,* Doubleday 2019

SALISBURY, Mark, *Alice in Wonderland: A Visual Companion*, Disney editions 2010

SMITH, Lindsay, *Lewis Carroll Photography on the Move*, Reaction Books 2015

WALLACE, Richard, *Jack the Ripper Light-Hearted Friend*, Gemini Press 1996

WINCHESTER, Simon, *The Alice Behind Wonderland*, Oxford University Press 2011

WOOLF, Jenny, *The Mystery of Lewis Carroll*, Haus Books 2010

www.library.columbia.edu/libraries/archives/resources/media/alice
(this link contains short recordings made during Alice's visit to America in 1932.)

# Index

Anime 57–8, 60, 64, 70, 116

Bandersnatch 104, 122, 152, 154
Bayne, Thomas 87–90, 92

Carroll, Lewis *see* Dodgson,
    Charles Lutwidge
Characters:
    Caterpillar 56–7, 100, 112–13,
        119–20, 126–7, 132, 145, 176–7
    Cheshire Cat 32, 57, 59–60, 69, 76,
        100, 102, 107, 110, 113, 121, 123,
        126, 133, 135, 143, 150, 164, 167,
        172–3, 176
    Dormouse 108, 110, 115, 132, 146
    Gryphon 116, 126, 135–6, 170
    Hatter 2, 58–9, 69, 71, 76, 95–9,
        102, 108, 110, 113–15, 122–3,
        126, 128, 131–3, 139, 143, 148–9,
        152–3, 155–7, 163–4, 169, 171–3,
        176–7, 181
    Hearts, King of 71, 92, 98–9, 116,
        132, 168–9
    Hearts, Knave of 116, 123, 168, 173
    Hearts, Queen of 2, 73, 76, 78,
        98–101, 104, 112, 116–8, 123–4,
        143, 145, 148–9, 153, 156–8, 161,
        163, 168, 173, 177
    Mad Hatter *see* Hatter
    March Hare 2, 57–8, 76, 98–9, 108,
        113, 115–16, 131–2, 149, 157
    Mock Turtle 112, 135, 170–2

    Red Queen 70, 76–7, 98, 100, 146,
        149, 153, 161–2
    Tweedledum and Tweedledee 12,
        66, 73, 76–7, 98–9, 102, 124–5,
        139, 143, 155–7, 164, 170
    White Knight 138, 141–2, 146
    White Queen 98–9, 117, 120, 161,
        169–70
    White Rabbit 1–2, 57, 60, 67,
        69–70, 76–7, 98, 105, 110, 112,
        120, 123, 130, 142, 145–6, 152,
        157, 163, 168, 172, 176–7
Christ Church, Oxford 1, 5–9, 11,
    16–17, 19, 29–30, 32, 39–40,
    86–7, 97, 113, 178–80
Clarke, Henry Saville 2, 35

Dabbs, Dr George 82, 93
Dali, Salvador 133, 136, 138–9
Dodgson, Charles Lutwidge 1, 7–8,
    11, 80, 82, 86, 88–9, 91, 93–4,
    109–11, 117, 119, 131–2, 159–60,
    166–8, 173–4, 178–84
    *Alice in Wonderland (Alice's*
        *Adventures Under Ground)* 2,
        4–6, 9, 12–13, 32, 107–108, 113,
        116, 161, 169, 177, 179–80
    *Alice Through the Looking Glass* 9,
        66, 68–70, 73, 110, 116, 121–2,
        126, 129–30, 135–6, 139, 141,
        149, 152, 160–2, 167, 169–70
    Child Friends 16–37, 146

Index    185

Dodgson, Skeffington  16, 86

Film and TV  64, 68–70, 97, 132–3,
      144–5, 148, 149, 150–2
   *Alice in Wonderland* movie
      (Tim Burton, 2010)  66, 112,
      114, 116–17, 155, 174
   *Alice in Wonderland: XXX Musical*
      movie (1976)  70–3
   *Alice or the Last Escapade*
      movie (Claude Chabrol
      1977)  73, 150
   *Alice Through the Looking Glass*
      movie (Tim Burton 2016)
      122, 163
Forster, John  180–1

Hargreaves, Alice *see* Liddell, Alice
*Hunting of the Snark*  11, 88, 92–3,
      108, 134–5, 137

Isis, River  1, 6, 9, 29

*Jabberwocky*  88, 87, 104, 117, 121,
      123, 139–40, 161, 170, 177
'Jack the Ripper'  3, 80–94
Japan  56–61, 64–5, 67, 103, 166

Liddell, Alice  1, 3, 6–8, 10–11, 13–15,
      28–34, 36, 39, 42, 44, 96, 122,
      141–2, 179, 182

Liddell, Dean Henry  1–2, 7–9, 11,
      18–19, 29–30, 32, 39–40, 43, 142,
      178–9
Liddell, Edith  1, 7–8, 10–11, 13,
      29–32, 44, 179
Liddell, Harry  7–8, 29, 39, 42, 44
Liddell, Lorina  1, 7–11, 13, 18,
      29–32, 42, 44, 55, 179
Liddell, Mrs Lorina  2, 7–9, 11,
      29–33, 40, 42–3, 142, 178
'Lolita'  1, 4, 56–65, 79
Lutwidge, Robert Skeffington  38,
      107–108, 180

Manga  57–8, 60, 64, 70, 116
Murder Mystery Games  95–106

Photography  8–9, 12, 22, 28–30, 32–4,
      38–55, 68, 77, 108, 158, 179

Steampunk  148, 163, 173–4, 176–7

Tenniel, Sir John  2, 4–5, 15, 105, 113,
      115, 126, 135–6, 138, 140, 149,
      164, 167, 169–70, 176, 179

Wonderland  2, 10, 13, 58–9, 61, 69–71,
      73–4, 76, 78–9, 95–8, 100–102,
      104–105, 107, 112–13, 115–19,
      122–4, 131–3, 137, 142, 144–5,
      147–52, 154–7, 163–4, 167, 171